RED EVA McMURROUGH

GHOSTS
IN
IRISH HOUSES
A Collection of Ghostly Folk Tales

JAMES REYNOLDS

DOVER PUBLICATIONS, INC.
Mineola, New York

To the Memory of
Count Frederick Eric von L

*A Norwegian friend who related to me
many stirring tales of Viking ghosts,
to match my stories of the haunted Gael.*

Bibliographical Note

This Dover edition, first published in 2009, is an unabridged republication of
the work originally published by Creative Age Press, Inc., New York, in 1947.
The nine original color plates have been reproduced here in black and white. The
original endpaper map printed in green ink now appears as a double-page spread
in black and white on pp. xviii and xix.

Library of Congress Cataloging-in-Publication Data

Reynolds, James, 1891–
    Ghosts in Irish houses : a collection of ghostly folk tales / James Reynolds.
— Dover ed.
        p. cm.
    Originally published: New York : Creative Age Press, 1947.
    ISBN-13: 978-0-486-47171-6
    ISBN-10: 0-486-47171-3
    1. Ghosts—Ireland. 2. Ghosts—Northern Ireland. I. Title.

BF1472.I73R48 2009
133.1'22—dc22

                                                              2008042990

Manufactured in the United States of America
Dover Publications, Inc., 31 East 2nd Street, Mineola, N.Y. 11501

Introduction

Amongst the picturesque pages in *Lavengro* are the few in which the youthful author, George Borrow, looks out on, and in one case leads us into, the ruined castles of Ireland; in this case the castle is in County Tipperary. "The face of the country appears studded with them, it being difficult to choose any situation from which one, at least, may not be descried. They are of various ages and styles of architecture, some of great antiquity, like the stately remains which crown the crag of Cashel; others built by early English conquerors; others, and probably the greater part, erections of the time of Elizabeth and Cromwell. The whole speaking monuments of the troubled and insecure state of the country, from the most remote periods to comparatively modern time."

Young George (he spoke Gaelic at the time and was known as Seorsa) made a trip to one of these massive ruins. "I entered the keep by a low and frowning doorway; the lower floor consisted of a large dungeon-like room with a vaulted roof; on the left hand was a winding staircase the thickness of the wall; it looked anything but inviting; yet I stole softly up, my heart beating."

And there he came on a lone denizen, an old woman, at least eighty. She was seated on a stone, "cowering over a few sticks burning feebly on what had been a right noble and cheerful hearth." He continued:

" 'Is this your house, mother?' I at length demanded, in the language which I thought she would best understand.

" 'Yes, my house, my own house; the house of the broken-hearted . . . my own house, the beggar's house, the accursed house of Cromwell.' "

Borrow tells us nothing more about her, but that old woman seated on a stone becomes one of the memorable personages in *Lavengro*. She is memorable because we recognize that she is representative. She is one we would find beside a ruin in Ireland that the powerful once abode in and have gone from. And she is completely articulate.

"Speaking monuments of the troubled and insecure state of the country." A commentator on James Reynolds' anthology of stories about these castles would have to indicate why there are so many, why about all of them there is a sense of the disastrous, why every one of them has been endowed with a legend by the people, and why the legend is so often gloomy and even sinister.

When one talks about castles in Ireland, one begins with the Normans. The first thing they did after their easy entry was to build themselves the keeps that afterwards became castles. To be sure, there were stone-built strongholds in Ireland before the coming of the Normans; Cashel is directly from the Latin *castellum,* and the kingship of Cashel goes back to the eighth century. But the great houses of Gaelic times were of timber: King Cormac's hall of Tara, of which only the marks of the foundations can be traced, was of timber with copper ornaments. The Normans, wherever they got a foothold, put up a keep and afterwards a castle. The Irish princes soon did the same. The picture of Ireland changed.

Inconclusiveness has been the curse of Irish history. Had the Normans invaded Ireland a century before they did, they might have been able to lay the foundations for a Norman-Gaelic state as they laid the foundations for a Norman-Saxon state. In the earlier time they had no territorial predilections; their land was any land in which the Norman could acquire lordship. But, although they knew that England had no love for them, the Normans who went into Ireland in Henry the Second's time were beginning to be English: they did not want a kingdom detached from England. And the imperial-minded Plantagenets facing towards Europe did not want to have a state ruled by the politic Normans at their back. Henry the Second took care that none of his earls or barons should have supremacy in Ireland.

The battle of Athenry halted the Norman push towards the south and west. The Normans, without a new influx, could not dominate Ireland, and for various reasons that influx was not to come. And there things stood: the Irish now without the high kingship that had given them enough national unity to repel the Scandinavian attacks, and the Normans with great lordships here and there but with no national dominion. Whatever enhancement of power there was, was on the Irish side. O'Neill had castles as well as De Courcey; MacCarthy as well as Fitzgerald.

Great Norman families who found themselves at a distance from Norman centers, such families as the De Burgos and the De Birminghams, adopted the Irish language and the Irish law, and set themselves up as Gaelic magnates. "They became more Irish than the Irish," the English said tartly.

"They exchanged their churlishness for hospitality and their rudeness for a pure mind," the Irish said more indulgently. A Norman king was defeated in Scotland. True, the leader of the Scots was of Norman descent; the Irish had intervened in that war, and the English poet Chaucer, rather than give credit to the Scots for the victory, was willing to hand it to the Irish. Anyway, a kingdom had been established in Scotland with a Bruce at the head. Another Bruce might be able to do the same for Ireland. And so the Northern Irish princes invited Edward Bruce to set himself up as king of Ireland.

But the Irish were by no means united in support of Bruce. The war dragged on. It ended by Edward Bruce being killed in battle. But the old Norman and the old English settlements were laid waste. And now ruined castles stood everywhere as speaking monuments of the troubled, insecure state of the country. And, doubtless, over some right noble hearth a lone survivor cowered with words about "the house of the poor, the house of the broken-hearted."

The Gaelic families and the Norman-Irish and the old English—especially the old English of whom the poet Richard Stanyhurst was a good representative—remained Catholic. Two generations after the Elizabethan wars they were made to forget their racial competitiveness. The rise of aggressive Puritanism forced them into a Catholic League. The English dictator Oliver Cromwell, with the declaration of "thorough," invaded Ireland. His laureate, Andrew Marvell, told of his triumph:

> And now the Irish are ashamed
> To see themselves in one year tamed,
>   Such things a man can do
>   Who can both see and know.

The leaders who opposed the Puritans had names that showed different racial strains—O'Neill, Preston, Castlehaven, O'Moore.

Cromwell's soldiers had to be paid, and they were paid in Irish land bonds; there were confiscations and expropriations on a scale greater than ever before. New men took over. Poets like O'Bruadair lamented and were satirical about the grim visages that now looked from the castles. Elizabeth Bowen tells us that the Cromwellian founder of her family in Ireland "pulled down Nicholls' lean-to and demolished two of the Desmond Castle towers."

Two generations afterwards, it looked as if a Catholic dynasty might come back to England. The war that ensued was fought out in Ireland with French assistance. The Irish who rallied round a Stuart king in the hope of securing the lands that had been left them, or getting back titles to the lands that had been taken, or obtaining a moderate freedom in the exercise of their religion, were defeated at Aughrim and capitulated at Limerick. Again the surrender was, in fact, unconditional, for the treaty the army leaders made was torn up.

After that, the Irish were without an aristocracy. Their lands were taken from the survivors of the old order, their religion was outlawed, and everything was done to give them an inferior status—they might not carry a sword, they might not own a horse worth twenty pounds. Great numbers of them went abroad, taking service in the armies of France and Austria. Swift, who himself was a "new" man, wrote to Chevalier Wogan, the representative of the old Irish order on the Continent, that the Catholic aristocracy was the only one that Ireland ever had and that the new people had no interest at all in Ireland.

The new owners built many grand houses in the eighteenth century, a surprising number and surprisingly grand considering the economic state of the country. Many of these great houses remain as splendid and gracious dwellings. But ruin came on many more of them, this time not through war but through the operations of the Encumbered Estates Court. Like the keeps and the castles, many great houses of the eighteenth century stand in ruins.

About these ruins—keeps and castles and mansions—there is a sense of something disastrous. The imaginative relation of the people to a particular ruin is singular. These buildings in the memory of the people did not stand for an established native dignity; the people have no such amiable feeling about them as, one believes, the people of Sweden or Denmark have about their castles. Being an imaginative and articulate people, naturally they have legends about them. But the legends, generally containing something of a real history, are ominous and even sinister. These places are haunted, and the legend related of them is of an episode that led to the haunting.

James Reynolds is the first who has gone widely into this great section of Irish legend. He is interested in ghosts, and interested, too, in the places that are likely to have such visitants: houses in which grim things came to pass. In old Japan, such stories as he has collected would have been given classical expression in the Noh play. "The Bloody Stones of Kerrigan's Keep," for one, has the setting, the characters, the retrospective action of a Noh play. And indeed Yeats, in his *Purgatory*, has written something like a Noh play about such a house as we often come on in these stories:

> *Great people lived and died in this house;*
> *Magistrates, colonels, members of Parliament,*
> *Captains and governors, and long ago*
> *Men that fought at Aughrim and the Boyne.*
> *Some that had gone on Government work*
> *To London or to India came home to die,*
> *Or came from London every spring*
> *To look at the may-blossom in the park.*

INTRODUCTION

They had loved the trees that he cut down
To pay what he had lost at cards
Or spent on horses, drink and women;
He loved the house, had loved all
The intricate passages of the house,
But he killed the house: to kill a house
Where great men grew up, married, died,
I here declare a capital offense.

Yeats shows us here that such a house is haunted and must be haunted:

But there are some
That do not care what's gone, what's left:
Their souls in Purgatory that come back
To habitations and familiar spots.

Besides being ghost-conscious, James Reynolds is castle-conscious. What would be to the rest of us only a picturesque pile has for him measurements and a significant design, with insides as well as outsides. He can describe what a man with the eyes of a painter sees, and his descriptions have the rare merit of being workmanlike.

In one place he says, "This mass of violet-gray stonework looms flatly against the leaden sky if seen from the battlemented gate house which flanks the road from Oughterard to Galway." He writes in another place, "Shallardstown stands deeply embowered in trees, mainly Irish oaks and beeches. It is a gracious house of soft white Connemara stone, not too large, but spacious. The flight of stone steps leading to the portico is a miracle of line and balance."

Or elsewhere,

Dunluce rises today against the scudding clouds, a ruined dream of power. To many, this castle with its delicate pinnacles and pointed chimneys is the most beautiful ruin in Ireland. It is the most dramatic, surely. Compared with the majority of early Gaelic castles, which were built more or less to pattern, Dunluce seems remote from this world, something out of Norwegian lore, "East of the Sun and West of the Moon," perchance the palace of the North Wind King's Daughter.

I have seen Dunluce from an off-shore island near Benbane Head against a vivid sunset with purple, magenta, and crimson clouds massing against a sky of acid yellow. In silhouette Dunluce takes on a strangely Eastern look, a skyline like the *kasbah* of a Berber sheik in the fastness of the High Atlas, flanked by truly Gaelic fortress towers. It seems a pagan cenotaph to the ancient dead, where time stands still.

INTRODUCTION

We must remember in reading these tales that they are legends and not local histories; they may or may not have a core of historic truth. Some experiences of my own come into mind as I think this over. In a county that I lived in as a boy, a broken building stands on a little hill. Inside, I was often told, is a marble table split down the center. When the Catholic gentry were getting ready to fight for King James, the hero of that part of Breffni, Myles O'Reilly, called upon Fleming, the owner of that place. Fleming was not at home; he was in hiding, waiting to see which way the wind would blow. "Tell him that O'Reilly came." And with that the brave Slasher struck the marble table with his sword, splitting the table to leave the mark of his rage and disdain.

In another house, the daughter of the family was so ugly of form and feature that no one would marry her. So she was put on one side of a scale and bags of gold were heaped on the other; the man who would marry her would get her weight in gold. The scales are still there.

And it is not to be doubted that the people who lived in these houses did things in a striking, in a picturesque way. Below the Fleming ruin is an eighteenth-century house, now deserted, with a garden and demesne now wasted and overgrown. But in that wild place scores of peacocks and peahens run around or roost in the trees. A herdsman attached to the place told me that, when the house was being given over to another family, there was an article in the lease that peacocks and peahens should always be kept there. No story is told about the Nesbitts, whose house this was, at least no story that I heard, but the making of a picturesque one is there.

It is impossible for an imaginative people who seldom read a book to refrain from developing stories about the places that are always before their eyes. They paid rent to, they were forced into service by, the people who lived in the great houses; there was tension in their minds when they thought about them, and this tension caused the people in the castle or the mansion to seem larger than life to them; they were fabulous beings. Some happening amongst them remembered by a retainer was retailed over a turf fire and then taken over by the men and women who tramp the Irish roads and worked up into such stories as we read in this collection. If the ballad pattern had been familiar in Ireland, they would have been made into striking ballads. Periods are mixed up. Events are related as having happened in one century when it is much more likely they happened in the succeeding or the preceding century. The time of the stories? Well, it is the Irish past as seen and felt by men and women who, whether they lived in Victorian, Edwardian, or Georgian days, had the eighteenth century with its strongly marked character, its sense of class, its consciousness of house, furniture, and gardens in their bones.

INTRODUCTION

It would not do to write about haunted Irish houses in the manner of today or yesterday. With an admirable feeling for his subject, James Reynolds has gone back to the eighteenth century. The values of that century are the values he takes for granted. The house, the family, are everything, and social obligations, except to one's own class, amount to very little. The houses belong to the landowners, and, in a curious way, he makes the landscape seem to belong to them, too. It is always an eighteenth-century landscape with "Gothic" effects.

How well the Ireland of the ruling class, the Ireland of that century that has left such a mark on the capital and the countryside, is brought over to us in such a passage as this:

> Italian architects, workers in stucco, upholsterers and cabinet finishers, brought to Dublin by Lord Leinster to build and decorate his magnificent Leinster House in the city of the Liffey, and "Carton" of three hundred and sixty-five rooms at Maynooth in the springy-turfed County of Kildare, were engaged by Lady Elizabeth to build for her a splendid country house on the foundations of Rathmoy Keep. She loved the wild sweep of the Atlantic spread out before her on three sides. The sunsets along this dramatic stretch of coast are the finest in Ireland, surely; and the air is a renowned tonic. That there was not a tree or bush in sight of Rathmoy mattered not a whit to Lady Elizabeth. If she wanted verdure, she had only to drive three miles inland to one of her numerous farms, and there a perfect eden of greenery prevailed.

In his painting of horses and his writing about horses, James Reynolds is able to communicate the excitement he receives from these nervous creatures. And the quality that is in his accounts of ghosts and houses is the rare quality of excitement. The writing is in the period and has the character of the vigorous men and women who move through the great rooms, ride along the avenues, appear in the windows of their rocking coaches. This is a book which brings over to us, even in its legendary content, an authentic Ireland, an Ireland that exists in the memory of the people.

PADRAIC COLUM

Preface

When setting down the following chronicles of ghostly manifestations which I call *Ghosts in Irish Houses,* I found myself swept along a rushing current of Irish history. The truly fabulous legends of the Gael form overtones and undertones to most of the stories of supernatural happenings one hears in every county in Ireland.

For many years I have searched for material to incorporate into this book. Ghosts, and the houses they inhabit or visit on occasion, and the impact of their presence on various types of minds, have always captured my imagination.

In this search I have traveled all over the world. I have collected hundreds of ghost stories, for every race of people has its visitors in haunted houses. The yield of data, collected in huge portfolios, is immense, varied, and dramatic. It is especially interesting to note, when looking through these data, how closely a given country will follow an accepted pattern—almost, one might say, a formula.

For example, dwellers in the Carpathian Mountains and in the numerous countries touching any part of that savage, beautiful range favor stories of werewolves, male and female.

In India, particularly in the Rajputana and Hyderabad, the ignorant, superstitious natives keep clay images of any animal they fancy in small cupboards in their houses. They call these effigies, *Bahnus.* Like the voodoo worshipers in the African jungles and the bayous of Louisiana, the Indians stick pins and flame-hardened splinters of wood into the vital parts of these crudely made effigies to destroy their enemies by slow torture. Notwithstanding the fact that the torturees come back to haunt their persecutors, the practice goes merrily on.

Spain and France are rich in ghosts. They frequent lonely castles and medieval houses in remote mountain villages. In France these hauntings, more often than not, are the result of an ancient and bloody *crime passionnel.* In Spain I find ghosts sinister, often stemming from excruciating tortures visited upon unfortunates by Inquisitors of the Escorial.

Excepting Ireland, I venture to say that Italy has more ghosts to the square inch than any other country on earth. Italian ghosts, in the main, have grand sweep and color. Revenge, greed for another's gold, and power to rule keep these unquiet spirits active. In northern Italy, there are many religious ghosts, as well.

Scotland and England abound in ghosts, particularly Cornwall and Devon in England. Hosts of tortured women ghosts seem to have begun their horrendous careers during the infamous lifetime of John of Gaunt. A crofter near Carlisle told me once that many of the stark, square towers, devoid of windows, which dominate the landscape along the Scottish border for many leagues are called "Ghost Towers." Built originally by chieftains as watch towers, they are now the gathering place for myriad ghosts, witches, and their familiars.

The American scene is alive with many very potent ghosts. Virginia, Louisiana, in the part along the Mississippi River, and the hazy mountains of Tennessee harbor many singularly vital stories of family feuds. The victims of these feuds are "rampageous critters," as an old, corncob-smoking woman told me. After having heard some of these tales of mountain "hants," I believe her. Diabolical ingenuity is shown by the ignorant in their developing of plot and counter-plot. Some of the famous European medieval ghosts could well take a leaf from the American book.

The New England states offer a great list of superb ghost stories. Many are stark as Greek tragedy is stark. Implacable hate raises its head; in many cases, hate with stature. Maine derives most of its ghost stories from tragedies visited upon seafaring men or their families.

If anyone asked me to give one reason why ghosts in Ireland hold my interest more than any others, I would say it is because they are immediate and glowing in intensity, like the shining figures of kings and queens of Gaelic legend. Every day of your life in Ireland you may see "in haunted Connaught, a dead King walk."

In the telling of ghost stories, the Irish countryman and the People of the Roads surpass themselves. I once asked an incredibly old Woman of the Roads if she knew any stories about an ivied ruin of Gaelic splendor called Bunratty Castle. She lifted her weather-beaten old head majestically and said, "Arragh, I'm God's own authority, and why wouldn't I be now? I've trod the auld, ancient roads of Ireland since the day I was born—and before."

Country people in Ireland, living in the back counties of Monaghan, West Meath, Tipperary, and Roscommon, incorporate legend and the deathless exploits of Gaelic heroes as part of the daily round.

Houses are vastly important in Ireland. They are the pulse, the blood stream, the "heart's heart" of Irish life. The Irish are an agricultural people, surrounded by astounding beauties of nature. Yet it is his house the Irishman thinks of as he works the land, and it is there he returns at the end of day.

The house may be Russborough, grandly Palladian, or grim, impressive Rahee Castle in the Antrim glens. It may be a whitewashed stone "long farm" in the magic Vale of Aherlow, or a coteen of wattles and rain-drenched thatch in Connemara. No matter where or what his house, he stands proudly before it, regarding his possessions, the mountains, the sky and the sea.

Ghosts in Ireland are no respecters of persons. They appear in whatever mood they elect, at the "great house" or the coteen.

The ghosts in "Mickey Filler and the Tansey Wreath" chose a mood taken straight from Shakespeare's *Midsummer Night's Dream*. The exquisite Comtesse Adèle de la Tour-Vérrière, in "The Lady of Moyvore," spreads such enchantment that it seems a pity not to have known her. For unbridled venom and revenge, I give you Angelica Parrott in "Shallardstown and the Orloff Whip." "The Ghostly Catch" and "The Bloody Stones of Kerrigan's Keep" depict truly dangerous ghosts.

"Ghosts appear only in houses which have known great happiness or great misery," a well-known writer once told me. The reasons for their reappearing at a given place are legion. From over two hundred stories of ghostly visitors in Irish houses, I have selected the twenty-two that appear in this book. The stories of events which led up to these supernatural manifestations are, in many cases, human documents.

The stories I have chosen present a panorama of the infinitely varied Irish scene. They are, I believe, representative of the intensely personal Irish ghost.

JAMES REYNOLDS

Started:
    Ballykileen,
    County Kildare,
    October 9, 1937.
Finished:
    Laurel Hill,
    Province of Quebec,
    October 22, 1946.

Contents

Squire Bannott

"Old Pomp and Circumstance"
A Gourmand's Ghost

COUNTY CORK

SLIEVE DONARD

Squire Bannott

DISTANCES · HAVE PLAYED A GREAT PART IN adventures. A man coming out of a narrow valley looks off and away to blue or purple-green distances. Perhaps there will appear a gleam of the restless sea between a gap in the mountains. The man will be seized with a longing to range the world. Adventure clasps his hand. Eagerly, a little breathless, he strikes forward.

The man who never leaves the floor of the valley in which he lives is hedged-in his life long. He plods always in a cage. His initiative is strangled by lack of perspective. Walled-in physically, his soul becomes walled-in as well.

This is the story of two brothers who started life, walled-in. One escaped early on, in time. The other later in life. Too late.

Corcoran and Jason Bannott lived in a disheveled house with their father and a raft of slatternly servants. At the back of the house were broken-down kennels full of half-starved hounds. The oddest thing about this extremely odd establishment was that half the time the dissolute owner occupied the kennels with a few drunken cronies and the house was romped over and nested in by dogs.

The two brothers Bannott were as unlike as it is possible for two human beings to be, both in appearance and in ideals. They lived in a dark, damp, shut-in valley called the Vale of Bartoe in County Monaghan, near the border of County Louth. Everything about the daily round in this dismal bit of valley disgusted Corcoran Bannott. As for Jason Bannott, he was too lazy to care, too occupied in guzzling the endless plates of badly cooked food that he demanded be set before him at all times of the day or night, whenever his seemingly insatiable hunger was roused. Shambling old Annally Bannott, the father, seldom appeared in public; indeed he was seldom sober enough to walk. Life on any count was a pretty disheartening show at Clonannally Court.

One day when Corcoran was twelve years old he ran away from Clonannally. He did not go far; far enough, however, to set his pulses throbbing with an idea. This idea lay dormant, but not dead, in Corcoran's breast. At night sometimes, in the four years before he put the idea to work, he would take it out of his heart. Yes, it was sprouting leaves. One fine day it would burst wholly into flower.

The day Corcoran was sixteen, it was a typical Monaghan late spring day. There was a carnival of demented wind and weather, with a hint of clearing along the western edge of the horizon; even a brilliant sunset was promised. During the day, however, with hours hanging heavy, Corcoran took stock. He made a tour of his father's house, which he would inherit—or what was left of the sagging, sorry pile. First he walked around the house outside. Once-beautiful ornamental cornices were broken and mildewed. Gutters and drain-pipes hung in rusted swags. Stone chimneys lay strewn all over roofs that were as full of holes as a baudeen's shawl. Chimney pots were mere shards of terra cotta. "A derelict house," thought Corcoran. He wanted none of it.

After a tour of the inside of Clonannally, he was even more convinced that the house was on its last legs. In the drawing room which had once been so handsome and so stately the pear-wood floors were greasy and shored-up in places by pylons from the cellar below. Red-eyed rats, as big as ferrets and twice as savage, bared evil teeth at him as they scurried into the holes of the wainscoting. Corcoran could remember how, when he was a little boy of six or seven, his tall, chestnut-haired mother always sat behind the huge silver tea urn in the afternoons. Curtains would be drawn across the windows looking out across the park, summer and winter. No matter how bright it was out of doors, Mrs. Bannott liked to pour tea by candlelight. When Corcoran's mother died he was ten years old. That was the beginning of the end. One would find it hard to believe that in five years a house could disintegrate to the extent Clonannally had. Neglect and damp rot could rule, in this dreary valley, given half a chance.

There was slight difference in the ages of Corcoran and his brother; he was one year older than Jason, but that was enough to cause unbridled jealousy in the mind of devious Jason Bannott. What Corcoran had decided after his runaway journey up-valley was that Jason could have the demesne of Clonannally, if he could endure it. And the devil's luck to him.

The end of July, in Corcoran's sixteenth year, was so hot and stifling that the Vale of Bartoe was like a vacuum. Not a breath of air stirred in this pocket between the Dooney Mountains.

The stable-yard bell had rung for lunch. Lunch or dinner, any meal at all, was a procedure hardly to be called a meal at the hands of the shifty crew of servants at Clonannally. Corcoran usually went in to the sideboard and cut himself a slab of ham or beef, took a sour pickle in one hand and went to the terrace under the rotting portico to eat. As he started to go to the house from the stables, the hounds broke into song. They were ravenous and dashed at the broken wire of their runs in a concerted frenzy which showed Corcoran, only too well, how badly treated they were. The hounds knew perfectly what the clatter of the bell meant. Food. But not for them.

Corcoran surveyed the dining room. A revolting place, surely. Stacks of dirty plates from late breakfast were still on the spotted table. Food, and little enough of it, except for greedy Jason, came to the table half-cooked. A slovenly old ex-stable groom named Jocko made a stab at serving, but, crippled with rheumatism, he slobbered everything that was liquid down one's back. Corcoran, standing undecided at the sideboard, looked the room over. It was a shambles. Just as life as lived by the Bannotts at Clonannally was a shambles and a deep disgrace. Filth in every corner of this room, and in all the others. The mumbling old groom. The inedible food. The wildly hungry hounds that made the hot day hideous. He could stand no more of this life. Corcoran turned from the sideboard; all thought of food had vanished. Without a word to anyone he walked out of the room and out of the house.

All afternoon Corcoran Bannott walked. At evening, an hour before sunset, he came to a pass over the steep Dooney Mountains. Involuntarily the boy's breath caught in a sob in his throat. Far off, like the edge of a dream, were the blue-violet Mountains of Mourne that come down to the sea. Piercing the sky, or so it seemed to the bewildered Corcoran, rose the rounded point of Slieve Donard. At the foot of this mountain there appeared to be a gap. Through this Corcoran saw the late sunlight playing upon a blade of the sea. A great change came over the boy. Something that had irked and bound him ever since his mother had died fell miraculously away. "Adventure," called this wedge of sun-bright sea. "Come away out of that blighted valley, boy, come range the world."

From Marseilles, where the merchantman on which Corcoran had worked his passage lay in for supplies, he wrote a long letter home. He renounced every right to inherit Clonannally Court. It was all to be Jason's. Freedom was all he asked. Freedom was what he had.

When old Annally Bannott died and left his dilapidated house, his horses and sorry hounds—not much more than bags of bones—to his pompous son Jason, people wondered. "What will happen now?" they asked each other. "That great lout, with his grand ideas, will he live on in that old shebang?"

Jason had no intention of living on in the mouldering old house of his ancestors. It would take the Bank of Ireland's surplus to repair it. In any case he blamed the shut-in dampness of the valley for his bad health, which was due mostly to the trial of carrying around the vast quantities of heavy food stuffed into his belly.

In a few weeks Clonannally was sold for the proverbial song to a tenant farmer who promptly destroyed most of the miserable horses and hounds. Jason Bannott disappeared from the countryside forthwith, unmourned and certainly unsung.

Because Jason Bannott was so supremely self-indulgent and vain, he cared nothing for acquiring a house in a more open country. He simply took the first pretentious house he saw. True, the demesne was in the lovely County Cork, and, although it was in a shut-in valley, it was bright and arable, not dank and barren as had been the Vale of Bartoe. It was devoid of distances, just as Jason Bannott's soul was devoid of vistas. The dreams that sprang full-panoplied from the head of Jason's brother Corcoran, at the sight of pulsing, blue distances—dreams which gave him wings—were as impossible to connect with Jason as was the idea that he would ever refuse a plate heaped with steaming food.

When Jason Bannott saw the Palladian house called Temple Trilla, set back a mile or more from the Ballyvourney road, he was en route to Banteer, over and beyond the Boggeragh Mountains. A visit to a distant cousin of his mother was indicated. Roherboy House, where lived his cousin, the immensely old Lord Kinkarrnan, had a bad name, as had the old peer. But Jason, whose eye was ever on the main chance, hoped that his cousin could direct him to a pleasant property in this valley. He wished to settle near Cork, for he had invested a great deal of his patrimony in shipbuilding shares at Ballycotton across from Cork Harbor, and he did not wish to be too far away from his money. Lazy as Jason Bannott was about most things in life, watching his money work was not one of them.

As the open phaeton which he was driving came to a crossroads, Jason hailed a farmer leading a red Kerry bull to market. "Good morning to you, is the road forking to the right the direction to Roherboy House?" The farmer looked searchingly at Jason. "It is, surely. But why any man in his right senses 'ud be going to see that auld divil Kinkarrnan, I'd not know. If all else was well, the stinch av the auld goat 'ud knock ye flat."

Driving away from Roherboy in the early evening shadows, Jason wrinkled his pudgy nose and decided the farmer of his morning encounter had been right. Everything about the house had repelled him. The odor of death swirled through the air. When first he had looked at his old cousin he had thought him dead. But that extraordinary woman, Mrs. Dangan, had noticed his confusion and said: "Don't alarm yerself, yer honor. Sure the creature is next and nigh the grave this minute. He'll be a hundred, does he live a month out. Though I doubt that. I'm told be yer footman ye want a grand house and a woman to manage it. Is that true?" Jason told Mrs. Dangan it most certainly was. The quicker the better. "I've the very house for ye," she replied.

6

"It belongs to the Desmonds. Temple Trilla, they call it. It's wantin' a purchaser, and welcome it 'ud be to Lady Desmond, sure she's rubbed the bottom of her purse till her fingers 'er raw, like all the Desmonds." Jason hesitated to commit himself. He had spent all his life with men, his brother Corcoran and his father, though precious little influence they had been. Dominating women of the class of this dragoon-like Mrs. Dangan appalled him. Only waiting to catch her breath, the strapping woman continued, "I'd not leave his old lordship, mind, while he's still alive. But that won't be long, I can promise ye. Though I'll not lift a finger to hasten the end. As soon as he's dead I'll come to you. I hope ye'll take my advice and buy Temple Trilla. Did I say I'd cooked fer the Desmonds?"

That had started it. Every hour of the day, it seemed to Jason, Mrs. Dangan reminded him that she had worked for "the Desmonds." One would have thought the clan Desmond was the Alpha and Omega of the human race. No history or anecdote was ever started in Temple Trilla without Mrs. Dangan appearing on the scene, as if by magic, and adding, "When I worked for the Desmonds . . ." and on and on.

Once settled comfortably in Temple Trilla, Jason fell into his gluttonous ways again. Food, food, and more food wound in a never-ending parade to his table. Jason was never tardy to welcome it. He grew to be so fat he could not sit in an ordinary chair, nor lie in a bed that was not built especially for him. He was a gargoyle, a grotesque, a wallower in food.

He created a strange, an abominable vice. As food was brought to his table, to his bed, wherever he screamed for it, he would lose all control of himself. Tearing and slashing his clothing, which, as time went on and Jason became more and more obese, was only a kind of brocaded robe, the demented man would rub great gobs of food over his naked body. Screaming obscene endearments to his Mistress Food, this epicurean voluptuary would finally subside in complete exhaustion, his passion spent. Incredible as this exhibition was, Mrs. Dangan took it all in her stride. She had a sinecure. She knew it. What was a little exhibitionism? It was no worse in the long run than acting as chamber-nurse to his old lordship, and he in his ninety-ninth year.

After a year of these gustatory bouts, Jason's fatty, degenerated heart decided to call it a day. Without consulting Jason Bannott—"Old Pomp and Circumstance," as his neighbors called him—the Bannott heart stopped. No more Jason. The vast heap of flabby flesh which had been "Old Pomp" was buried without any ceremony in the Trilla churchyard. Outside of Mrs. Dangan and Jason's thieving valet, Maundy, there were no mourners. The hearse was afloat with black funeral plumes and the gigantic casket was a wonder of the undertaker's art. So richly elaborate were the silver handles on this casket that Maundy's fingers itched fit to kill him, all during the service. Late

7

that night he pried the handles loose from the casket, which rested on wooden horses in the chapel vault until ready for shelving in the crypt. Maundy was off and away, like the rook he resembled. He was never heard from again.

This of course left Mrs. Dangan the lone survivor in the field, the Field of the Cloth of Gold, as it seemed to her, for there was no "next of kin" that she knew of. Lord Kinkarrnan's daughter, Jason's fourth cousin, was in India, in some mountain outpost where her husband was stationed, or so she had heard when Lady Rintoule was informed of her father's death. It was unlikely Lady Rintoule would interfere, for a long time at any rate.

Mrs. Dangan was preening her rusty plumage with the utmost satisfaction—when Corcoran Bannott appeared on the scene. In all her life, Mrs. Dangan had never heard of Corcoran Bannott. In Corcoran Bannott's life he had never heard of Mrs. Agatha Dangan. The meeting of these two personalities was formidable—an irresistible force meeting an immovable object. Neither gave an inch.

Jason Bannott died intestate, so it was quite natural that his only brother Corcoran should inherit Temple Trilla. Mrs. Dangan knew when she was licked. She packed her bags and left the scene, not that she would not have stayed had Corcoran wanted her. But the fact that he had brought with him two Spaniards, a man and wife from Segovia, signified to Mrs. Dangan that "ther'd be no peace in it, with that class of foreign stravangers about," her term for undesirables and shrews. Before she swept from the door of Temple Trilla, she had the last word. To Corcoran Bannott she said, "I'll not give ye the rough edge of me tongue, it's not yer fault yer the brother of that livin' terror, Jason Bannott, and God'll not rest his soul. Mark me that. Ye'll rue the day ye ever stepped foot in this house. Fer all its smilin' face, it harbors the filthiest ghost in Holy Ireland. Yer skin 'ull prickle at the sight of 'im. I saw 'im, the night after he died. Came back fer his dinner. Arragh, it'll be a great treat to ye, and thim skittish Spanishers." With that Parthian shot, the widow Dangan was gone.

This return of Corcoran Bannott was in the year 1865. It was no prodigal's return. No fatted calf had been expected. He was a vastly rich man, and had returned to the land of his birth because, after ranging the world, he found he loved his own country most. Corcoran had intended to pay his brother a visit, look around for a suitable house, and settle down. From that long-ago day when he walked through a pass in the Dooney Mountains and saw the beckoning distances of the Mourne Mountains and the hint of the sea, Corcoran had been a free man. He still was a free man, and a man able to indulge any whim which presented itself. Temple Trilla was not his last choice in houses. He would stay here for a while. Later he would sell the house or put it up for let. He might even marry. Time enough and to spare. After all he was only thirty-nine.

A few nights after Mrs. Dangan had shot her bolt and walked out of Temple Trilla, the night was uncomfortably warm. It occurred to Corcoran, recalling only too vividly the stifling days and nights in the Vale of Bartoe, that he hoped to God this valley of the River Bride would not prove as hot. The hour was just on nine o'clock. Soon Jorita, his Spanish cook, would be ready to serve his dinner. The habit of extremely late dining, as is the Latin custom, was strong in Corcoran, for he had lived a great deal, in the last years, in Italy and Spain. His fortune had been made in exporting olives and their oil, and cork.

It seemed to Corcoran as he came downstairs that there was an unease rampant in the house. He had felt it since coming in from a ride around the Trilla demesne, late in the afternoon. Twice, while trying to sleep before dressing for dinner, he thought someone was in his room. Once Tomóz, his man, had knocked at Corcoran's door, asking if he had pulled the bell cord. Corcoran said he had not. Tomóz muttered a few unconvinced *gracias* and went below stairs.

The room which Corcoran had taken for his own had been Jason Bannott's, the finest in the house, surely. The spread of fertile valley and the reaches of the Bride made a superb picture from the front windows. He noticed the bed hangings and primrose carpet were disgustingly stained, but he would alter all that. Corcoran was just entering the library to offer himself a glass of the very special Amontillado Poria he had brought back from Spain, when a horrible cry rang through the house. Corcoran knew, instantly, that it had come from his bedroom. Leaping up the stairs three at a jump, he ran through the open door of his room.

An incredible sight met his eyes. The bell cord beside the bed had been yanked from its hook and was wrapped around the fleshy neck of Tomóz, who lay sprawled at the foot of the bed. The man's face was purple and his tongue and eyes hung from mouth and sockets. What was most stupefying of all was the condition of the man's clothing and the floor surrounding him. Great stains of grease and pools of what looked like spilled food saturated the carpet. As Corcoran gaped incredulously at this scene, there was a rustling sound near the window and he turned just in time to see the mountainous figure of a naked man step through the window and merge into the humid night.

So unnerved by this tragedy and its overtones of bestiality was Corcoran Bannott that he closed his house and, after sending Jorita back to her home in Segovia, took a small hunting lodge near Dublin in the County Kildare. The next year Corcoran sold Temple Trilla to an Englishman who was a great racing man. This Colonel Markham lived happily at The Temple for five or six years. Except for the fact that it was impossible to leave any food outside the locked pantry press without finding it strewn about the floor the next morning, half-eaten and then stamped upon, there were no signs of the ravenous ghost of Jason Bannott. The Colonel's ex-batman, who cooked for him, laid all this food stealing to some huge sort of Irish rat.

When Colonel Markham went back to England, Temple Trilla was vacant for ten years. Corcoran Bannott, except for a visit in the daytime now and again, never entered the place.

In his fiftieth year, Corcoran was killed in his paddock, savaged by a renegade horse he was trying to break. Temple Trilla was sold to a Dublin magistrate, one Mr. Justice O'Fogarty. Two weeks after he took up residence in Temple Trilla, he was found one morning strangled with the heavy silk bell cord, torn from its hook at the head of the bed. O'Fogarty lay half in, half out of the tumbled bed. The bedclothes and person of the Dublin magistrate were in a most shocking state. Smeared with gobbets of half-eaten food, the bed sheets formed a greasy trail from his body to the window.

Today Temple Trilla still presents a smiling, unlined, unscarred face, to admiring passers-by. From one spot along the Ballyvourney road, in particular, one sees the house through a ride cut in the park. It is a dream house. No one lived at The Temple when I last saw it, a few years ago. No caretaker lives at the house. It is a house sinking slowly to ruin. But the ruin so far is only on the inside. As Mrs. Dangan so rightly said, it houses "the filthiest ghost in Holy Ireland."

The Weeping Wall
Drumshambo

COUNTY LEITRIM

The Weeping Wall

SOMETIMES IT HAPPENS THAT GHOSTLY VISIT-
ations run in parallels. At a given time of day or night, either simultaneously
or a few minutes apart, the identical manifestations will appear in two or
more houses, many miles apart, even in different countries. This is true
in the case of the occurrences at Castle Śczriny in Poland and Drumshambo
in County Leitrim in Ireland.

That part of the story began in 1873, when a young Irish woman named Considine of Drumshambo, a late Georgian house standing in a run-down waste of
parkland on the Lough Allen near Ballyfarnon, married a young cavalry officer whom
she met at the Dublin Horse Show.

The young man, a younger son of the Polish family of Śczriny, fell madly in love
with the handsome Irish horsewoman, paid ardent court to her, and, a few weeks
after their meeting, the two were married at ancient Castle Bran, near Dunkineely in
Donegal, the house of Miss Considine's grandmother. Thus were the Hispano-Irish
House of Considine and the Polish House of Śczriny united.

Count Alexander Śczriny took his bride to Paris on their honeymoon. While in
Paris the new Countess met various members of the Guise family, related to the
Śczriny by marriage. In Italy she met members of the powerful Gonzaga. Here again
there were family connections, for in 1660, Louise Marie, daughter of Ruggiero
Gonzaga, Tyrant of Mantua, had married the King of Poland. In turn her daughter
had married a Śczriny. So by the reading of marriage vows, and a ring slipped on her
finger, the rather hoydenish, gray-eyed daughter of an unimportant Irish squireen
from a remote house in the back country of County Leitrim found herself related by
marriage to a number of the most important families in Europe.

The erstwhile Miss Considine was to learn that these families had long histories
of dark doings. Treachery and murder were rampant on the Gonzaga rolls. Greed for
power and overweening arrogance which made many enemies were on the side of the
Śczriny.

The Śczriny grandson of the Gonzaga queen of Poland came into the family

13

fortunes at sixteen. His grandmother signified she wished him named Stephan. A volatile, handsome boy, he showed early signs of mental instability.

Count Stephan Ŝczriny repudiated the authority of his mother and guardian, his father's uncle, Prince Oransky. He listened to no one and rode roughshod over nobles and peasantry alike. He squandered such vast sums of money on debaucheries of every kind that at last a family conclave convened. Somehow Stephan must be restrained, else the Ŝczriny fortune would soon melt away. Hoping he would listen to reason, his uncle invited Count Stephan to the Oransky Castle near Crakow, where he planned to entertain a hunting party and gradually to show his nephew that living off the rich lands of the Ŝczriny-Oransky estates had immense attraction and security. But whatever hopes he harbored were destined to failure even before Stephan arrived. For he arrived in a drunken, surly mood, and if one watched him closely, stark fear lay at the back of his eyes.

In this year of 1714, it was the custom in Poland for a noble to carry a whip at all times, as a sign of power more than anything else, though in the hands of such as Count Stephan Ŝczriny the whip often drew a pattern of welts across the back or cheek of a serf slow to do his bidding. The night of his arrival at the castle he became so violent that Prince Oransky realized he could bear with him no longer. As the night waxed late, Stephan became so fuddled with excessive drinking that he lay back in his chair in a coma. It was then his uncle had servants half drag the drooling figure of his young nephew to an iron-barred room, high in a tower of the castle.

For days Stephan railed against his imprisonment to no avail; then, in a burst of rage and bravado, he told his uncle why he had indulged in this last debauch: fear— fear it was. He had raped a young village girl near Vornov, the village nearest to Castle Ŝczriny. He feared he had killed her. If she died, he feared for his life at the hands of the townspeople. He begged his uncle to go to Vornov and find out how matters stood. Prince Oransky recoiled in horror at this tale. He felt the power of his family would be able to weather almost any escapade indulged in by his irresponsible nephew, but murder of a young girl placed Stephan beyond the pale and within the grasp of the king's provost.

Before any action whatever could be taken by Prince Oransky, word was brought to him that a delegation of men from Vornov were in the outer court, demanding that he receive them. The proud but wretched man stepped quietly out on a balcony overlooking the court. He listened to a man who stood out from the group of fifteen or twenty villagers standing in the bright sunlight.

The spokesman, a tall old man, the patriarch of the village of Vornov, told his story simply and with eloquence. It was a dreadful story—a young girl of fifteen, pursued by Count Stephan, ridden down and trampled under the hoofs of his horse, then raped as she lay dying. The people of Vornov demanded he hand over his nephew for trial.

Prince Oransky bowed his consent. He had not uttered a word, though every word of the tall old man had burned into his brain.

Later that day a strange, grim party of men set out for Vornov. A few of the village men rode ahead of the prisoner, the remainder, behind him. Prince Oransky rode beside his nephew in stony silence.

As they came out of the shadowed forest, three of the men rode ahead to meet a number of villagers who came toward them. It was then Count Stephan made his bid for freedom. Being an excellent horseman and well mounted, he cast for freedom on one chance in ten thousand. Digging spurs into the horse's flanks, he streaked across the field in front of the gates of Vornov, but he did not count on the sure aim of a young boy standing a little apart, the brother of the murdered girl, who stooped, then straightened, with a jagged rock in his hand. Like an arrow from the bow, it curved and struck Count Stephan just below his right ear. His horse reared, threw him, and galloped off into the woods.

Next morning the village mob was swelled by recruits from outlying villages. Many were the outrages laid at the door of unfortunate Stephan Ŝczriny. The court-house where he cowered was stormed, and the terrified youth, bound with ropes, was dragged across the square. Mob rule is swift and terrible in its decisions. It is an army with banners. Count Stephan, repudiated by his family, was strung up to a crossbar erected for the purpose near the village inn.

A cart bearing Stephan's weight was just about to be drawn out from under him when a distraught woman stumbled out from the crowd—the mother of the girl who had been killed. Pointing her finger at the prisoner, she shrieked, "Never will the Ŝczriny find peace. Misfortune will follow every bearer of that name, but, because your mother was always kind to me, I will say this: before disaster strikes, the Ŝczriny will be warned. Yes, they will be warned; if they can stave off impending fate, let them in their arrogance try. Let them try. They will be warned."

The woman was led away. The rope tightened around the neck of Count Stephan Ŝczriny, who had brought ruin on his House.

The Wall that Weeps appeared at Castle Ŝczriny more than a century before the phenomenon was seen in the library at Drumshambo. The first time was on a June evening. The moon had risen and the sky was littered with stars.

A servant, bringing food on a tray to a member of the Ŝczriny family who lay ill in an upstairs room, felt a strange dampness rise from the floor of a small salon through

15

which he was passing. Looking up at the walls, he was amazed and terrified to see streaks of water, like great tears, coursing down one wall from cornice to chair rail. The wall was distempered a dull green, and the dampness had already stained it in long points which made a design very like icicles hanging from a roof in winter.

Hastily placing the tray of food on a side table, the servant ran through the rooms seeking some member of the family. In the library he found Prince Paul Oransky, son of the Oransky who had delivered Stephan Śczriny to the mob at Vornov a decade before. Prince Paul followed the manservant cautiously, not knowing, from his chattering description of what was happening, just what he would find.

Dark runnels of moisture coursed down the wall—not the four walls, but only the wall opposite him. On this wall hung a large painting of a wolf hunt. Already the canvas seemed waterlogged and bulging.

Then the most curious thing of all happened—the strange manifestation which is seen only by members of the Śczriny-Oransky families at Castle Śczriny, or the Considine family at Drumshambo, never by anyone not a member of these two families who may chance to be in the room at the time the wall weeps. A slow tracing appeared on the wall as if a huge, invisible finger were writing a name, the name of some member of the family. As Prince Paul gazed transfixed, the unseen finger slowly wrote L-A-U-R-I-N. For a second only the name Laurin seemed to blaze upon the wet green wall. Then, as intimation of disaster to one of his family raced through Prince Paul's mind, the name dimmed and faded altogether. The sagging canvas of the wolf hunt tightened. All became as before, a plain green wall on which hung a gold-framed painting in oils.

Quickly he must find Laurin, for he knew that the heir to the Śczriny estates was not at home. Concealing his anxiety, Prince Paul sought out Laurin's mother in the music-room. From Countess Śczriny he learned that his nephew was in Warsaw, but that he was returning that evening. A coach had been sent to meet him at the house of friends about fifteen miles to the north. He had broken the tiresome journey from Warsaw by stopping to dine at Castle Bielāny. The Feast of the Pentecost, a three-day festival held each year at Bielāny, was in full swing. Many guests came and went at the castle. Laurin Śczriny would lay a wreath of myrtle and place a wax taper at the foot of the "Shrine for Travelers."

Even now, past eleven o'clock, he must be on his way to Śczriny.

No coach appeared that night. During the forenoon of the following day, word was brought to Śczriny that Count Laurin had been in an accident. Returning by the forest road, the horses of his coach had become frightened when suddenly sprung upon by hungry wolves, who searched continuously for food in the dry summer woods. The runaway horses had flung the coach against a tree, overturning it. In the wreckage Count Laurin had been found badly crushed. The coachman was dead and the young count was too badly hurt to move from the forester's cottage to which he had been taken.

Later in the day the heir to Śczriny died—so was fulfilled the curse of the mother of Count Stephan Śczriny's victim.

Within twelve years, the curse struck again. It was a hazy evening in late September when the little son of Count Laurin (who had been killed in the runaway coach) was returning through the park at Castle Śczriny with his nurse. Small Stephan was eight years old, and was to celebrate his birthday in a few days.

Passing the gates to the paddock enclosure, the nurse was alarmed to see the gates open, for she remembered hearing at lunch that a new stallion bought at Pörtöśk was kept in the paddock awaiting transfer to the farm, three miles away. She called to the boy to hurry, and they were just passing the open gate when, in a cloud of dust, slaver streaming from his mouth, the great red stallion galloped straight for the terrified woman and child. As he came to the spot where they crouched, he rose on his hind legs, pawed the air in rage and sprang upon the cringing woman who sheltered the little boy in her arms.

No one was about. The cries of the nurse went unheard as the wildly plunging horse savaged them both until they lay dead in pools of blood, torn beyond recognition by the powerful iron-shod hoofs. Snorting in the exaltation a maddened animal finds in the kill, the blood-flecked stallion raced across the park and away over the brow of the hill.

When a stable boy found the horrible remains of the nurse and the little Count Stephan, the sun was sinking beyond the hill over which the killer stallion had disappeared. Night came quickly over the tragic house. This was the story told by the mother of the dead boy:

She had gone to her bedroom after lunch to rest for a while. Then, as it neared teatime, she had ordered the special cakes that were so greatly enjoyed by her small son. Later, as Stephan and his nurse did not return, she had taken tea alone in a sitting room across the hall from the Green Salon, which, because of its sinister memories, was seldom used unless many guests were in the house. As she sat there, drinking her tea and looking down a ride of trees in the park, hoping to catch a glimpse of her child, she had felt a cold, damp wind play about her feet. A door must be open somewhere. But the day being warm, and it not yet late, how could the current of air be so tomb-like? An open door leading to the great wine cellars under the castle, perhaps. The countess had risen to investigate, when her eye was drawn to the room opposite where she had been sitting. There, in the Green Salon, the wall wept. Her knees seemed unable to support her weight. Cries froze in her throat. She seemed paralyzed, for all within Castle Sczriny knew what this lacy pattern of water descending the dull green walls presaged.

The countess tried to close her eyes so not to see the name that must inevitably appear. But she could not. Some power held her staring at the dripping wall. There—there it was. Slowly, letters so large they covered half the wall appeared: S-T-E-P-H-A-N. For a moment only, the word stood out clear and bold. Then down came the tears, obliterating the name of her little son. The countess wept, miserably, as she staggered through the hall towards the outer door.

It seemed ages before the distracted woman found anyone, for it was the harvest, and all except the house servants were in the fields. Finally, calling down an areaway, she drew the attention of a footman who came to her. More men were found and hastily dispatched to find Count Stephan and his nurse. It would almost have been better if they had never been found.

Many years later Moira Considine married Count Sczriny and went to Poland to live. The "Irish Countess," as she came to be called, fitted into life at Castle Sczriny with ease, as one fits a well-made glove to the hand. There has always been a similarity between the Poles and the Irish—their love of horses, freedom, and living in the country and their enjoyment of the sports and rich fruits of the land.

Two children were born to Moira and Alexander Sczriny, a boy and a girl. On the widely spreading estates of Sczriny-Oransky, the children grew up to be healthy, handsome complements to their parents' happy marriage.

The year that young Peter was fourteen and his sister Maria was ten, they accompanied their father and mother to Ireland to visit the Considine grandparents at Drumshambo. Neither of them had been to Ireland since they were babies and were eager to see their mother's rambling old house on the Lough Allen. She had told them much of the happy childhood that had been hers, running wild with the ponies and later with the big horses, and sailing a small red curragh of her own on the sparkling Lough.

She had rigged up a sail once, when her own could not be found in the boathouse. She had taken a white satin evening wrap belonging to Lady Barrymore, who was staying at Drumshambo. How beautiful it had looked, belling out in the stiff breeze! She had set her dolls in the stern and told them this was a royal barge and that only a Considine could manage satin sails. And then, that evening, the terrible hue and cry, the tat-a-ra-ra that had resulted, when the missing wrap was produced from the boathouse, sadly the worse for wear. Old Lady Barrymore had been very decent about it, but her father had whaled Moira properly. Her behind had been a very tender area for days.

Then, there were tales of hunting with the Tipperary and the Clonmel hounds, and the wonderful hunt balls, and the Dublin Horse Show, where she had had the grand fortune to meet their father.

Everyone and everything at Drumshambo looked exactly as they had pictured it, even to old Terry Bannery, the autocrat of the stable yard. He had ruled the roost at Drumshambo, lo, these many years, and had taught their mother to ride like a streak of lightning across the trappiest country and to take the great stone and sod banks in flying style. Terry was at the station in Ballyallen to greet them. This summer promised to be pure heaven for the two children.

The weeks sped on. Summer had proved even more satisfying than Peter and Maria Sczriny had hoped, if that were possible. In ten days now they must return to Poland. The count and countess were going to Paris with their grandmother a few days before; then their grandfather would take them to Paris later, where they would join their parents. The family would then return to Poland together.

Three days before the count and his wife were leaving for the Continent, it began to storm. A high wind whipped across the Lough, gaining in force as the second day set in, wild and wet.

The old house creaked and rumbled on its foundations and in every timber under the tiles. Grandfather Considine said that in a storm it always seemed to him more like being in an old hulk rounding the Horn than safe on land inside Drumshambo. "This old Ark," he called it.

For years repairs had been necessary at Drumshambo. The roof was noticeably unsafe. Squirrels had gnawed great gaps in the timber eaves that supported the heavy roof of the old Charles II wing. But life at Drumshambo followed the line of least resistance. One day, all needed repairs would be attended to. For the present, a new boat was needed on the Lough. Stone walls along the South meadows must be repaired to keep the Kerry cattle from straying. Let the roof leak for a while. The old wing was seldom used.

But it was in use now, for Countess Moira had chosen the huge bedroom with its sweeping view of Lough Allen and the Dowra Mountains, cradling the source of the River Shannon. Often as a child she had used this red and silver room, with its huge red-canopied bed, for a playroom. During this visit, she had installed the children in her old lavender and white room at the end of the passage, she and her husband occupying the room always referred to as "The Room With the View."

The storm continued unabated. The fury of the wind seemed to increase. Grandfather Considine made jokes about the old Ark, as the house wrenched at every blast of wind.

After dinner on the second day of this demented weather, Count Śczriny said the dampness had clutched at his throat all day. He would go to bed with camphor flannel wrapped around his throat, so that he would feel quite fit to start for Paris the next day.

Always after dinner, Peter and Maria joined their grandmother and grandfather in the library to listen to the stories of Gaelic deeds, ancient as the Mountains of Dowra, and as magic. Tonight, after making sure her husband was tucked comfortably in bed, their mother came in and sat on the hearth seat, her arm around Maria.

Just as Grandfather Considine was reaching the end of the story of Grain O'Malley, the wondrous pirate queen of the Isles, Peter Śczriny's arm shot out, pointing at the wall across from the fireplace where they were sitting. "Mother, look, the wall is wet. It looks like big tears. Mother, what is it?"

Every head turned. Then no one moved. No one spoke. In the tense stillness, the watchers saw a web of water spread across the gray wall. A large map of hunting coverts, insecurely tacked to the wall, bulged with moisture, sagged, and fell with a plop to the floor.

Then, slowly, inexorably, the unseen finger wrote the letters A-L-E-X-A-N-D-E-R. "Alexander," Peter spelled out the word. "Alexander," Maria repeated it. These two unhappy children saw the written but quickly obliterated name of their father, for they had Śczriny blood fused with that of Considine. To them the name stood out bold and bright.

The three others, being Considines, saw the writing only dimly through the moisture that stained the gray painted wall as it wept.

The full import of what this meant spread slowly in the mind of the countess. She sprang up from the bench where she had been sitting. "This is impossible," she cried. "Alex is not away from home, he is asleep upstairs. It always happens to a Śczriny who is away from his house. He is safe, safe," and she ran out of the room and started to mount the stairs.

A gigantic blast of wind struck the embattled old house of Drumshambo amidships, followed immediately by a crash of rending wood. The impact of wind and the crash above almost floored the five persons trying to crowd past each other on the stairs. Young Peter reached the door of the Red Chamber first. He threw open the door. Behind him grouped his mother and sister and his grandparents. The sight they saw was almost too heartbreaking to bear. Long-neglected old stonework had not withstood the impact of Atlantic gales of the past two days. A massive chimney, built when Charles Stuart ruled England, had crashed down, carrying the rotting timbers and broken tiles of the roof with it. Down it had hurtled through ceiling and bed canopy, crushing the life out of Count Alexander Śczriny, who lay half buried under soaking timbers and rubble. Through the gaping hole in the roof, storm clouds ripped away from a wan moon; the storm was over.

A few days later, a long letter arrived from Poland. The mother of little Stephan, the child who had been savaged by a stallion many years ago, now lived at Castle Śczriny, a very old woman, nearing ninety.

In this letter, the old countess told how she had been sitting in the room across from the Green Salon on the night of the fatal storm on Lough Allen, the same room in which she had taken tea that afternoon, so many years ago, when, looking up from her embroidery, she had seen the wall weep, and, horrified, had watched the finger write the name of her adored small son, Stephan.

This time the wall in the Green Salon had run dark with water, and for twenty minutes the cascades slanted and wavered as if blown by a high wind. The name Alexander appeared for an instant, then faded away in tears. It had seemed odd to her, she remembered, that, although her eyesight was impaired by her great age, the writing on the wall appeared crystal clear.

Later, when notes were compared, it was found the wall at Castle Śczriny wept at nine minutes past ten o'clock, the wall at Drumshambo, at ten o'clock.

Count Peter Śczriny somehow escaped the curse, but it struck again in 1940 when his nineteen-year-old son Count Casimir Śczriny was killed in an airplane accident in the Carpathian Mountains.

This time, the walls at both Castle Śczriny and Drumshambo wept the night before the accident. Since Castle Śczriny was then a headquarters for a field marshal of the Third Reich, those who saw the wall weep did not see the name appear upon it.

At Drumshambo, an elderly man lay crippled by age in an upper chamber. Only servants saw the wall weep. A dampness rose up from the floor, quenching the fire in the grate and causing a smudge to drift through the house. No name was seen.

As recently as 1943 the gray wall in the shuttered library at Drumshambo dripped tears, for a much longer time than ever before, it is said, and a dampness pervaded the room for days. As no word of any kind has been heard from a member of the Śczriny-Oransky family since the end of World War II, it is not known where the curse of Śczriny struck.

The Bridal Barge of Aran Roe

Sligo Rock

COUNTY SLIGO

SLIGO ROCK

The Bridal Barge of Aran Roe

CROSSING THE ATLANTIC BETWEEN NEW York and Galway in the late spring of 1932, I was standing at the rail of the steamer a little after dawn on the morning of the day we were to arrive at Galway. A fine, brilliant morning it was, I remember, the ocean in a calmer frame of mind than is usual along this North Atlantic sea lane.

At the first crack of sunrise, I had come up to the top deck, for we were just passing the Headland of Mallin More in County Donegal. Ireland spread its burning green mountains on our left, and I had a very special reason for my early vigil. The night before, as we were off Rathlin Island Light, which guards the northeast extremity of Ireland, I had seen, moving silently along the starlit horizon, slightly ahead of our own ship, a ghostly escort—the Bridal Barge of Aran Roe.

This was the third time I had seen the ghostly barge. Once before, during a mid-winter crossing, the cold clear night had seemed to open its indigo portals and in almost the same place, near Rathlin Light, the Bridal Barge had appeared, pursued its unhurried way slightly ahead of my ship, and disappeared again into the night, leaving no wake.

Always at night I had seen the Barge, for the second time was a night in August. A full moon bathed all Clew Bay in Connaught in luminous light. Suddenly I stood spellbound, for into my line of vision, about a mile out to sea, sped the dazzling gold and red of the Bridal Barge. For only a moment, the moon pointed up the gilded shields on the prow and turned into fiery streamers the crimson pall flung across the bier high upon the stern; then, silently gliding into the middle-mist whence it had come, the phantom ship passed into the night.

Many people tell of having seen the Bridal Barge in full daylight. Fishermen gathering their catch off the rocks of Erris Head and Inishmurray say the Barge sometimes looms out of the sea spray or early morning mist, so close that it seems almost to scrape the sides of their small fishing curraghs; so close that the gaping fishermen clearly see the set faces of the fifty golden warriors who forever guard the corpse of Aran Roe.

Realizing the morning was ripening into breakfast time, and since I'd seen no sign of the Barge on either side of the ship, I started down to have coffee. Standing at the inshore rail on the deck below was a man who turned as he heard my footsteps on the companionway and came towards me. "Mr. Reynolds, let me introduce myself," he said. "I am Charles Tyrell, professor of history at Notre Dame. I am on sabbatical year. Mostly I shall be at Trinity College doing research on Gaelic legends. I wonder if you would answer a question for me." He paused, seemed undecided, then smiled, "Well, here goes. Did you ever hear of the Bridal Barge of Aran Roe?"

I looked at the man for a moment; then, without batting an eyelash, replied, "But of course. I saw the Barge last night off Rathlin Light."

For a moment the professor looked around, up and down the deck, out to sea, bewildered. Sitting down on the foot-rest of an open deck chair he said, "So it's true. I saw it as well, last night, all red and gold, just the way I had heard about it. I've been told I'd see plenty of ghosts in Ireland; now, even before I set foot on the sod, I see the phantom Barge of Aran Roe."

Here, I realized, was a perfect listener, and, what was even better, a believer. I suggested we ring for a steward, order breakfast brought us there on deck, drink our coffee slowly in the freshness of the lovely morning, and then I would tell him the story of Aran Roe.

Sometime in the early part of the eleventh century there lived on Rathlin Island, an expanse of craggy, barren rock off the Antrim coast, a young warrior prince. Men called him Aran Roe, Aran of the Red Hood, partly because of the scarlet hood of heavy wool which Aran wore thrown back from his brow, but more, perhaps, because of the dark red of his long hair, worn, as was the manner of the time, hanging to his shoulder blades in a thick mane. In front it was cut across in a line with his eyebrows.

The people of Rathlin were vastly proud of their handsome young prince, for he was fearless in battle, could sail a ship unfalteringly among the perilous channels along the coast, which only Rathlin men knew, and was of happy disposition into the bargain. The day he became king would be a fine, wide day.

At this time Arghan, King of Rathlin Island, was nearing the end of his coil. He sat the day's length in front of a roaring fire, for his bones were always cold. Wasted and brooding, he pondered upon his long reign, a masterpiece of ill-fortune. It would not be long before the Old Woman of Gonn would beckon to the king. Then young Aran Roe would take the helm and Rathlin would again prosper.

In a measure the wish of the Rathlin men came to pass. One wild night, surely, the Old Gray Woman of Gonn rode into the bedchamber of King Arghan and flew away with him on her back.

The next morning the day broke bright and clear. Arghan's death was discovered. Aran Roe donned his scarlet-hooded cape and fastened it on one shoulder with a heavy gold and bronze lanula. He put studded bands of gold upon his arms. Grasping the great Sword of Rathlin in his right hand and a square shield of gilded oxhide in his left, he strode through the halls of Castle Roe.

In the wide courtyard before the Sea-Wall Gate, Aran was proclaimed King of Rathlin. Every man on the island cheered until his throat cracked.

On the day the men of Rathlin Island were cracking their throats with joy over the young king, a barge with twenty-four oars was setting out from Sligo Bay. It was the marriage barge of Mourne O'Glanney, one of the most beautiful and powerful women in the West of Ireland. The O'Glanny were an ancient clan, even in 1115. Soldiers of fortune, they had pirated most of their wealth, raiding lonely castles along the coasts of Ireland and Scotland and plundering Spanish merchantmen. The O'Glanny coffers had been greatly swelled by the dowry brought to Nial O'Glanny by a rich woman from the Glen of Mourne in County Down. This probably explains the first name given to Nial's daughter, Mourne.

A year before this story opens, the Battle of Clontarf had taken place, the great battle in which Brian Boru drove the Danes out of the South of Ireland. O'Glannys appeared in great array at the Battle of Clontarf, and with their spoils they next appear as lords of Sligo Rock in County Sligo. Just why Sligo Rock continued for centuries to arouse men's greed remains a mystery. A vast, ungainly barracks of a house, it has never had a shred of architectural elegance, and is not impregnable, for it has changed hands, time out of mind.

Sligo Rock dominates a formidable seacoast position and overlooks a fine small harbor. Its iron-spiked walls and steep stone staircases have run with so much blood, down the centuries, it is small wonder that, like ancient Castle Swords at the mouth of the Liffey River in County Dublin, it reeks of treachery. Its walls exude a stench of dried and clotted blood of saint and sinner alike.

From this perfidious house set out Mourne O'Glanny in her wedding barge, painted purple, green, and gold, loaded with wines, spices, richly dyed stuffs, beaten gold gorgets, and sharp bronze spearheads. The finest gift of all, she thought, were bales of softly tanned hides, to wear under armor, and thick animal skins, shaggy with warm fur, for cold stone Antrim floors.

In Ireland in the days of Aran Roe and Mourne O'Glanny, marriage customs were as rigid as they were flamboyant. Every move made by the man and woman, once they were betrothed, was according to tradition. Woe to the one who broke it.

The ceremony of the Bridal Barge took months, even years, of preparation.

ARAN·ROE
THE BRIDAL BARGE

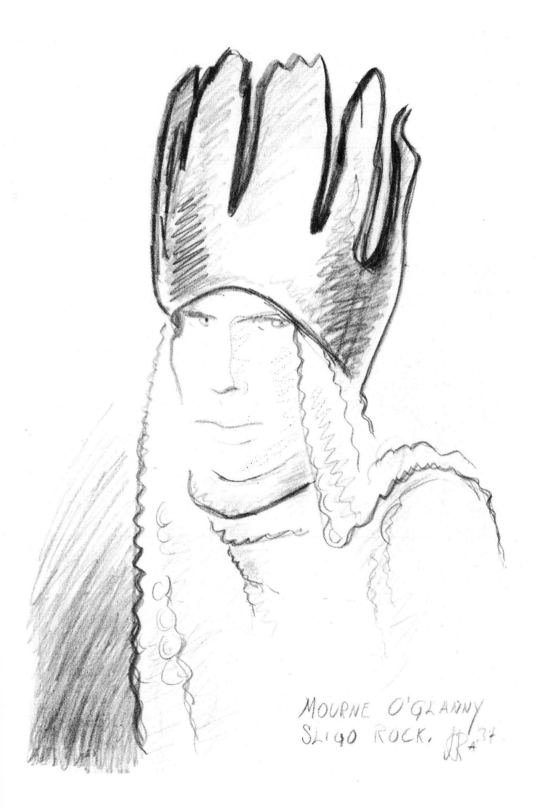

MOURNE O'GLANNY
SLIGO ROCK. JR.37.

In eleventh-century Ireland the procedure ran thus. The betrothed woman loaded a barge with her household gear, as well as with splendid presents for her future husband and his family. Naturally this display must be as fine as she could afford. On an appointed day the woman set out from a point of her own choosing. Half way to the place where her future husband lived, her barge was to halt and await his arrival in a magnificent ship with an imposing display of men-at-arms. The woman joined him at this stage. They then returned to his castle, her well-laden barge following behind. These barges were carved and painted in brilliant colors. Ancient Gaelic runes were embroidered on ribbon-like banners which streamed out behind. Manned by twenty to forty oars, these craft attained a fair speed and moved over the water silently. A high platform was erected in the stern and richly colored cloths were flung over it. Couches were arranged on the dais. Bards and minstrels grouped themselves about the deck. Lutes and harps made music. It was a veritable *Tristan und Isolde* tableau.

For two days, through cool, golden weather, the purple barge of Mourne O'Glanny noiselessly split the waves in the direction of Rathlin Island. It had been arranged that Aran Roe should proceed from his castle to Dunaff Head, put in at the walled village of Dunaff, and await Mourne O'Glanny at Ballyliffin Castle in Donegal.

Three days out on her journey, when they were off Dungloe, Mourne awoke to broad daylight and a clamor. Voices rose in confusion in the prow of the barge. Looking away over the sea Mourne saw small, swift sailing curraghs, the kind that have red latteen sails and dart among the rocky inlets of County Antrim. When she asked what this was all about, a page boy ran toward her. She hastily took the rolled parchment from his hand and, spreading it on the broad handrail, she read:

> *Fair Mourne O'Glanny—*
> *Come no further towards Ballyliffin.*
> *Turn and make with all speed to Sligo*
> *Rock. The O'Flaherty are abroad again,*
> *pillaging the North Coast. In a battle*
> *on the mainland at Dunluce Castle I*
> *was wounded. Soon I will come to Sligo.*
> *Aran Roe*

Springing from warrior stock, Mourne first thought to continue on her journey. If she encountered the Black O'Flaherty she would engage them. She had hundreds of spears and small arms in the barge, and thirty men-at-arms. When her mind calmed, she realized it would be useless. She could never overcome the O'Flaherty with her small force. Sadly, and in black anger at this bitter turn of fate, she ordered the barge turned round. As the sun sank in a riot of flaming clouds behind the Bloody Foreland, her oarsmen pulled all out for the protection of Sligo Rock.

Day after day and far into the nights, Mourne O'Glanny paced the spray-wet stones on the battlements of Sligo Rock. Always her eyes searched the miles of dun-gray Atlantic for some sign of Aran Roe. No messenger had come, either by sea or land. It was autumn now; high winds prevailed, and storms attacked the coast, scattering driftwood and cordage from wrecked ships along the beaches.

After waiting for weeks, with no word, Mourne had sent couriers by inland roads and secret goat tracks to try and find what was happening in the North. Two couriers never returned; a third was sent back to Sligo Rock, mutilated and gibbering, the O'Flaherty cattle brand of a black spearhead burned into his cheek.

As months strung out, and no word came, Mourne O'Glanny became desperate with anxiety. When finally snatches of news came to her lonely house, it was bad news, surely.

The O'Flaherty had sacked the Castles of Dunluce, Armoy, and Carnlough. O'Flaherty himself, with his savage men-at-arms, had holed up for the winter in a glen in County Down, near the smoking ruins of Portglenone. Still no news of Aran Roe.

The long winter dragged on, a winter of iron cold. Few men walked the roads and no ships were seen in the bay. Even the gulls were frozen stiff on the pinnacles of Renvyle. Mostly, during these drear days, Mourne O'Glanny sat huddled in a cloak before a leaping fire. Flames and sparks roared up the flues; her thoughts soared with them, speeding on to Castle Roe.

One night Mourne O'Glanny barred the doors of The Rock, as the fishermen thereabouts called the castle, took a flaming oak-knot from the banked fire, and mounted the stairs to her chamber. She had chosen this room, bitterly cold as it was, because from its one great window she could look away to Rathlin Island, hidden behind the Dunamanagh Mountains. She lay staring into the shadowed vaultings of the room for a while, then fitfully she slept. Often during the night the clash of wind wakened her, the sound of bumping, and the drag of chains rasping against rock. "Wreckage," she murmured to the night, and sank into sleep. Before dawn, she wakened sharply and rose from her bed. That bumping again. Pulling aside an oxhide curtain which hung across a window in the wall facing the sea, she looked down. Dawn had not cracked yet. In the foggy darkness she saw a storm-driven hulk, with lines of chains dragging away from it, bumping against the ramp of Sligo Rock. Some hapless ship sucked in by the strong currents. Well, when morning came the men-at-arms could deal with it.

When morning came there was more than a hapless ship to deal with. After a disturbed night, Mourne slept soundly. She stirred, slowly wakened, hearing the sound of clamor, just like that morning last summer when her wedding barge lay off Dungloe and a messenger from Aran Roe had come aboard. This time the clamor seemed more intense, with loud shouting and the sound of many running feet. As she lay listening, there were hurrying feet on the stairs and in the passage, and then the door was flung wide. Garda, her serving woman, stood there, her eyes wide with fear, one hand clutching her mouth to stifle tearing sobs.

Mourne O'Glanny leaped from her bed, flung a cloak across her shoulders. "Garda!" she cried. "What is it—where?" Garda only moaned, pointing outside towards the sea, "Aran Roe—Aran Roe."

Mourne O'Glanny stood motionless on the top step of the water gate, looking down. Thud, thud, bump, bump, in the ebb and flow of the ocean swell, this she had heard all night, a broken barge dragging seaweed-crusted chains.

Servants and men-at-arms crowded below her on the steps and looked hard at Mourne O'Glanny. Not a sound came from their lips. They watched to see what she would do.

Tall, she seemed, in her dark red cloak, lifted like wings in the morning wind. Tall, straight, and very fair. Tawny, the bards called her, with golden eyes. Some said she was more beautiful than Maeve. Who could tell? Mourne of the Fair Girdle. Her body was as a young tree in a wood, round and sweet with sap.

Mourne O'Glanny came to the landing stage. Alone she stepped aboard the barge and walked to the shattered dais where, bound round and round with heavy chains that cut cruelly into his flesh, lay the naked body of Aran Roe. Between his empty eyesockets and on his broad breast, burned black and deep, was the spearhead brand of O'Flaherty. Plundered bridal chests lay heaped in the prow, and the red hooded cloak by which all men knew Aran Roe lay soaked in blood across his mangled feet.

Mourne O'Glanny, with a face as bleak as the Rocks of Moher, walked twice round the ship. Blood, blood everywhere. Each chain ended in the drowned body of a man, Aran Roe's guard of honor numbering fifty men. Fifty chains, fifty men. Standing in the center of the barge Mourne O'Glanny called to her men-at-arms. "Wrap the body of Aran Roe in my cloak, bear him gently to my house, follow me."

For seven days Mourne O'Glanny kept silent vigil at the bier of Aran Roe. Washed and anointed with the oil of olive from Spain, rubbed dry with pungent herbs found in the glens of Finncairn, she wrapped him in a cloak of scarlet wool cut in full circle. She had dyed the wool and fashioned the cloak herself for their wedding day. Now she drew the hood well down to hide the despicable spearhead brand. The barge she had had repaired, well caulked, and painted scarlet, with white antlers at the prow, the device of Arghan, the name of his house.

Then with much ceremony did Mourne O'Glanny prepare what she had to do. The fifty Rathlin men who were slain with Aran Roe and bound in chains to the gunwales of his ship were wrapped in shrouds of heavy linen, only their faces exposed. An old Warn Woman from out beyond the Kyles of Rah in Mayo mixed a brew. This mixture was rubbed upon the faces of the fifty Rathlin men, and on the face and body of Aran Roe. Then they were gilded with the dust of mountain gold. Nor time nor weather would destroy their look of youth. Age or decay would touch them never.

When this was done, Mourne O'Glanny opened her bridal chests; forth she drew bolts of cloth and mantles, red and gold and white damask, threaded through with copper, gold, and yellow. These she threw across the dais high in the stern of the barge. On this dais, wrapped in his bridal cloak, was laid the body of Aran Roe. A bronze shield and the great sword of the O'Glanny were placed upon his breast, flagons of spiced wine, oaten bread, and fruits piled at his feet. The fifty gilded Rathlin men were bound upright in the prow, holding their spears at ease. They would gaze always to the chosen course, would guard forever Aran Roe.

When all was ready, Mourne O'Glanny called to her servants and her men-at-arms: "Fetch to the battlements of the castle bundles of wood and dry rushes; erect there a bier, cover it with the purple mantle in my marriage chest, then wait upon my orders. When the new moon shows in the sky tonight, I will light my bridegroom on his way, for Aran Roe starts out upon a journey—a journey that will never end."

Dark descended. The new moon appeared, a pale saffron crescent in the sky. As the moon appeared, so came Mourne O'Glanny from her chamber, robed for her Viking funeral. Tawny hair hung in ropes, crossed with beaten gold and copper. On her brow sat a wide crown fashioned of golden alder leaves and flying birds. Beneath her purple mantle showed a habit of emerald damask heavily sewn in gold and copper threads. Many chains of carnelian, green matrix, and the ruby called "pigeon's blood" swung from her white throat. Her arms were circled with jeweled golden bands. All about Mourne O'Glanny gleamed, save her eyes. Her eyes were dull.

Unhurried, Mourne O'Glanny walked to the parapet. Looking down, she called, "Cut the ropes, send forth my bridegroom's barge." Mounting the dais, Mourne O'Glanny took a cup filled with wine which stood upon the last step. Holding it high, she drank, long and deeply. For a few moments she watched the scarlet barge ride out

33

of the bay, breast the little phosphorescent waves, shudder slightly as it passed the sand bar, then take gracefully to the open sea.

Mourne O'Glanny raised high her cup of wine, hurled it far out. It hung suspended for a moment like the moon, then fell into the bay. "A portent to you, Aran Roe! Sail ever through the years, a symbol of my everlasting love, and to the Black O'Flaherty the curses of all women ring with mine, the women you have robbed of all they love."

Mourne O'Glanny paused. The strongly poisoned wine would soon rob her of speech. Looking down at the weeping women and the somber men, she said, "Light the pyre. I am ready. And go you far from here." Lying down upon the bier, she closed her eyes.

It is doubtful if the O'Flaherty suffered greatly, if at all, from Mourne O'Glanny's curse. Individually they were forever reviled, but the accumulated blanket of curses may easily have helped in the downfall of the tribe. It is a fact that soon after this occurrence (the massacre of Aran Roe and his men in 1115) the O'Flaherty black star plunged hellward in rapid flight. The Tribe O'Scanlon overcame them at the battle of the Lifford Glen, and in 1203 they were routed at Connellan Castle by the Tribe O'Haggerty and fled to the Lakes of Menlo. Today their last stronghold, Castle Blake on the river Corrib in County Galway, is a ruin, and has been for two hundred years. Visit the ruin of Blake on a moonlight night, a "soft" Galway night; it has a brand of magic I have never encountered elsewhere, the haunted beauty of the lost and damned.

Any attempt to recount the various hauntings accredited to gaunt old Sligo Rock would be nearly endless. Down its long and bloody history legends have clung to its wall thick as barnacles on a tramper's hull. Shrieks and moans of torture are often heard, the crashing of chains and the sound of men in combat, and pools of blood eternally drip down the stone stairs. There is a tale told in the pubs in Portacloy, in County Sligo, of a sailor who once appeared at the fishing village of Kilglass, near The Rock. He said he was of the Tribe O'Flaherty and would sleep in his own castle "the night." He did. For months thereafter a half demented man coursed up and down the roads, from village to village. Always he was run out of whatever clutch of houses he entered; for the night the man had slept at Sligo Rock he had fallen in the slippery pool of blood on the stairs. He bore a great spot of this blood on the side of his face in the rough shape of a spearhead. At last, no longer able to endure the shame of this flaming brand, which no rubbing or washing could erase, the sailor drowned himself off the breakwater at Portacloy.

When Mourne O'Glanny set the gilded body of Aran Roe adrift in his scarlet

Bridal Barge, a timeless argosy, a symbol of their deathless love, she set the torch to a pyre high among the battlements of her castle and was burned to ashes. People say that often on calm nights spirals of blue-gray smoke swirl upward from the ramparts of The Rock as if to signal the ghostly barge. After this smoke is seen, sometime during the night, a fisherman hauling in his nets, the captain of a transatlantic liner, or a woman walking along the Sea Wall Road will watch in silent wonder, for on the horizon, seeming to skim the surface of the sea, lonely and serene, sails the gleaming Bridal Barge of Aran Roe.

Mickey Filler
and the Tansey Wreath

COUNTY CLARE

WHITE-HOODED WOMAN OF BALINASLOE

Mickey Filler
and the Tansey Wreath

Nor poppy, nor Mandragora,
Nor all the drowsy syrups of the world,
Shall ever medicine thee to that sweet sleep,
Which thou owedst yesterday.
Shakespeare (Othello)

A MAN, AND HE WALKING THE ROADS FROM Derrybrien to Crataloe in the County Clare, might easily, on a summer day, seek the dense green shade of the ash and alder trees which surround a small woodland pool midway between the villages.

A clutch of coteens near this pool is called Cloonara. In the smallest of the whitewashed houses lived Bridget Ruane and her grandson, Mickey Filler.

Around this shaded pool there hovers a kind of spell. It seems a plot of ground, "all the world away," a fragment of the forest of Arcadia. It is a perfect setting for the awakening of Bottom in *A Midsummer Night's Dream*. Peaseblossom and Mustardseed cannot be far away. Cloonara Water, as the place is known, is the spot where Mickey Filler, the young country boy, whose mind was "away," built his house and made his curious bed.

Mickey Filler was a more gentle, certainly a more vague version of Puck. When he built his house on the edge of woodland water, yet near a frequented road, he felt he was safely hidden, but could still watch the passing of the world. Mickey constructed his house by bending great fronds of fern leaves, arching them, one towards the other, until they formed a green canopy above his bed. This bed was Mickey's pride. It was his "heart's heart." Sheaves of yellow gorse and bracken, purple and rusty-pink, formed the springy mattress of this bed. Over the gorse he spread long stalks of foxglove, whose bells of wine and lavender were spattered with points of brown and deep red, the like of a thrush's egg.

Around this bed, which was always brightly glowing when the sun latticed

39

through the fern fronds, Mickey scattered the herbs he loved so well. His grand-mother had taught him when he was only a small child to recognize all the herbs which grew so abundantly and in so many varieties in the bohireens and meadows of County Clare.

After a long day spent by Mickey Filler rambling through the fields and shady places near Kilmurry, he would return with his arms full of herbs, even his pockets bulging with bunches of the deep green camomile ("the father of all simples," says the Clare herbalist, giving the herb its Gaelic name, *Athair-Talav*), primrose-root (*Bainne-Bo-Blathan*), the sweet-sharp, wild parsnip (*Meacon Buidhe*) and the pungent tansey. But most of all Mickey loved to gather the sleep-conducive mandragora (*Doriha-Thu*). When a mandrake is pulled from the ground, it shrieks in protest. This made the finding of a mandragora, or mandrake bed, exciting. Then too, the plant always fascinated Mickey because the forked root resembles a human body. Wreaths were woven of mixed tansey and mandrake, the tansey's rich, dark green and the red of the mandrake stems worked into a lovely wreath.

Mickey took these into Cloonara and Derrybrien, where he sold them for a penny each. His way of peddling his wares was very much his own. He would knock on the door of a well-cared-for cottage. (In the small coteens a penny was as much as a pound to the poor dwellers.) When the woman of the house opened the door, Mickey would bow gravely and say, "To all within, God's Peace. If ye've a pain in the head, or yer eyes are tardy in closing, come the night, put on this tansey wreath and lay flat on yer back and sleep 'ull lay down beside ye."

In all the countryside, even into the counties of Cork, Tipperary, and Kerry, the name of Bridget Ruane was a household word. The miracles of healing performed by Bridget were well known by all the poor and hapless. The priest in Corbytara, just over the Tipperary border, was Father Dumany. He said, "Bridgie Ruane is assured of a front seat in the ultimate heavenly company, if the people of this diocese, including the Bishop and myself, have anything to say about it."

The children roundabout did not call Mickey's grandmother by her right name; they called her Biddy Early. She would say to them, "If ye want to go with me huntin' simples and leafy plasters, ye'll have ta be up with the lark, fer I'm off and away before he's stopped his mornin' song."

One of the tales told of Biddy Early's skill is of the time when Timmy Rally fell into a pot of water after a potato boiling. She said, "There was Timmy, the skin near scalded off him. Red as a cockscomb from head to foot. I'd primrose-root and cardamon jelly bound on 'im, till he'd the look av a mummy found in Egypt. Well, he's alive this day, the father av tin childer."

Another time, Biddy related, "John-Thomas Mahon was dyin' and him a man in his prime, no later. But from drudgin' in thim peat bogs his heart was worn to a silk thread. I cured 'im with oceans of loose-strife and camomile tea, with a plaster on his heart of widow's wort. Glory be ta God, if he's not the strength av a Tyrone ox on 'im this livin' minute."

Yes, the cures of herbs and simples are greatly thought on, in the County of Clare, and Bridget Ruane was their high priestess.

When Mickey Filler was fourteen years old, the potato famine rode cruel and roughshod over the people in the southwest of Ireland. This particular famine of 1881 was not as widespread nor as devastating as many others have been; however, many died. A class of dry mold, poisonous in itself, blighted the potato crop and spread even to the livestock if they ate contaminated grass.

During these wretched days, Mickey seemed to live an enchanted life. His little house near the woodland pool was as ripely green as ever, and his bed was heaped with mandrake and wild verbena. One day a small child, a girl from Cloonara, was out looking for some kind of berries to ease the terrible hunger that continuously clutched her belly these days. She wandered into the circle of Mickey's house and, worn-out with weakness, lay down on his bed of herbs and fell asleep. Either the child fell on her face from sheer exhaustion or during her troubled sleep she rolled over and buried her face in the mandrake and verbena. No one knows. When Mickey Filler returned late in the afternoon from a prowl in the fields, he found the little girl asleep. Or so he thought. But the child was not asleep. She was dead, suffocated in her sleep by the strong fumes of the crushed mandrake in her nostrils. The mandragora of the ancient Greeks had worked fearfully.

Mickey was not in the least frightened. He turned the child over on her back. She was pretty, he thought, like a doll in the window of Miss Bunora's shop in Kilmurry. Yellow hair and staring, sky-blue eyes. Mickey sat a long time gazing at the dead girl. Then he carried her small, stiff body into the bracken. There he dug a hole with a shard of rock. In the hole which he lined with ferns he laid the small corpse. Over this Mickey strewed earth and bracken. No one would know a grave was there. He would keep her for his secret.

The small village of Cloonara was hard hit by the famine. Many villagers wandered afield in search of food and never returned. In some remote place they died either of hunger or exposure, many times of both. People became numb to this sort of thing. There was no hue and cry after the disappearance of a child from Cloonara. Many had wandered away.

A few weeks later, as Mickey was sitting in front of his house, he noticed a child, about eight years old, walking along the road which ran close to the savannah of ash trees surrounding his house. Mickey picked up the shepherd's pipes he had fashioned from a handful of hollow marsh reeds. Upon the pipes he played a tune, of great simplicity, probably very like the tune heard by Chloë which caused her to turn her head and first see Daphnis. The child stopped and looked across the fern-edged water. Mickey rose and went over to the little girl. He took her hand and said, "I have potatoes roasting in my peat oven. Are you hungry?" The child nodded her head and great tears hung out of her eyes. After the little girl had eaten as many of the hot, roast potatoes as she could hold, she became dizzy. Long days of starvation caused her stomach to rebel at so bountiful a meal. Mickey told the child to lie down on his bed. Soon she was asleep. He thought to himself, "A black-haired doll, this one." Mickey went out and sat beside an ash tree facing his house of ferns. He watched to see no harm came to the sleeping girl and played very softly on his pipes.

The autumn season was close at hand and Mickey Filler felt a gust of cold, evening wind blow across his shoulders. He shivered. Winter would soon be here. He hated winter, for then there were no ferns, and the golden gorse was golden no longer, and the scraggy black branches rattled in the wind. Mickey never came to this glade in the winter. He got to his feet and, walking stealthily, like a creature of the woods, he looked at the sleeping child. He was afraid she would be cold. He was mortal cold himself. He went to the forked stick where he hung the tansey wreaths he had woven that day. These he had planned to peddle in the High Street of Kilmurry on the morrow. Carefully, Mickey selected two of the finest. Each had a little plume of mandrake leaves at the front. Kneeling beside the little girl, he lifted her head and placed one of the tansey wreaths far down on her pale forehead. With the other wreath he encircled his own brow. Mickey gathered big armfuls of tansey, verbena, and mandrake, which he kept in a pile near the door of his house. He lay down beside the sleeping child and piled the herbs upon them, the like of a coverlet. Mickey lay on his back for a time until he was done with shivering. High in the green-blue sky which gleamed through the ferns he saw a cloud of black rooks wheel noisily overhead. Becoming suddenly drowsy, Mickey pulled the tansey higher about his chin. He put his arms around the dark-haired little girl's shoulders. Soon, lulled by the overpowering herbs, Mickey Filler slept.

Mandragora, Mandragora, how deeply will I sleep?
Pindar.

A man out shooting rooks (which many were reduced to eating in those days of famine, be they never so sour and tough) found Mickey and the unknown little girl. They were still lying in each other's arms, quite cold and stiff.

Today, people passing near Cloonara Water tell of hearing the shrill music of a shepherd's pipes. Usually this is at dusk, though some have heard it late in the evening when all is dark in the savannah of trees. If one is curious and looks closely, he sees Mickey Filler in his battered little gaumeen hat and ragged breeches. He'll be sitting in front of a stand of tall ferns, playing his reed pipes. Weaving in and out among the foxgloves will be two little girls who dance buoyantly, as if their feet scorned the grassy turf. The hair of one dancer is golden fair. That of the other is raven black. Encircling the head of each child is a wreath of tansey.

The Headless Rider of
Castle Sheela

COUNTY LIMERICK

The Headless Rider
of Castle Sheela

COLOR IS A MAGIC QUALITY IN THIS WORLD.
Color takes many forms. There is the color spectrum. There is the aura
of color surrounding a given person or place. The name of a family is
often synonymous with colorful and exciting happenings in a house or
locality. This is very true in the case of the "Marvelous Mallorys" of
Castle Sheela. The family of Mallory, once Mael-ora, is large. Its ramifications are
formidable and far flung. The term "marvelous" is in effect a title. It might almost have
been conferred by some monarch of a realm. Instead it is bestowed by all sorts of people,
mostly with awe, now and again with jealousy, even with hate, as this story will
bear out.

The village of Galtymore is near the demesne gates of Castle Sheela. The post
intended for the Mallorys is sorted and dropped into "the Castle bag" by old Mrs.
Carmody, the postmistress. It is she who best applies the word "marvelous" to the
Mallorys. One day, holding at arm's length a rose-colored, crested envelope, covered
with foreign stamps, postmarks, and forwarding addresses, the captivated Mrs. Carmody said, "Great marvels happen in the lives of all those Mallorys. Half the time
they're walkin' the world, and the rest of the time they receive letters from it." Hitch-
ing her square-cut spectacles a shade higher, she continued, "They get letters from
kings and potentates. In me mother's day, old Lady Mallory'd a letter from the Pope
in Rome."

Mrs. Carmody seems to have capped the issue squarely. Marvels follow some
people, to color their lives, as ill-luck trails the less fortunate.

To Mrs. Carmody I am enormously indebted in more ways than I can name.
During my gathering of notes for this story, she answered a thousand questions,
answered them with authority and great good humor, a wide smile or a tch-tch-tch,
as she thought proper to the mood. Her wit is expansive, crisp, and boundless. Color
and graciousness enfold this Irish countrywoman, the like of a richly embroidered
cloak.

47

With the early Mallorys we are not concerned in this narrative. The family flourished early on, in Irish history, and stems from antiquity. As an old man of the roads once told me when I asked him where a certain family had come from, "Arragh, yer honor, nobody rightly knows the time. They rose out of a pile of stones, back and beyond in Fermanagh." The first Gaelic castle was a low, square pile of stones. The County Fermanagh is the antique cradle of many Gaelic families. With the exception of Turlough Mael-ora, who fought the Danes at the Battle of Clontarf in 1100, there is no early hero. The Mallorys have shone mostly under two crowns, which they adjusted on their handsome heads at will—sports and society.

In 1722, Brendan Mallory built a huge square house in the shadow of a half-ruined tower which had been built originally by Turlough Mael-ora to quarter his men and horses during the Battle of Clontarf. Later it was made habitable, and various members of the family lived there. One was an abbott; Brother Constantine he called himself. This Mallory abbott was a man of great piety, and it is said he founded an order of monks who lived in the tower for years. After he died and the present Castle Sheela was built, his forbidding presence was still felt. The gaunt, ivy-hung tower points a finger skyward and a shadow across the façade of Castle Sheela, as if to remind the gay, heedless, riotously living Mallorys that frivolity has no lasting substance, is but a pitfall for the soul. It is as if the old abbott continuously reminds his relatives that a seat in the Kingdom of Heaven awaits them, but only by the skin of their teeth will they make it.

In the vicinity of Galtymore—indeed, as far afield as Waterford, Cork, and Dublin —if one so much as mentions the name Mallory, some listener is bound to look up and ask sharply, "The Mallorys? Which one? What have they done now?"

The family reached its peak of brilliant showmanship during the century between 1740 and 1850. During that period two of the male Mallorys contracted marriages with European women. These alliances brought Latin and Tartar-Hungarian blood into the family, thereby adding a veritable rainbow of color to the already dazzling color chart of the Irish Mallorys.

In 1739, Galty Mallory, the eldest son and heir to Castle Sheela, made the Grand Tour on the Continent. At that time Budapest was, to most European travelers, like a city on another planet. Travel over tortuous, brigand-infested mountain passes was a thing only the most daring and hardy man would attempt. The heavy spring and autumn rains in that part of the continent made long coach journeys unthinkable for three-fourths of the year. Budapest, therefore, sat in red, gold, and white barbaric splendor on the banks of the swiftly flowing Danube, brushing herself free from Turkish occupation, which she had endured for many years, without losing a sliver of her unique quality. Spread out behind Budapest, the like of a fabulously long train, billowed the Puszta, a vast, flat, mirage-haunted plain.

Galty Mallory decided he wanted to visit this storied city of the Magyars. No roads of this world held any fears for Galty, so one spring day he set out from Vienna for Budapest, traveling by coach and later on horseback. For a part of the way the mud was nearly impassable. Then, as he came out of the Carpathian passes, down into the flat stretches of the Hungarian plain, oceans of spring greenness assailed him. He crossed the Puszta through acres and acres of wild flowers and waving spring wheat. Sitting astride his tired horse outside Budapest, Galty knew instantly that all the hardships of the long journey behind him had been worth it. Seen even from far off, Budapest beckoned him with a magic peculiarly her own.

In Budapest all was splendor. Galty hastened to present a letter of introduction to a great friend of his father, Count Bāylor Bātoik-Illy. Count Bāylor immediately set about arranging entertainments for the young Irish gentleman with the wide, engaging smile and a magnificent appreciation of fine horseflesh. Count Bāylor bred the Hātor-Orloff strain, beautiful and swift as any horses on earth.

Count Bāylor had also bred an extremely beautiful daughter. His daughter and a stallion named Dragoro were the two living things he loved most. In the vaulted banquet hall at Castle Tata-Tóváros near Debrecen hung two huge portraits. One was a life-size painting of Dragoro, black as night. The other was of a tall, slim girl descending the green turf steps of a terrace. Behind her spread an arc of tall ash trees whose massive gray trunks gave great power to the composition of the picture. The girl seemed a dryad emerging from the forest, but a curious dryad, with high cheek bones and slanting, almost Chinese, eyes. There was a look of not-too-well-controlled wildness about the mouth of this arresting face. The mother of Countess Hōja Bātoik-Illy was the daughter of a Tartar noble. There was more than a little of the furiously racing Tartar blood in Countess Hōja's veins.

Galty Mallory married Countess Hōja. After a year of travel, they returned to Ireland and settled, if one could ever consider the restless life of Countess Hōja "settled," at Castle Sheela. In any case, she made Galty Mallory a supremely happy man, for he understood and played up to the constant wild adventures which were the breath of life to Countess Hōja Bātoik-Illy Mallory, as she called herself. She bore Galty five children, two daughters and three sons. She was the mother of Ormond Mallory, wild as a hawk and handsome as Lucifer, whom in many other qualities he resembled—pride, for one. It is Ormond Mallory whose ghost now rides the staircase at Castle Sheela on Christmas night, a horseman without a head.

When Ormond Mallory's father died, the boy was eighteen years old. It was a madly dangerous age for a boy with the confused nature of Ormond to have so vast a sum of money at his command. Galty had, as he thought, very wisely provided for just this contingency. He had had no illusions about the waywardness, the arrogant pride of self, and the fiendish temper of the boy. All that was unstable and dross in the Mallory strain, coupled with the tempestuousness of his Tartar forebears, seemed to mingle in the blood stream of Ormond Mallory. Immediately Galty was buried, Countess Höja had called Ormond into her sitting room. She told him that, as the estate was entailed, it must go to him when he reached the age of twenty-one. What she proposed to do now was this: turn over to him at once the actual money that was to come to him. She and the three younger children would go for a long visit to her home in Debrecen. After placing the girls in a convent near Paris, she would return and take up residence at Knockrally, an old Charles II house belonging to the Mallorys at the harbor mouth of Waterford-Old City.

Ormond listened dutifully, albeit nervously, with one eye looking out the window at some of his hounds who were being taught the sport of coursing. His mother's absence would not cause him the slightest sorrow, for nothing in this world mattered to Ormond but Ormond.

As her son turned to leave the room, his mother said, rather bitterly, "The reason for my making this change is this, much as I hate to admit it. The life you are all set to lead frightens me. I do not wish to be a party to it. If I felt that I could do anything to stop it, I would try at least. I know I cannot. I have the girls to think of. If they lived in this house, no matter how closely chaperoned by me, they would be tarred by your brush. That is not a pretty picture. I will be blamed by many, I know, for deserting you at your age. But as you are already causing scandal in the village by forcing your attentions on young village girls, I see the way you wish to live, even while I am here. Your father is spared this, at least. It may be partly my fault. Your blood is dark with many crimes from my side of the family. Beware, Ormond, of the village men. However highly placed you may be, they will take their revenge."

Ormond flicked a burr from his leather legging, bowed to his mother, and left the room. Countess Höja thought to herself she might have spared her breath. Ormond had apparently not heard a word she had said.

Soon after this one-sided interview between Ormond and his mother, during which Ormond had said not one word, Countess Höja and her two daughters set out for Hungary. Before she left, her second son, Dominic, was placed in a Franciscan School at Lisdoonvarna. Dominic was fifteen years old. He was not nearly so outrageously selfish as his brother Ormond, yet he was rebellious against authority. It was hoped the

Franciscans would have a quieting influence. The third boy, born last of the Mallory children, died when a small child.

From the moment that Ormond Mallory had Castle Sheela to himself, monarch of all he surveyed, his affairs took a lively turn. For more than a year, he had indulged himself with a rollicking widow who lived in the busy market town of Killmallock. When Ormond had first met Moira Carmichael, she was not a widow, but the predatory young wife of old John Carmichael, a prosperous chemist. When Carmichael died suddenly and was hurriedly buried, a few months after Moira's meeting with the handsome squire of Castle Sheela, ugly rumors flew like October leaves in and out of the doorways of Killmallock. Moira, behind closed shutters, took stock of her chances. They did not look too bright if she remained in Killmallock. She sold the chemist's shop and her small house with all her belongings. One month after the death of old John, Moira arrived at the portals of Ormond Mallory's house. She was accompanied by many boxes packed to bursting with new dresses and bonnets provided by the infatuated and generous Ormond.

Moira's arrival was quite open. The old transparent dodge of "housekeeper," so often used by the gentry, was spurned by both Moira and the defiant Ormond. She came as his mistress. She might, if her cards told true, end up as his wife.

For a few years we find Ormond occupied mostly with his horses and coursing greyhounds. His knowledge of horses was supreme. As the years passed, he became a power in racing and thoroughbred horse-breeding circles throughout Ireland. However badly Ormond Mallory was regarded by his more conventional neighbors for his loose way of living, men respected him as a fine sportsman. Women secretly envied Mistress Moira, but would have died before admitting it.

Moira Carmichael was a shocking housekeeper. The beautifully chosen furniture, which gave such an air of elegance and comfort to Castle Sheela, was in a sad state of disrepair in no time after her advent. The rooms which had been the talk of the countryside in Brendan Mallory's day were now a shambles. Packs of burr-matted dogs trooped through the suite of drawing rooms on the first floor. Saddles, spurs, riding crops, saddle soap, coursing muzzles, and greasy horse bandages littered every chair and spilled over onto the floor. Fireplaces were never cleaned by the slack servants. Ashes lay in drifts on the floor and were ground into the pale amber rugs by booted feet. Whenever a door or window was opened, clouds of dust swirled through the house. If ever neglect rode wild, it was through the rooms of Castle Sheela.

Cheap, baudy servants were all that Moira could manage. The decent Irish servitor would not step foot inside the house.

It is told in the village of Galtymore that Countess Höja, on her return from

51

Hungary, stayed for a while with friends near Castle Sheela. One day she rode over to pay her son a call. The front door standing open, she walked in. Frozen with amazement and anger at what she saw, the Countess started forward to pull the bell cord. Deciding on another course, she walked through the rooms. Cobwebs hung in hammocks from picture frames to candelabrum and swayed back and forth in the breeze from the open door. A thick film of blue-gray dust lay on table tops and mantel shelves. Countess Höja sailed furiously from room to room, her anger rising at every step. As she came out into the entrance hall, she saw a blowsy, heavy-eyed woman coming slowly down the stairs. It was Moira, newly awakened from sleep. Without a word the Countess Höja approached the yawning woman and, raising her riding crop, she dealt Moira a slashing blow across the face. Turning, she walked out of the house.

In the Mallory stables was a young hunter which Ormond called Follow, for the simple reason that even as a foal he would follow Ormond about the demesne very much as a dog will follow the one person he picks out on whom to center a lifetime of affection and loyalty. Ormond fostered this trick, as he chose to regard it. He showed off Follow to his friends. One day, when Follow was a yearling, Ormond encouraged him to walk up the shallow stone steps leading to the entrance door of the castle. Ormond stood at the top and opened the door. When the young horse had successfully negotiated the steps, he walked through the door and without hesitation picked his way delicately up the rise of stairs to the door of Ormond's bedroom. This clever trick amused Ormond mightily. Next day he had a runway or ramp built at one side of the stairs. It was built in four broad, shallow rises and enabled Follow to mount the stairs and go down again with ease. At all hours of the day the horse would seek his master in this way. If Ormond was not in his room, Follow would return to the paddock. It came to be such a common sight to see the sleek sorrel horse marching up or down the ramp in the hall of Castle Sheela that no one even noticed. Certainly no one minded.

When Follow was four years old, Ormond started to hunt him with the Limerick Hounds. The horse was a superb mover, took his walls and ditches in a knowledgeable manner, and had a great heart. He endeared himself to the cold, sarcastic Ormond as no human had ever done. It finally got to the point that when Ormond was hunting and the meet was early in the morning, a groom would saddle Follow and the horse would walk out of the stable yard straight to the open front door of the house and march serenely up the ramp to his master's room. Then a little ceremony took place. Ormond would hold an apple in the palm of one hand and a stick of sugar in the other. Follow would look first at one delicacy, then the other. Undecided for a moment, he would finally choose. Ormond would then spring into the saddle, and they were off to the meet.

For two or three years this was a regular procedure. Moira had raged at the noise made by Follow's hoofs, of an early morning, on the wooden planking of the ramp. But Moira was gone from Castle Sheela. In the midst of one of her drunken rages, Ormond had packed her off. The last he had heard, she was living with a senile protector in Dublin.

For weeks there had been no one at Castle Sheela save Ormond, the ramping pack of greyhounds and terriers, and the constant visitor, Follow. In Ormond's tireless search for female companionship he roamed the countryside, playing the field. Playing the field spelled danger, the way Ormond did it. Flagrant and ruthless always, his complete disregard for another's feelings was his ultimate undoing.

Among the numerous women to whom Ormond paid marked attention was the boldly handsome but indiscreet wife of a neighboring landowner, a man so devious in his dealings and of so jealous a nature that at times his actions smacked of madness. One day this man encountered his wife walking with Ormond Mallory in a secluded lane near the gates of Castle Sheela. What took place in this lane is not fully known. Ormond, however, was laid up for months with a broken shoulder.

During these days of enforced idleness, Follow visited Ormond every day. He had another visitor as well—a surprise visitor. His mother, hearing that Moira Carmichael was no longer at the Castle, rode over from Knockrally to stop the night. Ormond was secretly glad to see her, and was charm itself. He even consented to sit for his portrait, which his mother had long wanted him to have done, to hang in the dining room at Castle Sheela along with portraits of his father and grandfather. An Italian painter named Cannorelli was living in Dublin. Ormond would ask him to come to the Castle as soon as possible. It would help pass the tedium of his inactivity. Besides sitting for his portrait, he could brush up on his Italian.

The other request his mother made was that he give a big Christmas party at Castle Sheela, a family party. He must ask his sisters, who had returned from their convent in France and were staying with their mother at Knockrally. Dominic, the brother, could come over for the party from Lisdoonvarna. Ormond told his mother to make whatever arrangements she desired. Countess Höja returned to Knockrally considering her visit to her son a most successful one.

The portrait of Ormond Mallory was painted and hung "on the line" in the dining room beside his progenitors. It had a certain dash and fluid grace the other portraits lacked. The picture shows a slender man in his early thirties with a rather highly colored face, little marred by dissipation. The hair is a light golden brown, unpowdered and tied at the nape of the neck by a wide black ribbon. He wears a dark green coat with silver buttons, and a black stock is loosely tied under the arrogant chin. The eyes arrest you. Cold, insolent, they are the hard, steely blue of a winter evening sky. It is an inscrutable face. No one living could ever fathom what Ormond Mallory was thinking. The decoration of the portrait is given great style by a touch of the bizarre. As a compliment to his Hungarian mother, Ormond has flung over his shoulder a Csikós coat of white wool, heavily braided and embroidered in green, brown, and black.

The Christmas holiday season approached. Castle Sheela was put as much in order as was possible considering the shattered appearance left over from Moira Carmichael's sojourn. The Countess Höja arrived accompanied by her daughters, Brigid and Caro. When Dominic arrived the afternoon of Christmas Eve, the family party at Castle Sheela was complete.

Late in the evening the Mallorys were sitting before the drawing-room fire. Goblets of light mulled wine were being passed around. Suddenly there was a sound of hoof-beats approaching rapidly along the hard, frosty driveway leading from the entrance gates to the Castle. The horse was pulled up sharply and the sound of an angry voice was heard at the front door demanding of a footman to speak to Ormond Mallory, "Or by the holy God he'll wish he'd never been born." Apparently Ormond recognized the shouting voice, for, as he hastily rose from his chair by the fire, his mother saw such a look of livid, intense hatred cloud his eyes that it frightened her. "Ormond, what is it? Do you know who that is?" But Ormond had flung out of the room. She heard the front door slam with a force fit to wrench it off its hinges. No more was seen of Ormond that night.

Christmas morning dawned cold and overcast. Follow was the first one up at Castle Sheela. Long before the front door was opened by a sleepy maid, Follow was nuzzling the doorknob, wanting to be let in.

The meet for the Christmas Day hunt was to be held at Rillantora Park, an old abbey but recently made into a habitable house by Sir John Ainsley, an absentee land-lord who had just inherited the place. The house had a dank, broody look even on a bright day. As the straggling riders cantered up to the abbey porch, assembling for the meet, many people shivered in their saddles, almost as much from dread of the house as from the biting wind. Through the densely packed trees of the park, the winter wind soughed and snapped off brittle branches. Horses champed at cold bits, riders banged gloved palms together to restore circulation, red noses ran unheeded. An unease was abroad. Old Lady Clonboy, atop a big raking gray, remarked to a man astride the horse next her, "How Sir John can live in this old shebang is the wonder of the world. The drains are clogged with so much trash left over from the dark ages that it defies moving. More murders have been committed in this house than there are chimneys in the roof."

At that moment a late horseman was seen approaching along a narrow ride cut through the trees in the park. It was Ormond Mallory, mounted on Follow. Ormond waved his crop, encompassing the entire group with one greeting. Some waved in return. The hunt moved off. But anyone looking closely at Ormond would have seen that he looked like death. His face was pale and drawn. His eyes shifted to right and left, nervously. His upper lip was puffy and there was a jagged cut at one corner of his mouth.

Christmas Day at Castle Sheela was far from a merry one. All day long there was a tension in the air that affected all within the house. Countess Höja's neuralgia assailed her, so she kept to her room. Caro and Brigid tried embroidery. No use. Late in the morning they took the terriers for a walk through the old rabbit warrens at the back of the paddock. This kept the girls busy until they returned to join Dominic for a late lunch. Dominic had spent the morning browsing among his father's books in the library. "Too cold to hunt," he said.

In Terrance and Brendan Mallory's day, Christmas dinner at Castle Sheela had been a meal in the great tradition. On this particular Christmas, dinner was set for six o'clock in the evening, with Ormond Mallory presiding at the head of his table.

The day dragged on. Six o'clock came, but no Ormond appeared. Everyone knew the hunt had found its last fox around four o'clock. Dominic had walked out to the gate house and talked with the huntsmen returning to Clonboy Castle. They told Dominic they had had a good day.

Mary Corty, the cook, was frantic. Dinner had been ready and waiting to be served these two hours. "It'll be a great ruin, and meself destroyed with the labor," she moaned. Then Kirstey, the maid who had opened the door early that morning for Follow, heard a noise on the stone steps of the entrance porch. It sounded like a heavy body stumbling. Then came the whinnying of a horse, a sobbing kind of whinnying, that of a horse far spent in wind. Kirstey ran to the door and flung it wide open. At the same moment Dominic appeared in the door of the library.

A foundering horse stumbled across the threshold of the hall door. His russet hide was streaked and matted with dried blood and lather. Astride his back rode horror, the very definition of horror—the body of a man, the legs tied with rope under the horse's belly, the wrists tied together behind the back. The dark green coat with silver buttons was torn and saturated with blood. Above the collar of this coat there was no head. Ormond Mallory's head had been severed cleanly from his body.

Too stunned by the shock of what they saw to move, Kirstey and Dominic sank back against the wall. Follow, his sides heaving in his last effort, slowly mounted the runway, as he had done daily for years. At the door of his master's bedroom he sank to the floor, dead.

The head of Ormond Mallory was never found, nor was his murderer ever discovered. Jason Fermoy, the neighboring landowner who had met Ormond in the lane and beaten him with a shillelagh, as Jason later told at the Assizes Court, fell under suspicion and was interrogated by Mr. Justice Callahan. Jason proved, beyond doubt, a watertight alibi. He was dismissed. A curious annotation on the margin of this phase of the case is that, for years after the murder, Mrs. Fermoy, heavily veiled, visited the grave of Ormond Mallory in the churchyard at Clonboy. After one of her visits a piece of paper, which she had tucked into a metal flower vase, was disturbed by an errant wind. The paper blew along one of the cemetery paths and was picked up by a lay priest who happened to be passing. Written in heavy black ink on a piece of stiff white paper was this:

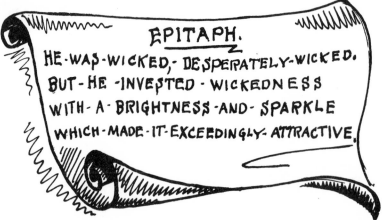

EPITAPH.
HE·WAS·WICKED,·DESPERATELY·WICKED,
BUT·HE·INVESTED·WICKEDNESS
WITH·A·BRIGHTNESS·AND·SPARKLE
WHICH·MADE·IT·EXCEEDINGLY·ATTRACTIVE.

Soon after his brother Ormond's death, Dominic Mallory went to Italy. There, in Venice, he married a Signorina Lydia Cannelleto, niece of the painter whose luminous pictures of the seventeenth-century Venice are world-famous. By this marriage Latin blood was infused into the Mallory strain. Countess Höja died at Knockrally, and the Mallory girls both married Irishmen. It is Caro's great-great-great granddaughter, Mrs. Torrance, who now lives at Castle Sheela.

When Dominic brought his Italian bride to Castle Sheela to live, the first thing he did was to remove the wooden ramp constructed by Ormond Mallory to accommodate his equine friend, Follow. But the mere absence of planking does not stop Follow from visiting his master's room as he always did when he was alive. Sometimes, just before dawn, the sound of hoofs hurrying rapidly up a phantom ramp is heard by persons in the house. If they listen they will hear (more sedately now, for the horse bears his master on his back) the iron-shod hoofs going down the ramp. Always on Christmas Day, after darkness has fallen, the front door will open suddenly and slam back against the wall.

Many people say they have seen a ghostly horse and rider mount the shadows beside the stair treads where the ramp used to be. The horse stumbles, as if nearly spent. The swaying rider has no head. Towards sunset on Christmas Day and on Christmas Day only, anyone looking at the portrait of Ormond Mallory, which now hangs over the fireplace in the dining room, will be rather astonished. A change takes place. The arrogant face with the supercilious mouth is no longer there. Above the black satin stock there is only a dim smudge, which seems to glow with lambent fire. Next morning the painted face is again there, the blue, wintry eyes inscrutable.

Mrs. O'Moyne and the Fatal Slap

Lough House. Ouhgterard.

COUNTY GALWAY

KELP GATHERERS OF COUNTY GALWAY

Mrs. O'Moyne
and the Fatal Slap

EMBRACING A GRAND VIEW OF THE LOUGH Corrib, whose restless waters are often sharply pointed by little whitecaps, called by Galway men, The White Horses of Rahilla, Red Queen of the Vales, is the village of Oughterard, a lively place, for it is here that fishing parties gather nine months of the year, enjoy the hospitality so freely offered, and then set out for the clear and sparkling rivers and loughs of Galway, Connemara, and Donegal.

To Oughterard one freshening evening in 1885 came a tall, buxom, and darkly handsome woman who established herself comfortably and in short order at Lough House, a small, unpretentious brick building, one story and a half in height, almost completely covered by matted vines of yellow cottage roses and white clematis. A small garden with many flower-bordered paths, which is enclosed within a waist-high wall, runs down to the lough in front, and on the west side of the house a graveled driveway swings in from Oughterard Common, ending at a small iron gate.

Accompanying the woman was her daughter, a tall, fair girl of pallid complexion and very light blue eyes. She seemed of nervous temperament, and anyone who had speech with her noted a high-pitched, rather hysterical voice and imperious manner which, her mother said later, was inherited from her father.

When the lady at Lough House sent her calling card to the village post office to be tacked above her post box, as was the custom, it appeared she was a Mrs. O'Moyne. Written in violet ink in a corner of the pasteboard square was "Miss Edith O'Moyne, and India Servant Rashina, post to be delivered to Mrs. O'Moyne, only." Life for the three women at Lough House then settled down to a quiet sequence of days.

Mrs. O'Moyne seldom came into the village. When she did, she was heavily veiled, though some men moving furniture into Lough House when it arrived from Dublin said she was "very handsome, in a dark broody way." Often the townspeople saw Mrs. O'Moyne, her daughter, and the Hindu servant sitting in a small breakwater-wall pavilion that had been erected at the end of the garden by a former tenant. Mrs.

O'Moyne seemed to enjoy her garden immensely, and had the "green finger" with flowers, apparently, for her garden was always at profusion pitch in color.

People passing the garden wall noticed that Mrs. O'Moyne worked her garden alone; no one ever saw the daughter or the servant enter it. Mrs. O'Moyne was always very gracious to passing people who wished a "Good day, God go with you," even asking the doctor's wife to stop a moment while she picked her a bouquet of flowers.

Outside her garden Mrs. O'Moyne was not so gracious. If she met anyone in the village street who seemed inclined to stop and talk, as is the manner of life in Ough-terard, she smiled, said a hasty word, and hurried on her way.

This attitude discouraged callers, which, the doctor's wife admitted to the wife of the jurist, was precisely what the lady of Lough House seemed to want. Mrs. Lacy, the veterinary's wife and a confirmed gossip, got as far as the front door one afternoon, but after ringing the bell and waiting a rather pointedly long time, she heard through the front door sounds of such violent words shouted at fever pitch, accompanied by uncontrolled sobbing, that she turned and fled—fled as far as the next house, that is, where she was admitted with alacrity and told what she had heard.

The summer passed and autumn was a series of wondrous days, with the light over the lough so clear and luminous that one could see the Twelve Pins of Connemara as close as if they were in the palm of one's hand; days that had the quality once written of Galway, where "The manifold mountain cones, now dark, now bright, alternate from rich light to spectral shade; and each dissolving cloud reveals new mountains while it floats away."

Late afternoons and early evenings, Edith O'Moyne and the Hindu servant were seen sitting in the breakwater pavilion, playing on a strange sort of instrument, a kind of zither, laid across the Hindu woman's knees. They sang eastern songs that floated softly across the water.

When the nights became chilly, and it was no longer possible to enjoy the pavilion, the house was always dark on the side facing the Common. A light showed in only one window, either an upstairs sitting room or bedroom, on the lough side.

It was this room that began to interest the villagers, for often at night someone taking a stroll by the lough could hear voices raised in shouting and the sound of slamming doors. One night John Teirney, a hostler at the Wily Trout Inn, a famous haunt for fishermen, was passing just as the door burst open and Edith O'Moyne, very lightly clad, pale hair streaming out behind her, her throat racked with shuddering sobs, rushed out towards the iron gate. Before she could reach it, her mother, like an avenging Fury, had grasped her by the shoulder with one hand and with the other she slapped the girl on the mouth so hard it resounded in the still night like a pistol shot.

John Teirney was so dumfounded he could not move. When he had gathered his wits, mother and daughter had re-entered the house and the door was slammed shut. After this little diversion was embroidered a bit by Teirney, the village began to seethe.

What was going on at Lough House, they asked each other? Was Edith O'Moyne being persecuted by her mother, or was this a family matter that was none of their business?

A few nights later another mysterious angle was added to the goings-on at Lough House, for a man arrived at the Wily Trout, having come by the Galway evening post chaise. He had no luggage and seemed very distraught. He inquired the way to Mrs. O'Moyne's house and asked when the next coach left for Galway or Clifden.

Both questions were answered by at least ten men who happened to be in the bar at the time, and the man swung off down the street and across the Common in the direction of Lough House. Actually he went alone, but the curiosity of Oughterard being aroused by the episode in the garden a few nights before and no one having been seen at Lough House since, he was followed at a discreet distance by three men posted as watchers to report any untoward incident.

Later in the night, when the stranger's wounds were being dressed in Dr. Channing's dispensary, he told this story.

His name was Martin Hanforth. He was from Cork, but three years before had gone to India as accountant for a firm of cotton merchants from Birmingham. In Madras he had met at the house of a mutual friend a girl whose father was a civil servant in Bombay. Her name was Edith O'Moyne. She told him she was approaching her eighteenth birthday, and in a few days must return to Bombay to her mother, whom she hated; and her father, who was dying of a strange malady. In her opinion, he was being slowly poisoned by her mother.

Martin and the girl with whom Edith was stopping were deeply shocked to hear this. They tried to persuade her that it could not possibly be true; there must be some other explanation. Martin even went so far as to say he would accompany her back to Bombay, and try to prove to her that it was all in her imagination. Then she shocked them still further by adding that they could believe her or not, as they chose, but that she felt very strange and lethargic at times, with hardly the will to move. India was full of obscure and subtle poisons, and, while she did not accuse her mother of actually trying to kill her, she thought she was putting some drug in her food to deaden her will.

Her mother told people she was only sixteen years old, and as they could see, dressed her as a very young girl; even her hair was still in braids. The reason was that, until she reached her eighteenth birthday, her mother had control of a sizable fortune left to Edith by her Grandmother O'Moyne of Belfast.

In a quandary, Martin, who had fallen deeply in love with her fragile, fair, prettiness, decided to ask the girl to marry him. Martin told her that, once married, they could return to England within a fortnight. He had been offered a post in London which he had hesitated to accept. Now all would work out perfectly. In three days Edith O'Moyne and Martin Hanforth were married. They went immediately to Bombay to tell Mrs. O'Moyne and to let Edith bid good-by to her father.

The good-by was never said, for as the bride and groom alighted at the house, they were stopped by a Pathan policeman and told they could go no farther. A man, hurrying up the path, said he was the landlord. Captain O'Moyne had died ten days ago in frightful agony, and under decidedly curious circumstances. An autopsy had been ordered by the Resident, and "poison" was given as the cause of death.

Mrs. O'Moyne had been removed to a prison attached to the Residency Compound. She denied everything, admitted nothing. The hot season was rapidly approaching. All who could, including the judge, wished to get away to the hills, so Mrs. O'Moyne's trial was rushed.

It soon appeared there was not a shred of evidence against her. She contended that her husband had been poisoned by a half-crazed Kashmiri servant who had been dismissed for stealing and had loudly proclaimed vengeance. Oddly enough, perhaps because the devil protects his own, this was partly true. Few servants in India are to be trusted. There were plenty of ways this one could have got poison to Captain O'Moyne.

Edith, now so happily married, was anxious to get the whole thing over. She cared very little, she said, whether her mother was acquitted or not. She was through with her. She did not admit she had ever had suspicions. She refused to testify.

The verdict was read. For lack of evidence, Mrs. Francesca O'Moyne was declared not guilty. The murder was committed by a person or persons unknown.

Martin went to Madras to wind up his affairs, promising to return in a week at most. Edith went with her mother and Rashina, a woman from Bengal who had never left Mrs. O'Moyne and had slept outside her cell door from her first night in prison.

Mrs. O'Moyne expressed a wish to take a small house in Calcutta. Edith would help her mother pack her belongings, see her and Rashina off, and await Martin's arrival in Madras. In five days Martin returned but found no trace of Edith, her mother, or Rashina. No one knew where they had gone. From that day on he had hunted them down.

Through a letter sent to him by a doctor friend in Dublin who knew of Mrs. O'Moyne, he had traced her to Oughterard. That night, when he arrived at the gate of Lough House, he had found it on the latch, and, to his surprise, the front door as well. He encountered Rashina, who recognized him instantly, in the small dark hall. Sensing that his sudden arrival meant trouble for her mistress, she tried to push him out of the door, saying there was great illness in the house.

A door opened on the landing and Mrs. O'Moyne appeared, carrying a branch of candles. Her face grew livid. She stood still, calculating her next move. "Go away, Rashina," she said. "Martin, come up to the study. I will talk to you here." She motioned him to enter the small room facing the lough from which she had just come. For a moment they looked deep into each other's eyes, implacable hate in hers, an awareness of impending violence in his. Her first words were what he expected: "How did you find us?"

Martin told her he returned to Madras after her acquittal to find her, Edith, and Rashina vanished without a trace. For three years he had searched for them; now that he had found them, he wanted Edith. He would take her to London, where he was established in good circumstances. He wanted no unpleasantness, although it had been a long, agonizing time for him. He was willing to forget everything. He would like, however, to hear her version of how she had managed to induce Edith to leave him three years ago.

Mrs. O'Moyne smiled bitterly: "It was not difficult; I simply told her the truth, that she has an incurable malady—some give it a more dreadful name—inherited from her father. Edith is an epileptic, and her mind is diseased. She needs care, constant care. Only Rashina, who has been with me since Edith was born, can give her that care."

Martin was horrified. "You are lying," he said. "She is delicate but perfectly well; you are deliberately keeping her shut away, clouding her mind for your own ends. She told me as much in Madras. Where is she? I am her husband and I demand to see her."

Martin told the doctor he had never seen such a sight—the gamut of all the baser emotions fighting for supremacy on the face of Mrs. O'Moyne. If it were possible for a face to go "blue" with hate, hers most surely had.

After a moment she quieted and said, "Very well, follow me." She took him to a heavily curtained room across the hall. On a bed, under a canopy of pale blue muslin, lay a young but terribly ravaged girl. It was Edith, his wife; no doubt of that, but so cruelly changed. Her pallor was that of the grave, with no color at all to her lips. Her closed eyes seemed buried in great purple hollows. Martin was appalled. How could this be? *What* could it be?

Mrs. O'Moyne spoke: "For days on end she lies like this. Sometimes she rallies enough to sit in the garden house with Rashina and me. Then, after a few days, her spells take her and she becomes abusive, hysterical. She must live completely away from the world. You will do well to leave Oughterard tomorrow and forget you ever heard the name of Edith O'Moyne."

It was then, Martin said, that he lost all control of his feelings. He realized the enormity of this "death in life" existence being forced on Edith by the degraded woman before him. His voice rose to fever pitch: "You shall not do this thing! I will go to Dublin and tell what I know from Edith herself, and what I have seen. I never believed your acquittal was just. You poisoned your husband and now you are poisoning Edith!"

Martin said that he started to leave the room to return to the Wily Trout. He would think over what course to follow in Dublin to attain Edith's release. As he reached the head of the stairs, he felt a powerful blow between the shoulder blades. Clawing wildly at nothing, he pitched forward down the stairs.

When Martin came to, he was lying on the cobblestones of the high street in front of the iron gates to Lough House. A passer-by helped him to the dispensary.

Dr. Channing asked, "Was anyone in the hall who could bear witness to your accusation that Mrs. O'Moyne deliberately pushed you down the stairs?"

Martin replied, "I saw no one. That is the trouble; it is my word alone."

The next day, bandaged and aching in every joint, but with no bones broken, Martin set out for Dublin. Before he left he asked Dr. Channing to post a watcher across the street to see that Mrs. O'Moyne did not attempt another of her disappearing acts like the one from Madras.

This was duly done, and a village deputy, one Barney Dalton, ensconced himself at the foot of a big oak on the Common, read the *Irish Racing News,* and waited, watching. Two days he watched, relieved at intervals by the loquacious John Teirney.

The second day, a Friday, was sultry hot. Not a ripple scalloped the dark blue surface of the Lough Corrib. Barney lay with his hands behind his head, thinking that he had not seen hide or hair of any of the people at Lough House since the beginning of his vigil. He noted as well that the once-bright garden seemed to droop in the heat. For the first time since Mrs. O'Moyne's arrival, it had an untended look.

A dozy feeling came over Barney, but it was suddenly nipped in the bud by a high, piercing scream from the shuttered house. The door burst open, and Edith, fully dressed, ran towards the wall skirting the lough. Striding behind her was her mother, looking as if she had just been roused from sleep. Her hair was disarranged and she clutched a yellow tea gown across her breast. Edith Hanforth seemed to have little strength as she ran along the garden path. She suddenly put out her hand and grasped a tree for support.

It was then that Mrs. O'Moyne overtook her daughter. Catching Edith by the shoulders, her mother swung her around. A distracted look, plainly seen even from where Barney sat, spread over the girl's face. She opened her mouth to scream as Mrs. O'Moyne's flattened hand descended with smashing force against Edith's cheek. The impact was so shattering that Barney Dalton, across the Common, leaped to his feet as if he had been slapped himself.

Barney watched for the next move as in a trance, and what he saw he was never able to forget to his dying day: Mrs. O'Moyne standing there in yellow disarray, in the hot, overblown garden, across her powerful, outstretched arm the limp, dragging body of an emaciated young woman whose head lolled from side to side as if no bone held it to her body.

At eight o'clock that evening a delegation of six people prominent in Oughterard, headed by Mr. Justice Lacy, the jurist, knocked at the locked gates of darkened Lough House. Repeated knockings brought no response. Finally both the gate lock and the front door had to be forced. A house in utter confusion received them.

Oxhide and canvas-covered boxes and hand luggage, bearing such labels as Cawnpore, Madras, Calcutta, Paris, Rome, Santander, Nice, Monte Carlo, Vienna, lay helter-skelter on all sides. Here was proof of disorganized wanderings over half the world. But where was Mrs. O'Moyne now? Neither she, nor Rashina, nor the dead body of Edith O'Moyne Hanforth was anywhere in that house.

When in Ireland, I go very often to Galway, motoring from my own house near Castledermot in County Kildare. The road leads through Oughterard. A glass of ale at the Wily Trout is in order. The Lough Corrib always draws me to its shores. The infinite variety of cloud shadows drifting in from the Atlantic, throwing a mantle of deep color across the points of the Twelve Pins in Connemara, has curious magic.

One sparkling day in June, 1938, I stopped in Oughterard. Striking off across the Common, I passed slowly along the garden wall of Lough House. The windows were shuttered, the door was heavily boarded. Matted vines covered even the chimneys. Rank grasses and weeds snarled the garden paths. A few perennials, with more vitality than most, managed to give a bit of color to the borders, but it was in no sense a garden. Neglect rode through the place.

Walking all round this deserted house in which no one had lived for twenty years, I decided to sit in what was left of the water-edge pavilion at the end of the break-water and try to evoke the entire picture of Mrs. O'Moyne's evil and lurid occupancy.

Dr. Channing had told me this story of the days following the sudden departure of the household, alive and dead, from Lough House.

DOCTOR CHANNING'S STORY

Search of house and garden revealed no trace by which the Galway constabulary could find Mrs. O'Moyne, Edith or Rashina, notwithstanding the dragging of Lough Corrib from shore to shore. It never gave up the body of the murdered girl with the broken neck.

Many people imagined that mistress and servant had bound the body in sheets or other covering and buried it at some point along the many miles of unfrequented lake shore. Someday, but probably never, her skeleton might be found.

Two fishermen told the constabulary that in the mist of morning they had been hauling in their nets close to the village of Cong, which is across the widest part of lough from Oughterard, when a curragh had suddenly appeared out of the fog. In it were two heavily shawled women; one, the larger of the two, was rowing; a third figure, or what appeared to be a figure, lay in the bottom of the curragh. It might have been luggage, they could not tell. One of the women seemed very dark-visaged, but so were many Galway women with Spanish blood.

The men thought nothing of this at the time, for the wives of Cong fishermen were often out on the lough early in the morning. It was not until days later, when they had heard in Oughterard of the runaways from Lough House, that they remembered the women who had appeared the morning after the murder. They had, the men said, come silently out of the fog and as silently gone into it, and, as far as was ever heard, out of the lives of men.

It is, of course, quite possible for persons in this unsure world to disappear utterly. One knows of many such cases. But it seems curious that these two women, so unlike in looks and birth, one a Bengali serving woman with no greatly developed quality, save blind loyalty to her mistress, and the other an Irish woman of birth and breeding, could find haven anywhere without detection. For, I learned, the case in the last years of the nineteenth century was a *cause célèbre*.

One wonders whether Mrs. O'Moyne, with her strong, handsome features and her dominant personality, found a place in the sun once more. Did her wanderings take her as far afield as Monte Carlo, Segovia, or Madras?

A few months after "L'Affaire O'Moyne," Lough House was occupied by a sporting man from County Waterford who, on an expedition to buy horses at the Galway Horse Fair, had seen the house, rented it, and installed his family, consisting of a wife a widowed sister, and two children, a boy and girl in their teens.

Possession was taken late in October. The winter passed most pleasantly. The family, named Lysaght, became greatly attached to the comfortable house and enjoyed the many pleasures afforded by the lough. June ushered in with a soft calmness that lulled the mind to rest.

Then, one evening, a horrible uproar broke out. Screams came from an upper bedroom. Running footsteps pounded on the stairs. The front door slammed shut with such force that it nearly rode off its hinges. Most sinister of all was the terrible sound of the unseen slap. It rang out, as if someone's hand had struck with great force against another's cheek. Then there was dead silence, more ominous than sound.

The family Lysaght was amazed and mightily upset. But as the months sped past, and no recurrence of this scene troubled their lives, it was all but forgotten by the hearty, sports-loving Lysaghts.

One still evening in December, with a pale, slender moon riding high above the gently lapping Lough Corrib, it happened again, but with frightening variations. Mildred Lysaght, the young daughter, was sitting at her open window looking out over the shimmering water. The night was wonderfully clear. Then her ear caught what she thought was a rustle of silk in the passage outside her room. The night being mild, she did not stop for a coat, but went hurriedly down the stairs and out into the garden. No sooner had she reached the path than she felt a stinging pain on her cheek, accompanied by a resounding slap. With such force was this ghostly slap delivered that it all but broke her neck. The frightened child ran sobbing into the house, to be met by her father and mother, who had distinctly heard the sharp slap in the drawing room.

A few days later the family Lysaght left Lough House and returned to County Waterford. And so it was for a number of tenants. Some more brave than others stayed for a few months. Some stayed only weeks. No one stayed a year.

Many people in Oughterard believe that Mrs. O'Moyne died in her wanderings and that it was her ghost haunting Lough House, in eternal pursuit of her unhappy daughter.

The owner of Lough House, a successful publican in Dublin, boarded up the cottage many years ago. It stands unwanted now, a rose-covered house, outcast, beside a lovely lough. The curious, like myself, fascinated by its moribund appeal, will sometimes push open the rusty gate and walk out onto the sagging breakwater. The once gayly airy pavilion where Edith O'Moyne and the sullen Rashina used to sit is derelict. The railings trail in the water.

On still nights, villagers in Oughterard say they hear the sharp ring of flesh striking on flesh. Then wild, wailing sobs come from the direction of the garden paths of Lough House.

Lady Mornington's Glove

Black Church Inn

COUNTY DUBLIN

Lady Mornington's Glove

THE CASHEL ROAD FROM DUBLIN TO NAAS is as old as Ireland itself. Over this ancient thoroughfare, built on living rock, history has been made countless times. On this road, a few miles out of Dublin, stands the Black Church Inn. It is a long, low building, approached by a semicircular graveled coach drive. The steep gabled roof still retains, among its heavy thatching, remnants of far older straw, laid in diamond and scroll pattern, when thatching was a fine art.

The Inn is whitewashed stone with black doors and window sashes. The black and white motif is carried out in two cages of magpies which swing in the breeze on either side of the entrance porch.

The name Black Church comes down the centuries from the time when this stone building was the storehouse of a priory known as Brothers of the Black Church. This order was burned by the followers of Sir Humphrey de Burgo during his depredations in County Dublin. Nothing now remains of this priory itself but turf-grown mounds. A few outlying stone buildings, with thick walls and heavy beams of blackened oak, are used by farmers as cow byres and barns. The largest is the Black Church Inn, which was converted to its present use in 1450.

When James II of England plodded along this historic road in his tragic flight from Leinster, it was at the Black Church Inn that he sought and received refreshment for himself and his weary, ragged followers.

The dashing Lady Castlemaine called her coach to halt one hot summer day at the gabled entrance of the Inn. She remarked on the excellent quality of the porter served by the host. He showed his appreciation by ordering his hostlers to strap a keg of the tangy amber porter to the back of her coach, to be enjoyed at her leisure. When she informed him she was driving to Dun Loaghaire to embark for England, the innkeeper said, "Madam, I ask one favor of you. Drink every drop of this porter on Irish soil."

Through the front door, under the porch pediment, you pass along a hallway, the

73

walls almost hidden by framed photographs of famous hunt meets at the Inn. Straight ahead is a black door hung with brasses which lets into the bar parlor, a spacious room where one may sit in comfort and be served the hospitality of the house. Paneled in hand-hewn oak slabs, thick as your wrist, the wood is jet black from centuries of peat smoke.

The mother of the present owner told me one day, and we lifting a tageen of good whisky to luck and a good hunt which was to follow, "That peat fire on the hearth has never gone out since I can remember, and I'm in this house next and nigh to seventy years." Winter or summer, a peat fire in most Irish houses is carefully tended through the day and banked with moist sods and ash at night. In the morning a fan of rook feathers is waved skillfully back and forth at the base of the smoldering cone and a strong fire springs up to boil the morning tea water.

Plentifully strewn with spotless Victorian antimacassars, the chairs in this parlor are deep and inviting, and one often spends an hour or two here on a rainy afternoon looking over its treasures. This room is the Inn Museum as well as parlor. In front of the garden window stands a large, round, marble-topped table. On it, under a glass dome, intended for wax flowers originally, but put to far more exciting use, lies a red velvet guest book. It is bound and clasped in gold filigree. On the opened page there is an impressive signature. In faded ink is dashed across the ivory paper, "Countess Hoenembs," the transparent incognito assumed by Empress Elizabeth of Austria. The Empress loved Ireland. She loved its friendly, witty people. Three different winters she took Lord Longford's rambling, rose-red brick house, Summerhill, so she might hunt with the Meath Hounds. Under her signature is the massive, almost illegible, scrawl of Bay Middleton, who was never far from her side or her thoughts during her Irish visits.

There are hunting crops with signed tags giving dates and names, the horse ridden, the length of the hunt, and where the kill took place. There are mounted fox masks, pads, and an occasional brush that have been presented to the host of the Black Church Inn to commemorate some outstanding day.

The chief pride of the owner of the Inn is not to be found, however, in the Museum. Instead, it reposes in a glass *vitrine* set in the wall behind the bar which is in the taproom. A curtain of faded wine-red velvet hides this treasure when not "on view," so to speak. When pushed back, this curtain discloses, lying on a silver plate, a pale russet leather glove, a riding glove, long in the gauntlet and buttoned with gold studs. Once this glove belonged to the Countess of Mornington, mother of Lord Arthur Wellesley, The Iron Duke.

Lady Mornington's glove has had adventures. It was lost for years. At any rate, no one ever confessed they had hidden it. One day it turned up in the same place it had been lost, but on a stranger's hand. The story of the russet kid glove was told me in this manner.

When Lord Arthur Wellesley was a young man, before he went into the army, he lived at Mornington House in Upper Merrion Street, Dublin. During his young manhood his constant companion was his beautiful mother, the Countess of Mornington. The pleasures of the country around Dublin are legion. Arthur tested them all: riding and hunting, fishing, sailing on the Liffey Estuary and choppy Killiney Bay, and taking long walks into the wildness of the Dublin Mountains. His favorite of all these was riding and hunting with the Meath Hounds or the Dublin Harriers. In this his mother joined him. She "had a way" with a horse, as so many Irishwomen have. Her hands on a horse's mouth were that soft she could braid a cobweb and not disturb the dew. As a lone tinker woman standing at a wall said to me one day of a woman riding past on a handsome thoroughbred horse, "They go strong together now. Like a picture. The heart of her and the heart of him are one."

The heart of Lady Mornington and her son were one, surely. Many is the long ride they took together. Later, in letters written by Arthur Wellesley when he was Duke of Wellington, he spoke of these spring and autumn rides, and of how he missed them.

Returning one day in early autumn along a bohireen near the Cashel Road, Lady Mornington and her son had passed the Six Crosses, a curious welter of lichen-covered rocks where, legend has it, six monks, each carrying a small stone cross, were waylaid and robbed by thugs. In panic, the monks fled, leaving the crosses in a pile in the middle of the road. These crosses were never moved because, it was thought, bad luck of the worst possible kind attended them.

Not far from this spot lay the arc of gravel in front of the Black Church Inn, always a favorite place for refreshment and a short rest after a long ride across country. The day, which had been cool and bright when they started the morning ride, had turned hot. As Lady Mornington walked through the passage leading to the bar parlor, she stripped off her russet kid riding gloves. Rolling them together, as she thought, she stuffed the gloves into a side pocket of her habit. Sitting in the window seat in the parlor, Arthur called to his mother's attention the masses of bronze and deep-yellow chrysanthemums so pungent in the hot sunshine. Lady Mornington, in turn, admired the swags of dark red creeper, with clusters of blue and purple berries, which swayed in the light breeze. The tangled, unkempt garden at the Black Church Inn never receives much attention but is always a miracle of color.

Soon the innkeeper arrived, bearing a tray on which was a green pottery jug brimming with the specialty of the house, porter. A plate of freshly baked barley bread and a napkin-wound Stilton cheese called forth exclamations of delight from Arthur and his mother. They made a good lunch. Before leaving, each drank an extra glass of porter to the health of the Inn and to all under its roof.

Later that day a footman from Mornington House galloped up to the Black Church Inn. He strode into the taproom and asked for Danihy, the host. Behind the bar was a slatternly young girl. "Just washing up. I don't belong here rightly," she said. She looked dirty and stupid, not the type you would expect to find at a well-considered inn like the Danihy's. The footman said sharply, "Go fetch Mr. Danihy, quickly. I've got to get back to her ladyship before evening." The girl slouched off. After a few minutes' wait, the footman went on his own to locate Danihy. When he found him, Danihy said the girl had not sought him out. He had not known he was wanted in the bar.

"What is it you want, anyhow, in such a hurry?" Danihy asked the footman.

The man replied, "The countess lost one of her riding gloves this morning. She thinks it might have been dropped here. This is where she took them off after her ride. Paris gloves they are. A favorite pair."

Danihy shook his head. "I don't think her ladyship dropped it here. I never saw it, and there's been nobody about the place since they left."

A search over the lower floor of the Inn and the grass-grown paths in the garden was fruitless. Finally the puzzled footman swung onto his horse and headed for Dublin.

Next day Danihy thought of the girl in the scullery. There was just a chance she might have picked up the glove. Half gone in the head as she was, there was no telling what she might do with it. Big, vacant eyes stared straight at Danihy as the girl listened to his questions. No, she had not seen any glove—what kind of a glove was it, red, or black? "A glove," she repeated, holding out one chapped red hand and stroking it with the other. "A glove." She kept murmuring this over and over in a demented fashion. Disgusted, Danihy gave it up.

It was not until a few days later, after the footman from Mornington House had come and gone again, that Danihy thought of the rather peculiar actions of the half-witted girl in the scullery and the way she had rubbed her hand and muttered "a glove."

The glove was never found. Many years passed. Lord Arthur Wellesley smashed the Grand Army of Napoleon at Waterloo. The British Crown heaped honors upon him. Men called him Duke of Wellington.

Lady Mornington was dead. So was Michael Danihy, who had served porter and a ripe Stilton cheese to Lady Mornington and her son in his bar parlor on a long gone day in autumn. Michael's grandson, Thomas, now owned the Black Church Inn.

A short time after Thomas inherited the Inn, an old woman died in a smoke-ridden little coteen on the edge of the oak woods behind his cow barn. The land was rightly his, but, like his father and grandfather before him, he let poor folk live in the coteens along the lane, rent free. The old woman, he was told, had once worked for his grandfather as scullery maid at the Inn. Well, that was that. He thought no more about it.

Late that night a scratching at the back door drew him to the area way. Opening the door, he saw a man covered against the lashing rain with a huge, dark blanket. The man was a tinker. He said he came from the wake of the dead woman in the woods. Would himself come and take a look at the corpse. Something was wrong. Catching up a heavy coat, against the night, Thomas went up the bohireen with the tinker man.

In the front room of the incredibly dirty coteen lay the body of a skeleton-thin woman. Straggles of greasy gray hair hung in a web about the bony face. She was dressed in a collection of as miserable a lot of rags as Thomas had ever seen, and literally hundreds of cheap rosaries were hung about her neck. Her misshapen feet were bare, but on her right hand, which was folded across her breast, was a beautiful French kid riding glove. The gauntlet was long and delicately scalloped. The glove was pale russet in color and as fresh as the day Lady Mornington had stripped it off her hand in the bar parlor of the Black Church Inn.

On the autumn day that the glove was dropped in the passage, Thomas Danihy, present owner of the Black Church Inn, had not been born. So, when he beheld this fantastic sight, he knew nothing of the glove's history. He turned to a middle-aged woman who looked less sodden than the rest and said, "Do you know what all these rosaries and that glove mean? Where did she get them?"

At first the woman glowered; then, hunching her shoulders, she replied, "The rosaries, yer honor, do be given her all her life long, all and others. Sure it's all the poor goneen ever wanted. The glove, now, I don't know the true or lie of that. Some say a grand lady gave it to her. Maybe she whisked it away for herself. Who knows, or cares?"

Something in Thomas' mind fought for recollection. Hadn't his grandmother once told him a story of the beautiful Lady Mornington who used often to come to the Black Church Inn with her son, and they out riding the fields? That was it, surely. He turned to the woman who had answered his questions. "Let me have that glove. How she got it we'll never know. It belonged to a friend of my grandmother's."

As one sees the glove now, resting so peacefully behind its ruby curtain, it seems never to have left the hand of Lady Mornington. It still smells faintly of orris root, a fashionable scent of the Regency period. The glove has a fullness of its own. It does not lie limp and flat as do most empty gloves. Thomas Danihy told me once that, lock the small glass door in the *vitrine* as much as he likes, it is often found standing open in the morning when he comes down to the bar. There is only one key. It is on his key ring among many others. And that ring never leaves a chain which he wears around his neck.

Near the *vitrine*, on the corner of the bar, there is always kept a portfolio type of writing case with a few sheets of Black Church Inn stationery and a pen and ink. One morning, a few days before Christmas in 1935, he was startled to see the glove lying on the bar counter. On the index finger of the right hand was a large spot of blue ink. The pen had rolled onto the floor, and on the blotting paper a letter had been blotted. Faint as it was, by holding it up to the mirror, he could make out:

Dearest Arthur.
    I trust y————.

Red Eva's Lepp

Kilkenny Castle

COUNTY KILKENNY

STRONGBOW

KILKENNY CASTLE.

Red Eva's Lepp

I N ALL THE BRIGHT ROSTER OF GAELIC HISTORY,
I'll wager there is no person accorded a background so magnificently caparisoned
as Red Eva McMurrough, of Kilkenny Castle and Red Eva's Tower on the
border of County Tipperary and County Limerick. The fortress of Kilkenny
Castle belonged to The McMurrough, Eva's father. The border tower Red Eva
built herself. She waged continuous war, and eventually lost her life defending the
tower against the Quinns of Limerick.

Schoolbooks make a great feature of Eva McMurrough being the "wife to Strongbow." She was that, of course. But the story of Red Eva blazes forth, up and down the
land, in so many other forms that it takes your breath. She is said by historians to have
been of titanic stature, and for some she has assumed a height towering out of all
reason; one chronicler says Red Eva was eight feet tall.

Another tells extraordinary stories about her cascades of dark red hair. He says
Red Eva would plait her thick red hair into two braids hanging on either side of her
face. Sometimes, as old stone carvings show, she would wrap these coils around her
throat and shoulders, the like of a wimple. When preparing for battle, Eva would
braid hunks of iron into these coils. The ingots hidden in her thick hair were invisible
to an enemy. Not wanting to kill a man, but perhaps just to stun him, she would hit
him a clout with this rope of hair in which were imbedded iron "knuckles." It would
seem an effective weapon.

Another device to which Eva McMurrough was partial, according to a series of
carved stone door panels which I once saw in Limerick, was her spiked cuirass, a kind
of metal jerkin, grooved and covered with flexible plates. A wide V of metal, running
from shoulder to waist, bristled with long, lethal iron spikes. They were razor sharp
and needle pointed. Her method was, it appears, to grasp her enemy firmly around
the body and crush him to her bosom, thereby impaling him like a fowl on a spit.

In an incredibly old volume of early Gaelic heroes and their doings, which I once
saw in a private library in Antrim, was this description of "Eva Roe" (in Gaelic, "roe"
means "red"): "A great cloud of dust shot through with silver sun balked the ap-

81

proach of Eva Roe. The wind came howling out of Duneen Glen. The cloud of dust ran off, shrieking down the glen. Eva Roe, mightiest woman in Ireland, trod biggly through the storm. Her armor ran with blood, for the hearts of men were stuck on prongs of iron. Iron spears that bristled across her breast."

The old towers of Kilkenny Castle rise above the darkly flowing River Nor. The busy market town of Kilkenny, which is the town of battling cats as well, sprawls about the walls and gate house of the castle on three sides. The keep of Kilkenny Castle is magnificent in its power. It lifts boldly against the sky. Built in 1192, it has housed the "Proud Butlers," marquises of Ormond, for centuries.

The enormous muniment room in the inner bailey is one of the finest in the world. The Ormond collection of arms of war, in every conceivable shape and form, from every epoch and every country, is a world in itself, a world where ingenuity and cruelty are masked by grace of design.

The Chapel, where lie a sleeping company of Plantagenet knights, smells of musty banners and rotting battle gear. The knights lie in rows. Fully armored, they grasp their long, two-handed swords. Between eye-slits in the lowered visors of their helms, they gaze with shriveled eyes into eternity. The Kilkenny man will say, "There's not one ave'um that wants to lay there. We like to keep an eye on 'em, so we pile their armor on 'em, to hold 'em down."

Little or nothing is heard of Eva McMurrough before her seventeenth birthday. But on that day she was married in one of the most outlandish ceremonies ever recorded in history, arranged and carried to an amazingly successful conclusion by The McMurrough, considering the tricky temper of Strongbow. "In the dying month of the year [November] in a dead city [Waterford] big Eva McMurrough was traded in for freedom from the Dane." So runs an old tag line in *The Far and Wide History Of Leinster*.

The events leading up to the curious marriage ceremony of Red Eva McMurrough and Strongbow in the smoking market place of Waterford were deeply involved in the conniving between Dermott McMurrough and one Richard Fitzgilbert de Clare, Earl of Pembroke, called Strongbow by the British.

Shortly after Dermott McMurrough's elevation to ruler of Leinster, which in 1161 included Waterford and Dublin, he started to create trouble and to cause every Irishman's hand to be raised against him—the "back of his hand," at that. Wherever the King of Leinster went he caused turmoil. A huge, gross man, with a flaming, murderous temper, he was unwelcome in the houses of his subjects. One day he forced his way into the Castle of Dromahair and carried off Tiernan O'Rourke's wife, Dervorgilla, a woman famed to the four extremities of Ireland for her remarkable beauty.

After this little diversion, Dermott retired, with an apparently not-unwilling Dervorgilla, to live down the act of wife-robbing. In the next year we hear of him approaching, in deceitful ways, the ambitious, impoverished Earl of Pembroke. Dermott visited Pembroke by stealth, in the dead of night, in some appointed bay off the Glamorgan coast. Ever expansive and generous with that which was not rightly his (but which, because of his kingship, was his for the taking), Dermott offered Strongbow "the greatest treasure in Ireland," besides a payment in gold and a patent of succession to the kingdom of Leinster. These evidences of generosity on the part of Dermott McMurrough were to be handed over to Strongbow on the instant that he delivered Ireland from the Danes.

"The greatest treasure in Ireland" was, of course, Dermott's handsome daughter, Aoife, or Eva. In October, 1170, Strongbow arrived suddenly at Wexford, the Danish stockade. He put the sprawling town, with its sloppily defended keep, to the torch. He massacred and pillaged the garrison and townspeople. Then, in an incredibly swift flanking move, Strongbow swept into Waterford Old Town. Here he slaughtered all of the inhabitants except seventy of the leading citizens. The next day, in an orgy of cruelty, Strongbow ordered these men bound together with chains. Their limbs were broken, and, only half-alive, they were cast over the cliffs by catapult into the sea below. By these two murderous strokes did Strongbow break the Danes' hold in Ireland.

Standing in the sacked, smoldering ruins of once-lovely Waterford, Strongbow called on Dermott McMurrough for his reward. He was mightily anxious to possess "the greatest treasure in Ireland." Responding, the King of Leinster walked through the gutted, black-scarred streets to what had once been the market place of Waterford. By his side was his daughter, Eva McMurrough. Dermott handed "the treasure" over to Strongbow, along with twenty bags of minted gold and a rolled parchment promising his succession to the kingdom of Leinster.

We are told that Eva was so streaked with soot from walking through the streets, where the air was heavy with black clouds, and her mouth was so choked with dust that Strongbow was angered at first, thinking a joke was being played on him. Eva, quickly sensing the cause of the trouble, seized a helmet from a soldier who was passing and filled it with water from a nearby well. Dipping her hands in the cold water, Eva scrubbed her face like a small child who has been bade, "wash behind your ears." In a few moments the freshened face of Eva McMurrough shone out white and clean. Smiling at Strongbow, she won him instantly. For all the wildness of the times, the alarums and excursions of war, and the bloodletting in which Red Eva and Strongbow lived, the marriage is described as a happy one. According to chroniclers, Eva bore Strongbow eight children, all boys.

In the latter years of her life, when her sons were grown, Eva was much occupied in building watch towers on the uneasy borders of Kilkenny and Limerick. A passion for erecting edifices of all kinds was also part of the many-faceted nature of Strongbow. Perhaps his finest and most lasting is the soaring beauty of Christ Church in Dublin, built in 1171. Out of remnants of the shattered chapel, which had been founded by the Danes, Strongbow erected the present church. It is in an amazing state of preservation. The raking centuries have weakened or defaced the building not at all. Vaultings and joists of oak are as strong as the day they were carved and erected. The preservation is said to be due to some mysterious chemical in the soil. Poultices of this soil are used for healing wounds and for preserving human flesh and bones.

When Strongbow died in 1176, he was buried here in a huge, oblong tomb of black slate. On top of the thick slab of slate which forms the lid is a crudely carved effigy of Strongbow in full armor of Norman design. Beside this figure lies the pitifully mutilated body of one of his sons who has been sculptured without legs. According to the *Leinster Chronicles*, this boy proved cowardly in battle, attempting to flee from encounter with the enemy. Strongbow had the boy's legs amputated.

The story of Red Eva's "lepp" varies considerably. If you engage one of the "licensed guides," and he loitering about the gates of Kilkenny Castle on fine days (I defy you ever to find one of these guides on a "dark, demented day of rain and weather," if you should want to show a visiting friend through the muniment room), he will have his own carefully befrilled version of the tremendous "lepp" taken by Red Eva McMurrough in her deadly anger against Decies, O'Rourke, and their men.

Flicky Twohig's original account of this epic leap is far and away my favorite. Let me state right now that Flicky is as engaging and chancy an individual as ever trod the cobbles of Kilkenny or any other town, and is the doyen of the licensed guides at Kilkenny Castle. I believe Flicky's baptisimal name is Brickley.

On one particular visit, I happened to ask him how he got the nickname of Flicky. He replied, "It's a class of title, or other. The flick av me tongue scalds the lot of blatherers that do be trying to tell me all about the great lepp. Sure I was all but there meself, or so ye'd think to hear me tell it."

Flicky was limping a bit, so I asked him if he was up to showing me the spot beneath the keep. For a moment the old buccaneer flared up; then, putting his hands on his hips, he said, "Ochone, I've the pain whippin' through me hips this livin' minute, that'd fall a horse." Flicky sighed and continued, "Some say I'm too old fer me job—well, I'll take ye to the tower if ye have to carry me back."

Flicky Twohig's account of Eva's Lepp is not learned by rote, where each syllable is in its exact place and never varies in the telling, like some of the monotonous ones I've heard. Oh, no! Flicky has the blood of Gaelic bards in his veins. The very essence of the raconteur in the grand manner courses through his whole being. After I had "pressed on 'im" a tageen of whisky at Doolin's pub across from the castle gates, we started along the Canal Walk to the foot of the cliff-like rise of the great circular keep.

Flicky stopped, came all over very professional, cleared his throat with a volcanic "hawk, hawk," and, favoring me with a rather dissolute wink, said, "Now, asthore, ye'll believe ivry word I say, or I'll not talk at all." I promised. Flicky proceeded. "Ye'll be after noticin' thim stones under that patch of earth in front the tower. Well, they don't lay quiet, at all. Sure, there's great auld names buried there. Decies, O'More, and O'Rourke. They lay folded away there these siven hun'red years, and still they weary their rest."

It seems that during a prolonged and wavering battle between Strongbow and Tiernan O'Rourke, which eddied at the foot of the keep of Kilkenny Castle, the tide was turning against Strongbow, who was hard pressed against the very gates of the keep itself. For hours Eva McMurrough had watched the fighting from the battlements of the keep. Having been told by her husband to stay out of the fight, Eva champed at the bit. Her emotions became so aroused that she called for her armor and two-handed battle sword, Og-Roe. Ignoring her husband's bidding, Red Eva clasped her sword in her two hands, raised it high above her head, and cried out to Strongbow below to heed her intention. Poised for a moment on the lip of the battlements, Red Eva leaped. Her famous red hair streaming out behind her, she sailed through the air. Like an eagle swooping for the kill, Red Eva plumetted down onto the heads of the astonished O'Rourke and his men. So swift, sudden, and driving was this assault that the weight of big Red Eva, plus her armor, drove the warriors into the ground ("the depth of the length they stood up in, and more," said Flicky). A pit opened under Red Eva's feet in front of the portcullis of the keep. She and Strongbow pitched the bodies of her enemies into the hole and covered them with stones. And there they lie, huddled and restless till this day.

For a few years after Red Eva maneuvered her famous leap, little is recorded in chronicles pertaining to the activities of this unpredictable woman. Her mind was occupied all this time, as it later appears, with the idea of annexing the division of land we now know as County Limerick to her already spreading demesne. It appears as well that Red Eva refused to accompany her husband to England, where he wished her to assume her rightful title as Countess of Pembroke. She never allowed anyone to call her by this title.

Battles raged back and forth between Strongbow and O'Rourke's sons before the English earl decided to visit his native land for a while. Then we hear again of Red Eva McMurrough. She had built herself a fortress tower at Cappamore, a walled town of fair size on the border of Tipperary and Limerick. The tower is built so close to the boundary line between the two counties that it encroaches on Limerick sod, "the breadth of yer foot, if ye've a foot as big as Red Eva's," a Limerick farmer once told me. Her intention was to reduce the chiefs of small tribes such as O'Murtagh and the Quinns, who held the Limerick borders and plundered far and wide. With a well-stocked town like Cappamore situated directly behind her from which to draw provisions and men-at-arms, Red Eva felt very confident of victory.

From the *Kilkenny Chronicles*, which are in the Castle Museum, one learns of Eva's tower: "Her chamber, from which she can watch any movement in the surrounding countryside, is hung with precious stuffs of silk and wool. In the like of banners, they are embroidered with scenes from the battle of Clontarf and tales of amorous dalliance. Fur rugs from the backs of animals killed in the Galty Mountains and the Nine Antrim Glens are spread upon the couches and add comfort and warmth to the stone floor." It would appear that Red Eva McMurrough did herself very well in the matter of her housing. And for all her warlike turn of mind, she liked reminders of the joys of "amorous dalliance."

Clashes between Red Eva and Desmond Quinn, her arch enemy, took place almost daily. First she would win a skirmish, then he would win one. Finally this jockeying for place, which was getting Red Eva nowhere, provoked her to arrogant fury.

She called Desmond Quinn to a hand-to-hand encounter to settle the feud. The stakes were to be undisputed hold over Limerick. He refused, saying he would not fight a woman, least of all a McMurrough. This retort drove Red Eva wild. The next day, from the arched window of her great chamber, she announced that she would pursue him into Limerick and force him to fight, or brand him a coward before his men.

Stung by this threat which mocked his courage, Desmond taunted, "If you do, I will kill you and bind your carcass to the topmost branch of an oak tree, to be pecked to shreds by rooks."

Shrieking and trembling in rage, Red Eva howled back, "If you kill me, I'll haunt you to your destruction."

Wearying of this battle of words, Desmond snarled, "I would know your ghost anywhere, and spike you."

But Red Eva had the last word: "You will not know me, for my ghost will take the shape of a red Kerry cow. Thousands of red Kerry cows roam the lands hereabouts. You'd never know which one was Eva McMurrough."

A year later, just as Red Eva was preparing to abandon the tower at Cappamore, one of Desmond Quinn's bowmen shot her in the throat as she conversed with her captain of the guard.

The spectacular Red Eva McMurrough is buried in the crypt of Kilkenny Castle. A red deer sculptured in stone lies quietly at her feet.

In many parts of Ireland it is common belief that animals are often haunted, possessed by the bitter, rampant souls of persons long dead. This may account for the strange encounter I had one summer afternoon at Red Eva McMurrough's Tower, near Cappamore. I had left Galway early that morning, stopping at The Mariner Hotel in Ballyvaughn for lunch. As I passed along the road near Bunratty Castle, I looked off and away across the fields to where, standing out sharply against the clear, robin's-egg-blue sky, loomed the gray stone tower where my favorite warrior woman had met her death so many centuries ago. Moved by some impelling force which took complete possession of me, I stopped the car and parked it off the highroad down a hawthorn-bordered bohireen. Getting out, I struck off across Farmer O'Bannon's fields.

As I approached the half-ruined tower, I noticed that there was some sort of movement inside it, for the rooks that always nested in the thick ivy patterning its walls were in high confusion. The rooks dipped and uttered the piercing ca-ca-ca-ca-ca which always strikes such a hysterical note. I approached slowly, not wishing to disturb any member of the O'Bannon family who might be in the tower. I stopped, as if I had been shot. Standing in the arched doorway of the tower was a red Kerry cow. "The ghost of Red Eva McMurrough, be the Holy," I whispered.

I went up to the Kerry heifer and put my arm around her neck. She seemed unimpressed, chewed her cud in the classic manner of all cows, Kerry or not, and blew jets of clover-scented steam through delicate nostrils. I asked Red Eva how she did and how was Strongbow the last time she saw him. Rolling a wary, purple-brown eye at me, she walked away and stood gazing reflectively across the Limerick plain, the plain she never conquered. As I left, I turned my camera on Red Eva and got a photograph of her contemplating the far horizon and the follies of this unsure world.

The Four Terrors

Rahee Castle

COUNTY ANTRIM

RAHEE CASTLE

The Four Terrors

AN OLD SONG OFTEN HEARD IN THE DUSTY alleys of Ballymoney and along the fish-littered wharves of Portrush in the County Antrim runs the like of this:

The high and mighty Grantleys
Live in terror of their lives.
Terror, Terror, Terror, Terror,
Comes in fours and never fives.

There are many families of ancient lineage in Ireland who, to this day, feel the weighty hand of disaster fall across their shoulders with dreadful regularity. Out of the dark of night it may come. Sometimes it approaches stealthily out of the sea mist. Another time, with no effort at secrecy, it strikes its victim down on a clear, luminous, moonlit night.

In many cases, this relentless and malignant persecution of a family is the fulfillment of a curse uttered in venomous anger inflamed by some real or fancied wrong. Usually accredited to "people of the roads," tinkers, and "foreign gypsies," there are cases where a member of the accursed family itself will call down a deathbed malediction on some other member.

The terrible "Stranglers Curse" of the Nunnally family of Lisroon Castle was started just after the battle of Clontarf in the eleventh century by a gallowglass, or mercenary soldier, who, perceiving that the Nunnally who owed him two years' pay was decamping from the field, robbed, then strangled him with the embossed bronze belt bearing the Nunnally device, a stag, rampant. As the belt choked the life out of Baron Nunnally, the gallowglass cried down on him a curse so potent that it has pursued the unhappy Nunnallys of Lisroon to this day.

The malcontent called on all to hear that in every generation of the direct descendants of this Nunnally, the eldest son would be strangled before he reached his majority. To doubly bind the bargain, he added that himself would come back and

91

do it. Always down the years, when the eldest son of the house of Nunnally is found strangled before his twenty-first year, the device of a stag rampant is incised in raw red flesh on his neck, just under the chin.

Three Irish family curses which rise instantly to mind because of their pitiless fury are The Curse of the Waterfords, The Fatal Cry of the Clanricardes, and, perhaps the most ill-omened and destructive of all curses, The Four Terrors of the "Grand Grantleys."

A synopsis of these curses in the order in which I mention them will afford the reader a picture of how diabolical these ancient curses can be.

The stalking, untimely death which hounds the male de la Poer-Beresfords, heirs to the Marquisate of Waterford and magnificent Curraghmore, usually takes the form of an accident—a fall in the hunting field or the collapse during a storm of a footbridge over a freshet-swollen river in the Curraghmore demesne. There have been times when the mental strain of watching and waiting proved too strong. Resistance cracked. The Waterford Curse was fulfilled by suicide.

The origin of The Cry of the Clanricardes is not clearly defined. No records are in existence for the reason of the far-reaching power of this curse, or when it was uttered.

The cry rang out one night in 1690 at Portumna Castle in County Galway. Next morning the Clanricarde heir was found weltering in his own gore. The body lay sprawled across a great four-posted bed. The head, completely severed at the base of the neck, stood propped upright on a table in the window bay. The staring eyes were gazing out to sea.

It is said that Clanricardes died mysterious and violent deaths long before 1690. However that may be, this is the first recorded. Described by those who have heard it, "The Cry" starts on a low gurgling note, rising to a chilling, fearful crescendo, then dies away again in a gurgle. The sound is as if some unfortunate was being strangled, or was in mortal agony from a sword thrust. It may well be the latter. Clanricardes have ever been warriors and met death on the field of battle.

In one instance this was not true. The eccentric Marquess of Clanricarde who held the title in 1870 was no soldier. He lived in abject poverty, hoarding an astronomical income and letting beautiful Portumna Castle fall derelict, a haunt for rats and rot. After his death, some say from miserly, willful starvation, his vast fortune was divided among many heirs. It brought them only misery and dread.

Surely the most signal case is that of Viscountess Boyne, an indirect heiress. The virulent curse seems to have singled her out, a frail and lovely woman, as victim of its fury.

G'AYNOR
NI-GRANTLEY.
RAHEE CASTLE. JR '88

One night she was awakened by two horrible cries, mounting on the night silence, then dying away—two cries, separated by minutes. Within a few days word was brought to Lady Boyne that two members of her family had been killed. Within a year she heard the exact two cries again. Shortly after, she received news of two more sudden deaths in her family.

A few years elapsed. The German legions were sweeping everything before them in Europe. Human fortitude was at low ebb. One night, just before Dunkirk, Lady Boyne heard the foreboding cries again. Loud and terrible, they rose and fell—three distinct cries. Within the week, word arrived that her eldest son, Gustavus, had been shot just as he was boarding a British destroyer at Dunkirk. Her second son, John, was killed in Africa by an exploding mine. A few weeks later her third son, Desmond, was crushed to death by a runaway truck in Sicily. Her youngest, Richard, a boy of fifteen, is still living.

The score of seven deaths chalked up on the roster of the family curse leaves Lady Boyne the greatest sufferer in the annals of Clanricarde.

The Four Terrors, the curse of the "Grand Grantleys," has a haunting quality of Gaelic legend hovering over it, apart from the actual haunt itself.

At the time Rahee Keep was built by Shamas Roe, head of the Tribe O'Hanlon, the building of a fortress was a long and serious business. "Stronghold" was the very definition of the word. The constant threat of attack from both sea and land caused a landholder to build the strongest possible walls to house his family and men-at-arms.

Danes, Normans, Norwegians, and Spanish pirates seemed intent on despoiling Ireland. Shamas Roe had as neighbor one of the proudest tribal families of the north, the Corballys of Dunluce Castle. Dunluce rose, a mighty rampart standing sheer from the same rocks which form the Giant's Causeway a few miles to the east. A vast pile of purple-gray rock, it seems one with the crag on which it is built, which, in fact, forms the tortuous dungeons and secret escape corridors that honeycomb the base of the castle. For so early a fortress, built as it was for strength and not for looks, Dunluce is of astounding magnificence.

It commanded, when built in 1009, as it does today, the land and sea for miles. One tower, a great hollow drum of stone used as a lighthouse, was built in the manner of the still-standing drum lighthouses of the early Phoenicians at Carthage. The Corbally impounded slaves taken in border wars or galley-bait captured from pirate ships wrecked on the devious Antrim rocks to haul bundles of faggots and logs from the densely wooded Antrim Glens. Gigantic fires were kindled nightly. Belching flames and reddened smoke, these leaping fires guided sailors far out at sea.

Dunluce rises today against the scudding clouds, a ruined dream of power. To many, this castle with its delicate pinnacles and pointed chimneys is the most beautiful ruin in Ireland. It is the most dramatic, surely. Compared with the majority of early Gaelic castles, which were built more or less to pattern, Dunluce seems remote from this world, something out of Norwegian lore, "East of the Sun and West of the Moon," perchance the palace of the North Wind King's Daughter.

I have seen Dunluce from an off-shore island near Benbane Head against a vivid sunset with purple, magenta, and crimson clouds massing against a sky of acid yellow. In silhouette Dunluce takes on a strangely Eastern look, a skyline like the *kasbah* of a Berber sheik in the fastness of the High Atlas, flanked by truly Gaelic fortress towers. It seems a pagan cenotaph to the ancient dead, where time stands still.

The Castle of Rahee was never comparable to Dunluce, either in beauty of line and proportion or in strength. Until 1410, the O'Hanlons held Rahee Keep against all comers. Fighting was constant and fierce along Ireland's northern coast. Rahee held firm, probably because of its position high on an escarpment which at high tide was an island.

The Corballys looked down on the Grantleys, no matter how "Grand" their reputation. Then one day, during the siege of Rahee Castle by Conn Grantley, his eldest son, Donard, took his longbow and went foraging for game in the woods near his father's camp. His way led to a hillock overlooking a path through the glen on the far side of a wall surrounding the Corbally demesne. Donard heard the clip-clop of horses' hoofs, and there along the path appeared Aultain Corbally, riding towards Dunluce with a woman companion. Forthwith Donard ni Grantley "Traded his heart for love— and disquiet," as the Connaught people say. Evening came and Donard returned to camp empty handed. In his breast was an empty place where his heart had been, as well.

Before winter settled on the land in the year 1411, the starving O'Hanlon made a truce with the "Grand" Grantley. Shamas, humbled by privation, asked a boon—that he, his family, and his household might emerge and disappear into the hinterland un-molested. This was granted, with the proviso that all able-bodied men-at-arms sur-render as prisoners. Thus the O'Hanlon and all his get take no further part in this story.

Grantley had gained his title of "Grand" because of the grandeur in which he lived, coupled with the loftiness of his ideas. Oddly enough, these ideas were usually successful. The Grantleys, like the "Daring Desmonds" and the "Fantastic Delavals," are synonymous with luxurious living. Their profligate and handsome persons em-broider with brilliant threads the pages of Irish history.

While the Goddess of Fortune has smiled upon the Grantleys down the years, they were not able to escape the curse of The Four Terrors, which has at times nearly caused the extermination of the direct male line.

The first gesture made by Conn Grantley after his victorious assault of Rahee Castle was to ingratiate himself with the proud and powerful Corballys. At first his advances were coldly received. Not to be put off, he persevered. He must swallow his pride in order to further the suit of his lovelorn son and heir, Donard, and the fair Aultain.

Boatloads of splendid presents and loot from the plundered O'Hanlon and other victims .robbed by Grantley were rowed to the water-steps of Dunluce. After a few months, Liam Corbally consented, in a rather patronizing manner, to the marriage of his daughter Aultain and Donard nì Grantley.

As far as was apparent, everything went smoothly at the wedding, and for years afterwards. But the "Old Woman of Gonn" was surely a silent and unseen guest at the ceremony, for it was Gaynor Grantley, the first son born of this union, whose evil deeds so mounted that they finally toppled him and his fortunes into the dust. It was Gaynor who brought down the dreadful curse upon the Grantleys forever after.

Five sons were born to Aultain and Donard. Morlan was the youngest. Gaynor, the eldest, was heir to Rahee Castle and the fortunes of his father and grandfather, the rapacious old Conn Grantley.

As Gaynor grew to manhood, a fear took root in his murky mind. It was the knowledge that, when his grandfather died, shares of his money would go to the four other Grantley boys, Morlan, Durmuid, Ronan, and Conn. A share of his mother's wealth would be divided between his brothers as well, since Aultain was a great heiress in her own right. Her dowry had been the talk of the north when she had ridden as a bride under the iron-spiked portcullis of Rahee. Her head held high, ash-blond hair gleaming like silver gilt in the spring sunlight, a sweeping cloak of gold-threaded, wine-red samite rippling from her shoulders, Aultain had looked the very heartbeat of a northern queen.

For hours on end, Gaynor would prowl among the rocks, brooding. He must think of some way to circumvent this natural course of events. Even as a small boy he had been devious, treacherous as the winds that blew the tall ships out of their courses to break their keels on Rahee Rock. Animals loathed him. Only by his prodigious strength and the quick and crafty brain of him was he able to tame a horse. Many times horses had nearly savaged him to death.

Gaynor's hate for his brothers grew with the advancing years. They, in turn, gave him a wide berth. They never included him in their games. He was never wanted when the boys went out with the trawlers and fishing curraghs to Rathlin Island or to

CONN MORLAN

THREE BROTHERS
of GAYNOR
N. GRANTLEY R A 38

RONAN

the wild Inishtrull, a towering pillar of serrated rock where the hunt for cormorant and gulls eggs was richly rewarded. Gaynor not only demanded, but took, the biggest share.

The younger boys were inseparable companions, for they were nearly of an age together. When Conn, the youngest, was nineteen, Morlan was twenty-three. Gaynor was twenty-six.

A few miles from Rahee Castle there extends a long, narrow belt of bog-land. Black and dread it lies. Shallow pools of brackish water wink back at the sky. Cardree Bog it is called. An ill-omened, stinking acre, Cardree's yield of good turf is nil. It is a blot on a fair countryside. Old men walking the roads, and they warily picking their way across the path that skirts the bog, spit in it and say, "Arragh, this is where the divil fouled the land, surely." A traveler enters the bog-acre just past Armoy, the great fortress-place guarding the approaches to the Nine Glens of Antrim.

Riding slowly across Cardee Bog one rainy evening, Gaynor Grantley was deep in thought. At last he had formed a plan of action, a monument to treachery, full worthy of Gaynor's circuitous mind. He must proceed craftily. His brothers were wary of him and his infrequent attempts at friendliness. He knew this well.

The ardor with which Gaynor threw himself into the campaign of winning over his brothers was worthy of a far better cause. He gave Conn his finest wolfhound bitch, Orra, long coveted by his young brother. To cautious-eyed Durmuid he gave a wide belt of hand-wrought red gold. Displayed on the clasp was a full, radiant sun, the Grantley symbol of their brightness and power. The boys accepted these gifts somewhat coolly. Gaynor smiled and back-slapped in high humor. He bided his time.

One day in early autumn, the sun blazed forth after a fortnight of dull days, soaking with rain and wet, misty winds from the sea. To Gaynor this seemed an omen of good fortune for his enterprise. The Grantley sun shone forth in all its glory.

There was feasting at Rahee Castle that night. Owen O'Curran, a chieftain from Galway, the City of the Tribes, had stopped at the castle with his retinue of huntsmen and gallowglasses. After the smoking roasts had been cut from the carcasses of ox and boar, the bones were tossed to the hounds who fought in corners of the room. Horns of light beer made from fermented wheat and honey were passed round. Owen O'Curran held his listeners spellbound with his stories of a great hunting trip, which had extended across the demesnes of friendly chieftains who had joined him in the hunt, all the way from Galway to Antrim. He had found the red-brown bear in the dense Sperrin Mountains, a rare trophy in Ireland. He had swelled the winter larders of all his hosts. This very boar they were eating he had speared. Tomorrow he would set out for the Nine Glens and swing east to Killkeel Bay, at the foot of the Mourne

Mountains. From there he would take ship, sailing north, then west, to Galway.

As Owen O'Curran finished his tales, there was a long silence. Then Gaynor spoke. "Neither my brothers nor myself have ever explored the wildness of the Nine Glens, though we were reared on great tales of the Giants and the Little People who hide there. We would like to ride with you tomorrow, returning at our will." And so it was agreed.

The days continued cool and fair. Banners of color unfurled and spread across the Glens. It was a grand sight, surely. Each boy carried a parchment scroll at his belt. In it he wrote the name of each Glen as they entered.

The retinue of The O'Curran camped outside the gates of Rathlarn Castle and, just after dawn the next morning, entered the first of the fabled Nine Glens of Antrim: Glenarm, sunny and spread with asters and wild haws; Glencloy, darkling, where the tall ferns rusted in the October air; Glenariff, small and pinched, haunted by the Dun Bull who slew Queen Raghilla's child and was in turn hunted down and slain by her; Glen Ballymon, where a lake lies still as death, and as black; Glencorp and Glendun, the twin glens, where the silence is more terrifying than clamor; then dark, dark, Glenshesk, the banshees' lair, where ten dead princesses lie under the Great Stone of Shesk; and last and darkest of all the glens, Glentow, where tall trees touch the sky and lean close together, forever telling and retelling old runes of the proud Gael.

At Ballyclare, the five brothers Grantley said farewell to The O'Curran and his men. Turning west, they circled Lough Neagh, the largest and surely the loveliest lake in Ireland. On the southernmost tip of the lough, near Lurgan, stands a round tower over a hundred feet high, wider at its base than the span of fifty horsemen riding abreast. Here the boys camped the night, setting out early next day for Dungannon.

Gaynor, quiet until now, took the bit in his teeth. He said that instead of going round by Tobermore and through the Glenshane Pass into Derry, they would make haste to reach Rahee by a shorter route. He added that at this time of year they might encounter the cold November winds screeching down the Pass. At first the boys, four against one, held firm. They would chance rough weather in the Pass for the great hunting it would give them. In the end, constant bullying from Gaynor wore them down. Setting out along the fringes of the lough they rode through Moneymore, heading for Kilrea and Rahee. What the four did not know was that this route, so blandly chosen by Gaynor, would lead them across the shunned Bog of Cardree.

Because the country around Maghera, in Derry, through which their way led, was wild, and marauding stragglers from Tyrone's battered army still lurked in the forests, the Grantleys wore half-armor. Hauberks of chain mesh reached to their knees, and pliant armor plate covered their breasts, backs, and arms. Each boy carried, besides his longbow, a stout sword and a small square shield of tough, fire-hardened oxhide. A light hunting spear, arrow tipped in bronze, was laid across the saddlebow. The young Grantleys considered themselves well armed for anything short of actual battle.

Gaynor took arrogant charge, spacing his four brothers in single file, he riding well ahead. The homeward journey was uneventful until the last day. A surprise awaited the boys at Carone Cross, where three roads meet. Waiting to join them and ride the rest of the way in their company was Roan Corbally, their uncle from Dunluce.

Returning from hunting, the uncle had heard from a messenger that the Grantleys were riding in his direction. Gaynor argued at first that they were in a great hurry; Corbally's mare could not follow the pace they must set to reach Rahee by midnight. Roan laughed at this. Finally Gaynor realized there was nothing to do but give him his way. He partly pacified himself with the thought that what he had to do could be visited on five as well as four. A meal was eaten hurriedly at the Cross Inn. By mid-afternoon they set out, riding furiously in order to cross the vicious bog before dark. When their uncle heard the road Gaynor insisted on taking, he said that if they did not reach the bog before dark, he, for one, would not venture across it until the next day.

On hearing this statement, Gaynor put his uncle directly behind himself. He could deal with him quicker that way. Riding well ahead, Gaynor found it necessary to stop twice as evening approached. Probing for an imaginary stone in the frog of his horse's hoof took time. Mending a broken saddle girth that looked suspiciously as if it had been cut took more time. Halts of one kind and another prevented the travelers from reaching the edge of Cardree Bog until night was settling perilously fast over the world.

Gaynor had spent years inspecting every inch of the bog road. He knew where the pools of stagnant water were deepest and which one covered a scum-pool far more lethal to a horse and man, weighted down with armor, than quicksand ever was. He even knew a spot, a quarter way across, where the shoulders of the road spread out over some rocks. A man might draw out of line here. The rock shoulders would prevent him from slipping off into the muck. Now, he made for this spot at breakneck speed. Looking back, he saw his uncle and four brothers, all lying low over their horses' withers. One thought, and one only was in each mind: to get across this hell-boil bog as quickly as a horse could run. Gaynor smiled evilly to himself. The hour he had waited for longer than he could remember had arrived.

He brought the flat of his sword in a sharp slap on his horse's rump. The horse leaped forward, so that Gaynor was yards ahead of his uncle. His brothers were strung out, fifty yards or so apart—Morlan, Durmuid, Ronan, young Conn last. As his horse reached the widest spot in the road, Gaynor swung out of line, yanking the horse into a position at right angles across the narrow road. The bog winked and sloughed on either side. All was deadly dark.

In a flash his uncle thundered up, reining in his horse. Livid anger and stark fear followed, one upon the other, across Roan's face as he sensed what was up. Gaynor's sword slashed at the hocks of Roan's horse. Letting out a piercing, womanish shriek, the horse plunged into the bog, carrying his frantic rider with him.

On came Morlan and Durmuid, almost abreast now. Both had drawn their swords, but Gaynor rushed upon them, gigantic in his lust to kill. With one lunge of his sword he pierced Morlan's throat. Morlan, choking on gushing blood, slid into the bog and was slowly sucked under. Durmuid's horse crashed into the dark water as Gaynor made a lunge at his rider. It was the deepest of the pools, for horse and youth disappeared instantly.

A snorting horse almost ran Gaynor down. As he quickly turned, Ronan slipped from the horse, and, grasping his sword and shield, prepared to make a stand against his demented elder brother. Over his shoulder he cried to Conn behind him, "Turn if you can, ride for your life, tell what you have seen. Ride, ride, Conn, save yourself."

Brave Ronan Grantley made a stand. He fought well, his rage and horror giving him strength. But he was outmatched by the incredible strength of his diabolical brother. Ronan slashed first at Gaynor's face. So true was his hand that a deep red gash opened along Gaynor's cheek from ear to chin. "One," cried Ronan. Again his sword slashed. "Two," he called, as another sword sweep curled back the flesh from Gaynor's cheek. "One for Roan, one for Morlan, and here is one for Durmuid," he shouted, as his sword ploughed across Gaynor's chin.

Although Gaynor was blinded by pain and blood, his first shock of surprise at Ronan's strength and fury quickly passed. Making a downward thrust, Gaynor caught Ronan in the groin, wrenched his sword out of his hand, and flung it far out into the bog.

As Ronan sank slowly to the ground, he was conscious of two things: the sound of Conn's horse galloping away, bearing his young brother to Rahee, and the thought of the dagger in his belt. Quick as lightning he pulled it out of its sheath. As Gaynor leaned over to lift him up and throw him after the others, he raked the hideous, blood-soaked face once again. A great slice seemed to come away. "Four," murmured Ronan. "Four murders; I curse you and yours forever." As he felt himself sinking into the reeking mud of the bog, Ronan lifted his arm. Bending his thumb back against the palm, he spread four fingers in the manner of gypsies. "Four you murdered. Four is your curse. Four will murder you."

Strange as it may seem, the tale told by Gaynor Grantley when he arrived, more dead than alive, at Rahee Castle was believed by his father. Young Conn had arrived on a foundering horse at midnight in a state so confused his babblings were fantastic.

Gaynor said that he, his brothers, and Roan Corbally had been waylaid by Tyrone's renegade gallowglasses, who prowled the countryside, robbing and killing all in their path. This was probable enough to give his infamous story weight. Overpowered, his uncle and brothers had been killed, robbed, and thrown into Cardree Bog. He, not Ronan, had called out to Conn to ride for his life. He had, of course, killed many of the highwaymen. It is said that Conn never again gained his reason. His mind was "away" forever after.

Gaynor Grantley, odiously scarred, married a daughter of the Tribe O'Flaherty of County Galway, a bleak, cruel woman who bore him ten children. Four were wiped out by the curse.

The Curse of the Four Terrors struck first after Gaynor inherited Rahee Castle, and in a most singular manner. After four of his finest stallions had been found with their windpipes cut, awash in their own blood, Gaynor posted men-at-arms as sentries at every door of the stables and castle. Then, one morning a sentry was found gibbering, clawing at his mouth. Weeks after, when he had regained his speech and could remember, he told of walking his beat along the battlements over the portcullis. Suddenly he heard a sound as of armor scraping together. Surrounding him, he saw four figures of men in rusty armor dripping with bog water. They reeked of decay and the nauseating stench of death. That is all he remembered.

Three times after that episode, guards were found in more or less the same horrified state, unable to talk or remember for varying lengths of time. When again coherent, they told a similar story.

When Gaynor's eldest son was eighteen years old, he was found lying dead in the bottom of a curragh he had been sailing. There were four gashes across his face. Three more of Gaynor's children were found dead. All bore the same four gashes.

In his sixtieth year, the torso of Gaynor Grantley was discovered on the rocks at the foot of his Castle Rahee. Both arms had been cut off at the shoulders. Both legs were cut off at the hips. Arms and legs were bound together around a rusted sword, in the manner of the fasces of a Roman lictor.

Apparently no generation of Grantleys, direct descendants of Gaynor, entirely escaped the curse. Yet the curse did not always mean death. Many instances were recorded in which the same ghostly apparitions seen by the sentries at Rahee appeared to members of the family. In all cases, however, the partial paralysis of vocal cords and mind were apparent. This state lasted anywhere from a month to a year. Three cases have been recorded where repeated visitations resulted in the persons' losing their reason completely and being declared insane. In 1772, a cousin of Georgiana, Duchess of Devonshire, married Hugh St. Ormond Grantley, direct descendant of Gaynor. Grantley brought her to "new" Rahee Castle, built in 1740. Two nights after her arrival she rose from her bed and went to the head of the staircase, which ascended in a spreading curve from a wide stair hall below. She was found next morning in a completely paralyzed state by her bridegroom. Since her mind was never lucid again and she never spoke, no one ever knew exactly what she saw. Considering the other cases, it must have been the Four Terrors in rusty armor, dripping with slime from Cardree Bog.

The present house called Rahee Castle is built of stone, whitewashed with lime. Designed in the Palladian style, it commands a splendid view of the romantic ruin of old Rahee Castle on its rocky, sea-drenched eminence, half a mile away.

In 1892 the eldest Grantley boy, heir to the estates, was found dead in the drawing room the morning after his return from India, where his regiment had been stationed. On his arrival at Rahee he told the assembled dinner party that an extraordinary thing had happened to him before he left Darjeeling. He had received three mysterious letters, weeks apart. They had been slipped under the door of a bungalow he shared with two other officers of his regiment. The letters were on fine quality white stationery and bore the Grantley symbol, a sun, radiating rays of light. Each letter was worded the same: "Do not return to Ireland, and Rahee Castle." Unsigned, they were written in a bold, dashing male script. He had disregarded them, thinking some joker was playing a bit heavily on the well-known family curse. He sailed. The day before his ship was to dock, he noticed an envelope slipped under his stateroom door. It was identical with the letters he had received in India, and with the same warning. Four letters.

In the case of the dead young Grantley heir in the drawing room at Rahee, there was a curious deviation in the mutilation of the corpse. There were no gashes, but four fingers of the right hand had been hacked off. The fingers were never found.

Shallardstown and the Orloff Whip

COUNTY WATERFORD

PRINCESS · ORLOFF

Shallardstown
and the Orloff Whip

O N A LATE DECEMBER AFTERNOON, JUST AS
it was approaching twilight, a heavy landau creaked along a lonely
marsh road in the back country of County Waterford. It is difficult
to imagine a more barren, desolate stretch of road anywhere. Certainly this winding road bordered by brackish pools and wind-rattled
grasses is an exception in the South of Ireland. Most people would avoid this part of
the countryside when taking a pleasure drive; for, as a man of the roads will say, and
you meeting him, "A scar on the lovely face of Waterford. The divil spit here for an
auld grudge, and he passing."

On this sharp, cold, November day the clop-clop of sixteen heavily shod hoofs as
they trotted along the road became so magnified that you would say a troop of cavalry
was approaching. On the iron-hard road, bright sparks flew from stones scattered by
the heavy yellow wheels of the landau. The rumble of the passing vehicle startled the
blue and white herons resting in the marsh grass. They rose with dripping wings and
flew off to quieter grounds at Dungarvan.

The landau swung round a curve in the road, and the lead horses strained forward
to breast a slight hill. Silhouetted against the cloudless, pale-green evening sky, the battered old carriage seemed about to fall apart. For all its look of clumsy durability when
seen close to, it appeared overlong and spidery in design when etched cleanly against
the flat, clear distance of sky.

This rather seedy equipage was an old Austrian court landau acquired in Vienna
by the Princess Orloff when she was returning to Ireland from her honeymoon in St.
Petersburg.

In Vienna, she and her husband had ridden in a landau of this design while at-
tending cavalry maneuvers with the Emperor. The Imperial landau had been drawn
by eight porcelain-white Lippizaners from Westphalia, four postilions up. Today this
battered old yellow and black carriage harnessed four dark-chestnut cobs. The horses
were old, showing a sprinkling of gray hairs in their dusty coats. Two postilions in the

107

Orloff livery of yellow and black leaned stiffly over their horses' withers, half perishing with the cold.

At the top of the rise, the carriage halted for a moment while one of the postilions sprang to the ground and busied himself repairing a broken breeching leather. The victoria top of cracked, varnished leather was pushed back. This gave a glimpse of the extraordinary occupant of the landau.

Sitting sunk in a swaddling mass of purple brocade and billows of Russian sable was a figure who resembled nothing so much as a sleeping Buddha. The outline suggested neither man nor woman. It was just a figure, an image, an idol. The face was obscured by a broad-brimmed flat hat of purple velvet, the crown encircled with dingy, matted, purple ostrich plumes. A veil of the same color swathed the lower part of the face. Only the shadowed eyes were left uncovered, and they were closed, as if asleep. The figure had the look of one of the gorgeously dressed marionettes one sees in Venice. *Persone Fantastichi*, Venetian children call them. They jerk into flamboyant life when their strings are pulled. This planted figure looked as if its strings had been forever cut.

The postilion leaped into the saddle. The cobs pulled back a little, going downhill. At the foot of the hill the rider of the lead horse turned for a second to catch the eye of the man astride the wheeler. Raising his hand to signify his intention of hurrying the pace, he winked and nodded his head towards the graven image huddled in the corner of the landau. The other postilion smiled and shrugged his yellow whipcord shoulders. A sharp cut with the whip and the four cobs broke into a gallop.

In the gathering darkness, the landau swung in at the gates of Shallardstown. Wheels sprayed the loose gravel of the circular driveway and groaned to a stop. Lights appeared in the lower windows of the house. A tall, thin man opened the great mahogany doors and stood waiting at the top of the steps. This man was Creed, the butler. After a moment's watching, he descended the steps and opened the carriage door. He put his hand on the arm of the silent purple figure. With the help of Creed, the cloaked figure slowly climbed the flight of wide stone steps. The two disappeared into the house. During this arrival not a word had been spoken.

SHALLARDSTOWN AND PARROTTSTOWN

In the year 1778 two brothers by the name of Parrott arrived in Ireland, accompanying their father, General Aloysius Parrott, who was returning to his native land from India. General Parrott was the fortunate heir to a large and rich inheritance from an uncle. Having also amassed a considerable fortune of his own in India in the Choppa silk trade, the general felt that his declining years would be happy ones indeed.

The first concern of the general was the building of a suitable house. For to enjoy properly a rich life, one must be magnificently housed. So the general built a large, rather windy edifice, with a vast frontage, a pillared portico, and no comfort. He called the house Parrottstown. His two sons—Cadogan, the heir, and Bartholomew—hated the house. They barely stepped foot in it from one month's end to the next.

Cadogan spent most of his time traveling in Spain and Italy. He bought a small Charles II house with the delightful name of Arhigadee Court, near Malahide, on the Irish Sea. Here he pursued the sport of cockfighting. Many were the famous mains arranged here.

Bartholomew held horse racing to be the prime sport for gentlemen. He owned some of the finest thoroughbred horses of his day, among them the history-making stallion Tambour. So little did Bartholomew think of draughty Parrottstown that he lived in two rooms in the stables. He named it Paddock House, and many fine toasts were drunk therein.

In lonely grandeur, the general tried vainly to keep up some sort of state in his unwieldy barracks. But Fortuna, who had so lavishly set him up in this house, now pulled it down about his head. Fortuna's sister Fate took a hand and dealt the bedeviled general a series of blows by straddling him with almost continuous illness. One bout of sickness after another laid the general low. Finally, in midsummer, the wretched man was stricken with "the Pox," as smallpox was called then. He recovered from it, but with a badly disfigured face.

Soon after this misfortune, Parrottstown burned to the ground. One windy, winter night the house caught fire. The pond at the side of the house was frozen over for the first time in years. This of course hampered the few servants and farmers who turned out to fight the blaze. The high wind fanned the flames to an inferno. In no time, Parrottstown, gaping at every seam, tottered to a pile of blackened stones and embers.

For two years after the loss of his house by fire, the general traveled on the Continent. In Venice he came under the spell, as had so many Irish gentlemen before him, of the houses along the Brenta Canal, built by Andrea Palladio. He secured a set of plans and elevations for a house in the Palladian taste. Returning immediately to County Waterford, he chose a piece of land on a gentle rise of ground. This rise was shaded by a woods of oak trees. Here he set about building the house he called Shallardstown, named for his late wife, who was born Lady Aileen Shallard.

Cadogan Parrott, realizing that he, as heir to his father's large estates, must inherit whatever house his grandiose father chose to build, attempted to prevent the dire mistakes which attended the building of ill-fated Parrottstown. Cadogan set out from Arhigadee for Ballymacorthy, the village nearest the Parrott demesne. Arriving late at night, he took rooms at the village inn. Next morning he went out early to the site his father had chosen for his new house. Workmen were just breaking ground, so he was in time. General Parrott was greatly pleased that he should wish to superintend the building of the house, for Cadogan's good sense and fine, sure taste were well known.

The Palladian elevations for Shallardstown pleased everyone who saw them. The house as it stands today is, in construction and intent, exactly as it was in Cadogan Parrott's day. The general, unhappily, did not survive a fit of gastric poisoning contracted in London and died before the house was completed. He had purposely gone to London to stay until the house was finished. He would, he said, return for the housewarming.

Shallardstown stands deeply embowered in trees, mainly Irish oaks and beeches. It is a gracious house of soft white Connemara stone, not too large, but spacious. The flight of stone steps leading to the portico is a miracle of line and balance. The portico itself is one of the finest in Ireland. Inside the house are a series of living rooms opening one into the other in the Italian manner. These rooms alternate in proportion with single cubes and double cubes. Throughout the house, the wide, beautifully spaced windows arrest the eye. To me, Shallardstown is a completely satisfying house on all counts.

Two years after Cadogan Parrott had taken up residence at Shallardstown, he married a woman at least fifteen years older than himself. Her name was Angelica Gammage and she hailed from Clonmel, in the County Tipperary. She was considered the finest horsewoman in Ireland at that time, which was the year 1806.

Mrs. Cadogan Parrott was a handsome woman, built in the heroic mold, the "classic" type, so much admired in the epoch known as Regency. She was, however, of a peculiar turn of mind. For days she would fight waves of a strange, overpowering melancholy. At times she exhibited a wild, sadistic streak. Often the high, east chamber at Shallardstown, which was her bedroom, rang with her hysterical shrieks.

She bore Cadogan two children, both girls, fifteen years apart. The first daughter was named Angelica, after herself. The second child, a sickly, spindly little girl, was called Rosaleen. It was a poor choice of name to hand this frail infant. For, as Angelica said later, "I'll venture that Mamma had 'The Dark Rosaleen' of Red Hugh O'Donnell's song in mind when she named my sister. But that Rosaleen was of the lusty, Black Irish of the West. My sister is golden-fair. She has a milksop nature, to boot."

After her second child was born, Mrs. Parrott set out to travel in Europe. She was gone from Shallardstown for three years. On her return she gave up any activities in the countryside. No hunting. No racing. She seldom went outside the gates of the Shallardstown demesne, even to drive her dogcart to a tandem of two spanking cobs. For years she had bred these cobs for just such showing.

Soon after her return from Europe her mental illness returned. One night, in a fit of rage, she tried to stab her husband. Next day she disappeared from Shallardstown, arriving breathless, late in the evening, at the house of her sister, Mrs. Delemere, who lived at Tramore. Her sister said later that Mrs. Parrott was in a very distraught frame of mind. She cried out that a terrible obsession claimed her. She craved to kill. Mrs. Delemere put her sister to bed, giving her a strong sleeping draught and hoping that a long night's rest would ease her mind. But in the morning the bedroom that had been given to Mrs. Parrott was empty. She had slipped out of the house sometime during the night. As she had arrived at the Delemere house with no belongings, it was thought she would not go far and would soon return. Two days later the battered body of Mrs. Cadogan Parrott was found washed up on the rocks off Hook Head, near Tramore Bay.

When young Angelica Parrott was told of her mother's death and how it had happened, she said an odd, cryptic thing, "I knew she would take her own life, somehow, sometime. I saw it in her eyes. I have eyes just like hers."

The tall girl who was now mistress up at "the great house" was known to everyone in the countryside as "Miss Angelica." She was not exactly popular. She was, rather, respected, even a little feared.

One afternoon Miss Angelica was entertaining the parish priest in the drawing room. Owen, the footman, brought in the tea barrow. Going out of the room, he forgot to close the big double doors. Later, Miss Angelica gave him a raking over the coals for his forgetfulness. Owen told of it below stairs: "The saints surround me. She's a scaldin' class of tongue. Just like her Ma. Do ye know, she gits more like her Ma ivry day she's let live."

In 1833, Rosaleen Parrott was sixteen years old. She was distractingly pretty, in a babyish sort of way. All her life, especially when evil days hounded her to the brink of insanity, her fair, violet-eyed immaturity won her great pity. But little else. The day after her birthday, Rosaleen was sent off to Mistress Dunnelyn's Conservatory For Musically Inclined Young Gentlewomen, at Dalkey, near Dublin.

The years seemed to fly past the Palladian windows of Shallardstown. A few months after her mother's death, Angelica Parrott went to Paris to replenish her wardrobe. She had inherited her fondness for fashionable clothes from her opulent mother, along with her strange eyes. While she was away, Cadogan Parrott died suddenly, leaving her sole heiress to Shallardstown. Since the place was entailed, it could never be willed out of the family. For her lifetime, Angelica Parrott would be an immensely rich woman.

It did not take long for the eligible young men of the neighborhood, and some not so eligible, to hear of Miss Parrott's good fortune. They flocked to her doorstep, laden with flowers and notes asking to pay their respects.

After a suitable period of mourning for her father, Miss Parrott began to entertain at Shallardstown. It was entertainment on the grand scale.

Among the suitors who paid the amazonian Miss Parrott ardent court was Dagan Ferritter, a handsome, aloof fellow from Lismore. He lived with his widowed mother, Lady Ferritter, at Clonbally Castle, an ancient, weather-beaten house, rapidly falling into ruin. Money was woefully scarce at Clonbally. Lady Ferritter bade her lazy, improvident son hasten his suit, lest another and more gifted man outstrip him.

Angelica Parrott looked Dagan over carefully, the way one does a stallion. She mused, "A fine, big body. He looks in great health. No faults there. Of course, the Ferritters haven't a penny, but that doesn't matter to me. He looks quiet and tractable, probably a little stupid. Well, I can manage him. I want an heir to Shallardstown. This man looks as if he could give it to me."

Forthwith Miss Parrott made a proposal to Dagan Ferritter. He accepted with suspicious alacrity. Perhaps, she thought later, she should have looked closer into the recesses of Dagan's mind and learned some of his habits. She would have learned that he was inordinately vain. He was extravagant to the point of idiocy. He was devious with women and bone lazy to the world.

The time of the year was December. Miss Parrott decided to give a grand ball on Christmas Eve. She would ask the entire county; all Ireland could come if it wished, so expansive did she feel these days. When the ball was at its height, at the stroke of midnight, she would stand beside Dagan Ferritter, on the third step of the hall staircase, and announce their betrothal. The wedding would take place at Shallardstown one week after the announcement.

Two days before Christmas, Rosaleen Parrott arrived home for the holidays. She had blossomed out considerably. Her wine-red velvet pelisse, trimmed with white fur, set off her fair beauty. At first glance she looked radiant, but only at first glance. The longer one looked at Rosaleen, the more one became conscious that she was vapid to a degree. Her eyes, so lovely a shade of violet, held a vacant stare that was upsetting. It crossed one's mind that if the top of Miss Rosaleen's head were removed, feathers would fly out.

The night of the Christmas Eve ball, Shallardstown outdid itself. Ropes of burnished bog ivy and holly garlanded the gleaming rose-marble columns of the drawing room. Huge Italian urns filled with red amaryllis lilies flamed against white walls and yellow curtains. Black lacquer trays of fresh and sugared fruits stood on tables in the corners of the hall. An army of footmen ladled out brandy punch and spiced toddies. Everyone hung upon the entrance of the Misses Parrott.

Down the stairs, glowing brightly in the light of hundreds of wax tapers, came the two sisters, arms encircling each other's waists. Miss Angelica looked a tall, raven-haired Artemis. Her gown of emerald velvet fell straight to the floor from her full breasts. She blazed with diamonds. Someone murmured, "A tour de force."

Rosaleen, on the other hand, was a spring flower, a Daphne in soft pink. Her pale gold hair was in ringlets, caught with pearls. Her lips were a little parted and the vacant eyes seemed to focus nowhere. At the sight of Rosaleen Parrott, Dagan's heart turned handsprings in his breast. A thought rose in his sluggish mind. He would wed Rosaleen Parrott, not Angelica.

The Misses Parrott mingled with their guests. At least, Angelica did. Dagan immediately possessed himself of Rosaleen's hand, and they moved swiftly out of the crowd and into a small room set out with tables for cards. No one was in the room, and there Dagan made love to her. Rosaleen, unaccustomed to violent love-making, was easily won. What simple Rosaleen did not know was that this sudden infatuation on the part of devious Dagan Ferritter was frosted over with his brand of reasoning. One day Angelica would die. She might die young—who knew? In any case, the estate being entailed, Rosaleen was bound to inherit it. So, he would get the fair young Rosaleen and, in the long run, Shallardstown as well.

Five minutes before midnight, Angelica Parrott called Dagan to her side. Taking his arm, they started towards the hall. As they approached the stairs, Dagan, feeling he had nothing to fear, whispered a few words in Angelica's ear. For an instant she stiffened and her wary eyes narrowed. Then, a slow, insidious smile playing about her lips, she mounted three of the steps. Raising her glass of punch, she called out in her deep, throaty voice, "Christmas greetings to all of you. Let me announce that on the day before the New Year, in this house, will be celebrated the wedding of my sister Rosaleen and Dagan Ferritter, of Clonbally Castle. You are all invited to the wedding. Let the dancing proceed." Miss Angelica then walked slowly down the steps and lost herself in the dancing throng.

The wedding ceremony at Shallardstown, which took place on the afternoon of New Year's Eve, 1837, was the talk of the county for years afterwards. Three persons stood out in relief: Miss Angelica Parrott, haughty and withdrawn; Dagan Ferritter, floridly handsome and self-satisfied; and simpering, bewildered Rosaleen.

The bride and groom were to leave Shallardstown next day. They would catch the Paris mail packet from Waterford Harbor. The morning of departure, as the three sat at breakfast, Miss Angelica smiled cordially at her sister and said, "Rosaleen, it is my wish that you and Dagan accept a quarterly allowance from me in lieu of a settlement. That will come later. I must consult lawyers. I suggest you take a house near Paris—Chantilly or Passy, for example. Send the bills to me. I will arrange everything. Whatever you both may want, pray, ask me."

Leave-taking was hurried, and the Ferritters were driven to Waterford in the Shallardstown barouche. Once on board ship, Dagan settled Rosaleen in their cabin and strolled out on deck. He radiated contentment. The first quarter of the promised allowance was in his pocket. It was princely. He stretched and yawned like a sleek cat. Life opened before him a series of tantalizing days. He had leisure, a lovely wife, plenty of money easily come by, and magnificent Shallardstown to come back to. Dagan saluted the future.

At Shallardstown the picture was somewhat clouded. Quiet settled over the house. For hours Miss Angelica would sit at the writing table in her sitting room beneath the portico. She posted innumerable letters, addressed to Dublin, Paris, London, even Rome. In the evenings she walked in the yew garden. The tunnels cut into the old trees formed a path of rich, aromatic darkness, well suited, she thought, to her mood. She was always heavily cloaked, for sometimes a gale whistled up the valley of the Blackwater. Up and down, up and down, she paced the dark path of the yew tunnel. Her eyes were narrow and hooded. Her gloved fingers tapped against the silver clasp which held her cloak. An observer would conclude that the mistress of Shallardstown had great plans. Like a mariner charting an unknown course, Angelica Parrott was setting a course from which she would never deviate as long as she lived.

The arrival in London of the regal Miss Angelica Parrott, early in the spring of 1838, caused something of a furore. She took a house in the much-coveted Carlton Crescent. The owner of the house, obliged to live abroad, was happy to find so desirable a tenant.

One night, from the vantage point of a box at Covent Garden, Miss Parrott swept the fashionable audience with her strangely brooding eyes. Behind her lorgnon, they were the eyes of a questing hawk. The London season, she believed, would be a gay one. The opera was *Flora*, sung by an Italian company but lately come to London. During the second entr'acte, Angelica's friend, Mrs. Imbolden, brought the first attaché at the Russian Embassy to present Miss Parrott to him. Prince Nicholas Orloff bowed low over Miss Parrott's hand. During the next act, Prince Orloff sat behind Miss Parrott's chair, and, when the opera was over, escorted her home. . . . After the

Prince had gone, Angelica stood at the head of the stairs in her Carlton Crescent house for a long time. Her eyes were hooded and narrowed. Barely audibly to herself she whispered, "He'll do—very nicely."

A few days later Miss Parrott received an invitation commanding her to Bucking-ham Palace. Victoria, the amazingly young English Queen, had only just ascended the throne, but even then, as always afterwards, Victoria was punctilious with the visiting Irish. When Miss Parrott was presented to Her Majesty, the Queen was most cordial. After wishing her a pleasant stay in England and inquiring in what part of Ireland she lived, the Queen thought to herself, "What curious eyes she has. They baffle one."

One guest at Buckingham Palace that night interested Miss Parrott more than all the others—Prince Nicholas Orloff. As she strolled in the Palm Gallery with the Prince, Miss Parrott mentioned the famous Orloff horses, knowing that his family had for centuries bred this superb strain of thoroughbreds. Angelica had the inveterate Irish love for horses and a surprisingly wide knowledge on the subject of their breeding. She and Prince Orloff got on wonderfully well.

As she told Mrs. Imbolden later, when asked by her friend how she had made up her mind to marry Prince Orloff so quickly, "I find Nicholas, as he finds me, agreeable. We find we suit each other."

Angelica Parrott and Nicholas Orloff were married in April. They set out imme-diately for St. Petersburg, via Paris. Prince Orloff was eager to present his wife to the Orloff family, whose ramifications were numerous and far-flung. The Orloffs stopped in Paris for a few days before setting out for St. Petersburg. One night, after dinner in their hotel, Angelica put down her coffee cup. She looked long and searchingly at her husband. "Nicholas, I look forward to meeting your family in Russia. There is one thing I must tell you, however. We must plan our visit so that I may be back in Ireland, at Shallardstown, before the end of this year. This is imperative. I cannot explain further. You must bear with me."

By all accounts the advent of Angelica Orloff in St. Petersburg was brilliant. The Orloff Palace blazed nightly with receptions. The Orloffs asked many guests to meet the graceful Irishwoman, a splendid addition to their family, they thought, with her freshly colored good looks. The young Orloffs fell immediately in love with her. They liked her wit. The older members of the family enjoyed her company vastly. Her strongly flavored views on life and world affairs stimulated them.

Late in November, Prince and Princess Orloff left St. Petersburg. Journeying to Paris was a slow process in 1838. Roads were all but impassable. Coaches broke down. Overtaxed horses foundered. Waits at remote country inns seemed interminable. On a day of howling blizzard, the Orloffs sat before a log fire in an old house on the Polish frontier. A new coach was being readied so that they might reach a large town to spend the night.

Nicholas Orloff looked for a long time at his brooding wife. Then he said, "Angelica, there is a strange look in your eyes these days. I often wonder about it. You seem to have a fixed purpose that weighs you down."

Continuing to gaze into the fire, his wife answered, "I have." Then she added, "But it does not weigh me down. On the contrary, I approach its fulfillment eagerly."

The Orloffs arrived in Paris the third week in December. The long, bitter journey, with the many detours that were necessary because of the appalling state of the Russian roads, had proved too much for Nicholas. He was desperately ill when they arrived in Paris. His lung cold increased. In four days he was dead. The funeral was held from the hôtel of his brother-in-law, the Duc de Choisel, in the rue Faubourg St. Honoré. Many people wondered at the lack of emotion displayed by the widowed Princess Orloff. Outside of a vast detachment, she acted as if nothing had happened.

On the Monday of the last week in December, Princess Orloff stood on the dock at Boulogne, waiting to go aboard the Cork packet steamer. The Duchess de Choisel, who had come to Boulogne with her sister-in-law said, "You returned from Russia with so little luggage. Didn't my family load you down with presents? Except for that desperately heavy oxhide chest, you have brought nothing to speak of."

A faraway look hovered in Princess Orloff's eyes. "I brought only what I need for my plan." She smiled grimly and nodded her head. "My plan—it will not fail."

Nor did it. In the long roster of tales of human vengeance, there has rarely appeared so concerted a plan for wrecking the human mind.

Princess Orloff arrived at Shallardstown on the last day of December. Events began to happen quickly. They never ceased to happen for many years. A sort of "mill of the gods" ground slowly, inexorably, and "exceeding small." To the outsider, it might have appeared that all was quiet within the white stone walls of this great Palladian house. But the mill was grinding. At the same time, Princess Orloff was separating and carding her threads of silk, the threads that were the warp and woof of the deadly tapestry which she was weaving to encompass the lives of Rosaleen and Dagan Ferritter.

The first move was to reorganize not only the way of life as hitherto lived at Shallardstown, but the entire household staff as well. The day after Princess Orloff's return, there appeared at the house a rather frightening-looking individual. Mary Finnerty, the hall girl, said, after opening the door to him, "Mary Mother, I thought it was some class of cadaver. Dead and dug up. The color of his face an' all, like an auld yella glove." This was William Creed, of Galway, half gypsy, the other half, God alone knew what.

As the years passed, Creed became the prop and mainstay at Shallardstown. He was butler, major domo, general factotum. To Creed and his ever-watchful snake eyes was due the extraordinary success of Princess Orloff's plan.

Under Creed's direction, the staff of servants, some of whom had been at Shallardstown since Cadogan Parrott's day, were sent away. A low-looking, dark-visaged crew arrived from Galway and Sligo—four men and two women. Except for Creed, none of them consorted in any way with people of the two nearest villages, Ballymacorthy and Clogheen. They lived a shuttered existence of their own behind the closed doors of Shallardstown.

Now and again Creed would go into Clogheen on some mysterious errand at the post office. It was there he heard that a great deal of speculation was rife about the heavy oxhide chest which the Princess had brought back from foreign parts. Johnny Trievy, who had helped unload it from the Cork packet steamer, had told all Clogheen a tall tale. It weighed so much that it took ten men to hoist it. Johnny asked Creed, "It's a coffin made av gold, maybe? Give to 'er be a king, maybe?"

"So!" thought Creed. "These villagers are beginning to wonder, are they? Well, they'll have plenty to wonder about. Bad 'cess to 'em."

On neither of her visits to Paris had Princess Orloff let her sister Rosaleen know she was there. The last time, on her return from St. Petersburg, Rosaleen and Dagan had been in Cannes. Angelica had good reason to know that. Her sister's bills and the lists of Dagan's gambling losses, which were awaiting her at Shallardstown, were gigantic. She had paid them all without a murmur. But that was all over now. She had, of course, deliberately fostered idleness and extravagance in the minds of the pleasure-loving young Ferritters. Thus she created the first spidery crack in the enamel in which to insert the thin edge of the wedge. Now she would deliver a heavy stroke on the hilt of that wedge, with the mallet of her hate.

By courier and fast packet, she sent a letter to Cannes summoning the couple home. She planned that they were to arrive at the gates of Shallardstown on New Year's Eve, one year to the day since they had been married under a bower of Christmas roses in the drawing room. But they should come no farther than the gates. The gates would be locked.

Her plans went slightly awry. When Rosaleen and Dagan finally received this peremptory note commanding them to return to Ireland immediately, they were enjoying the sun in Florence. It would be impossible for them to reach Shallardstown by the first of the year. In any case they had no intention of forsaking their enchanted existence in exchange for the fogs and whipping rain of an Irish winter. They posted a letter to Angelica to that effect. By return post she sent Dagan a letter that exploded like a bombshell in his hands. All funds would be cut instantly. No more money would be forthcoming. After an agonizing day, they gave up. There was nothing else for them to do. They returned to Paris and disposed of their house in Passy. Although deeply in debt, they made extravagant promises to their creditors and set out disconsolately for Ireland.

In the fortnight preceding the arrival of the Ferritters, Princess Orloff laid careful plans on her own behalf. She established the unalterable pattern of her days, which was never to vary a hairsbreadth so long as she lived. ·

During these days of waiting for the curtain to rise on a diabolical spectacle, Creed went more frequently into Ballymacorthy and Clogheen. A word here. A word there. A little talk with a villager in a pub or the cattle market set the man talking. According to Creed, the Princess was not well. A strange malady, brought back from Russia, had caused her to lose the power of speech, and her eyes were affected as well. She wished to see no one, and her only diversion would be a daily drive in the landau, which had but lately arrived from Vienna. Did any one know of four stocky cobs, immune to all winds and weather? The Princess must take the air every day.

The villagers raised their eyes to the saints. Calamity struck at the Parrotts with a downward stroke, surely. Poor, sweet Miss Rosaleen and her man were well out of it in a foreign land.

Voltaire once wrote a brochure entitled *Monotony*. In it he says: "There is a certain triumph in well-considered monotony. Constant repetition of a motif can so stupefy the beholder's mind that memory is held invalid." Perhaps Angelica Orloff once read this brochure. Certainly her design of considered monotony was a triumph. In the end, it so stupefied the minds of all who witnessed the daily passing of the landau that many people could not remember, for the life of them, whether they had actually seen it or not.

A few days before the arrival of Rosaleen and Dagan, Princess Orloff went for her first drive along the eight-mile stretch of lonely marsh road that spread out towards the seacoast near the Shallardstown woods. This drive was timed to take one hour to the minute. No more. Not a minute less. Timing was of paramount importance in Princess Orloff's plan.

A clock at the foot of the stairs in the hall struck three. The front door of Shallards-town opened. From out the shadowy hall came Creed. He walked to the top step under the portico. There was the landau, the black leather victoria top pushed back. Four chestnut cobs stood in the traces, two postilions up, in yellow and black livery. Creed walked back into the house. In a moment he came out again, walking very slowly. On his arm leaned a figure in a sweeping purple-brocade garment, copelike in its shape-lessness. A wide, flat purple hat and a veil wound tightly around the lower face hid the features. Looking neither to the right nor the left, Creed and Princess Orloff descended the steps, measuring each one carefully. Creed settled the Princess in the seat facing the horses. He tucked a fur rug about her feet.

In his left hand Creed held a whip which he gave the Princess, a short, stubby, braided-leather whip, such as Russian nobles use to chastise a disobedient servant. This whip was unique in that it had a thick octagonal handle of Russian malachite. Grasping this whip firmly by the braided-leather tip, the handle sticking out horizon-tally from the carriage door, Princess Orloff nodded almost imperceptibly to Creed. He raised his hand. The horses broke into a trot. Princess Orloff was away on her after-noon drive.

The arrival of Rosaleen and Dagan Ferritter at the gates of Shallardstown in a driving downpour was wildly dramatic. To the pair of drenched travelers, it was flab-bergasting. Locked gates and the sullen, adamant face of Creed blocked their way. They had expected an angry Angelica awaiting them, but nothing like this. To their demands to know why they were barred out, Creed repeated over and over again, "I have me orders from Princess Orloff not to admit either of ye."

When Rosaleen, wild with anxiety, appealed to Father Dabney, the priest who lived across from the Shallardstown gates, he said he dared not interfere. Princess Orloff would see or speak to no one, not even him. He tried to comfort the distracted woman, "Let ye quiet yerselves now. Come sit before my sitting room fire and drink a hot broth. In the morning we'll try and set things straight." Stiff with cold, they obeyed meekly.

But the morning did not put things to rights. Neither Rosaleen nor Dagan ever saw Princess Orloff again in their lives, excepting only, as everyone else did, when she drove in her landau out the marsh road at three o'clock every afternoon of the world. Once they ran along beside the coach crying entreaties, but if the solid, sunk figure in purple heard them at all, she made not the slightest sign. She might have been carved from purple quartz. Not an eyelid nor a feather fluttered. One day, after Dagan in a drunken fury tried to assault one of the postilions who prevented him from climbing into the landau, Creed took a hand. He went to the little house a mile or so from the gates of Shallardstown, where the Ferritters lived. Whatever he said to Dagan behind closed doors was never known. It had the desired effect, however, for neither Dagan nor Rosaleen ever went near the Orloff landau again.

Once every month Creed took a small sum of money in a leather bag to the Ferritters. It was all they had to live on. But for this niggardly allowance from the Princess, they were destitute. At first they had sought lawyers in Dublin. After listening to the circumstances of the case, not one would touch it. There was no chance of winning, they said. Princess Orloff was quite within her rights, however inhuman her methods. All the Ferritters could hope for was that, when the Princess died, Rosaleen would inherit Shallardstown and a considerable estate. The entail took care of that. This was the year 1841. Princess Orloff was rich and powerful. Being of the landed aristocracy, she had things pretty much her own way. Better let sleeping dogs lie, the lawyers advised Rosaleen. Wait.

But neither Rosaleen nor Dagan were of the stuff to wait quietly, no matter how bright the distant outlook. Dagan drank steadily and increasingly. He grew fat and slovenly. His debts rose as he deteriorated. Rosaleen gave birth to one rickety child after another. Five in number. Then one by one they died. The years passed by. Ten years, twelve years, fifteen years. Day after day, year after year, at three o'clock the landau rolled out of the gates of Shallardstown and took to the marsh road. At four o'clock it returned.

The whip with the malachite handle played its part in this daily outing. Cut into the handle were two long slits, opposite each other. By lifting the handle to eye level and squinting through the slit, one could see a twisted white ribbon, lettered in faded gold. A tiny dark crescent clung to this ribbon. The malachite handle was a reliquary containing a paring from the thumbnail of St. Stephen. Word of this holy relic had got about in the countryside. Women with babies in their arms would gather at the crossroads at Araghlin for a chance to touch the reliquary with their lips. They would also rub the babies foreheads against the cold stone, as well. St. Stephen's powers for good were well known. Each afternoon the landau halted for a few minutes at the Araghlin Cross. A postilion would hand the whip around to the women waiting there. When the daily ceremony was over, he would return the whip to the Princess. But this time the malachite handle was thrust into her gloved hand. So she held it on the return journey. No one was ever allowed to speak to Princess Orloff. She was very ill, the women were told.

There were never very many signs of life around Shallardstown. During the day all was deathly quiet. Then at three o'clock the usual action took place at the front door. Sometimes a group of children would stand by the gate as the landau spun past. They liked to see the horses. Few lights were visible at night. Like Miss Angelica's eyes used to be, the house wore a hooded look.

A few times a year Creed made a stealthy trip to Galway. In 1847, he traveled to London and was gone for a month. When he returned a man came with him. A few corded boxes arrived at Shallardstown at the same time. The man remained in the house for a few days, then returned to London via the Cork mail boat, as unobtrusively as he had come. No one in the villages nearby had seen or spoken to him. One of the Galway women, living in the house, took Creed's place while he was in London. She helped Princess Orloff in and out of the landau every afternoon.

At this time affairs at the Ferritter household were in a disgraceful state. One child was still alive, but nearly an imbecile. Dagan was a wreck of his former self, crawling from one pub to another. He consorted with tinkers and dock thieves along the wharves at Waterford Port. Rosaleen had sunk into a desuetude from which she never, in after years, rallied. Princess Orloff's plan was working monstrously well.

A fleck of interest was aroused one day by a gamekeeper in Creed's employ. The man supplied the Shallardstown kitchens with hare, snipe, and an occasional brace of pheasants. Once, after making a purchase at the Ballymacorthy chemist shop, he tried to pay for it with a gold coin which had a strange foreign look. It turned out to be a Maria Theresa minted piece, worth an English pound in the exchange mart. When questioned, the gamekeeper said that Creed always paid him in gold coin for the birds he delivered; he had changed such coins in Galway or Waterford before.

Among the dark Galway crowd of servants brought from the gypsy Claddagh, there had been changes from time to time. One or two of the men had become disgruntled with the monastic way of life imposed upon them by Creed. They would leave the "great house" mysteriously, in the night. In a day or two, another individual, equally smoldering-eyed and taciturn, would replace the man who had left. Soon after the episode of the gamekeeper and his Maria Theresa gold piece, which had caused the first ripple in these deep waters of deceit, a young footman, but newly come to Shallardstown, sought comfort at the Clogheen pub. Being more daring than the rest, and more sly, he slipped past the watchful eyes of Creed. He was a garrulous fellow, a boaster, and quick to take offense. Tim O'Forley, proprietor of the pub, took an instant dislike to the man and vowed to forbid him the premises.

One night there was quite a gathering at the "Sheaf of Barley." The harvest had been fair, so there was a bit of loose change about. Among the bar patrons was Dagan Ferritter, very fat and filthily drunk. In some way he angered the footman, who planted himself in front of Dagan and in a sneering voice said, "Stand up for yer rights, man.

Why don't ye and yer poor wife go up to the 'great house' and demand to live there? It belongs to yer wife, I'm told."

A sudden hush fell over the room; the footman, sensing an eager audience, continued. "The auld Princess is dead. Sure, she's as dead this livin' minute as I am alive. Yer all a lot of gaums. Ye've been hoaxed."

Dagan's mind cleared a little at this amazing turn. He flung at the man and said, "You lie. You're mad or drunk. Why, I saw her driving along the marsh road, only this afternoon."

The next morning a delegation of villagers, headed by Dagan Ferritter and Tim O'Forley, marched up to the black iron gates of Shallardstown. Oddly, the gates were unlocked, for the first time in years. Tim led the men up the stone steps under the portico and sounded the brass knocker loudly.

Almost as if he had been watching and waiting, Creed opened the door. No one had ever seen the man smile before, but smile he did. With a sweep of his arm, he said, "Good mornin' to ye, gentlemen. Come in."

Dagan demanded, "I want to see the Princess Orloff."

Simply, without a moment's hesitation, Creed replied, "You cannot see her. She's been dead for eleven years."

When Tim and Dagan tried to question Creed, he refused to say more than that he had simply carried out his mistress' wishes, her orders. For a long time he had expected the hoax to be discovered. That was the name the household had always called what went on, "The Hoax." He was glad it was over. Here was a letter written by the Princess a few days before she died. She told him to give it to the first person who discovered that she was dead. She was buried in the cellar of the house. A little altar had been set up there, and she had used the place for years for her devotions. He bid the gentlemen good day. The letter would explain everything.

PRINCESS ORLOFF'S LETTER

Shallardstown
Ballymacorthy
County Waterford
May 12th, 1861.

No greeting heads this letter for I know not who will first read it. He will be the discoverer of my plan, its exposer, if you will.

I have very little longer to live. The gnawing pains in my breast are becoming insupportable. I welcome death. At first I thought to give no explanation of my actions.

I have never done so before. Reconsidering, I feel I have done little to gain the notice of posterity. Perhaps my plan, if put down on paper, will be of interest to students of the human brain in the years to come. I can already hear the rumble of my detractors. There will even be a few admirers, I venture to hope. So be it.

My plan sprang full-panoplied out of the mouth of Dagan Ferritter. I have enlarged upon the main theme, of course, since that day years ago when, at my Christmas Eve Ball, Dagan whispered a few words into my ear. He said he wished to marry my sister Rosaleen, instead of me, when I was about to mount a few stairs to announce our forthcoming marriage. As I recoiled from his words, my plan was born. I wanted to kill him. I think I have succeeded, or so near as makes no matter. I have killed him by slow disintegration. Never having loved Dagan Ferritter in the slightest degree, I feel no remorse. I never loved Nicholas Orloff. But I admired and respected him. My interest in both these men was, that I had set my heart on producing an heir to whom I could leave Shallardstown. I cannot break the entail. It must devolve on a male or female of the Parrott line. As it turned out, both men thwarted me, one by treachery, the other by death. A few years after my return from Russia, a doctor from Paris came secretly to Shallardstown. He told me I was suffering from an incurable malady. Slowly, a hidden growth was eating my life away. I might live for years. I have, in desperate agony. My life, since my return from Russia, has been a long crucifixion.

For a year I deliberately placed unlimited funds at the disposal of my sister and her husband. I knew their weakness for pleasure in idleness. I have always despised Rosaleen, a poor creature. When I withdrew my support, excepting only enough to keep them alive, they both were lost.

The pains are mounting, as they often do at night. I must be brief. My plan was so to break my sister's and Dagan's will that when the day comes that Rosaleen inherits Shallardstown, it will be a mockery.

I want time. Time for them to suffer. Time to break their spirit. Two years ago I sent Creed to London on an errand of the utmost secrecy and importance. A Mme. Göldener has an atelier in the Haymarket where she makes an exact effigy of a person. A man from her establishment returned to Shallardstown with Creed. This man constructed and dressed a duplicate of myself. Many times, on cold days in winter, or when the pain in my breast was so violent I could not sit up in the carriage, I have substituted this doll for myself on the afternoon drives. The doll is jointed, and moves by pressing hidden springs. No one ever guessed that the purple figure was not Princess Orloff.

Daily, for years, I have watched, from under the brim of my hat, the gradual breaking of the Ferritters' spirits. I pass their unhappy house each day.

The heavy leather chest I brought back from Russia contained enough gold for me to pay my way for years, without resorting to legal means. My estates are therefore intact. The sight of gold before a man's eyes quiets his conscience. He will do anything, or so I have found. I have given Creed *cârte blanche*. He has paid the servants bountifully. Creed will stay on at Shallardstown after my death. Life will continue as if I were still here. One day, by some unforeseen chance, my plan will be discovered. I am prepared for that. I have ordered Creed to place the Orloff whip in a glass *vitrine* in the entrance hall. I curse anyone who removes it. This whip has given me the only solace I have known.

Adieu

ANGELICA ORLOFF

Rosaleen and Dagan Ferritter took possession of Shallardstown and the large fortune which went with it. But, alas, it was too late. Very much too late.

Dagan died within the year. Rosaleen lived for a few miserable years, a helpless invalid from rheumatism. At the time of her death she was childless. So the entire estate of Shallardstown passed to a cousin, John Despenser Parrott. This middle-aged man lived in England, where, after the Land Act Riots of ten years before, he had settled to join the insidious army of absentee landlords. He did not return to Ireland, but closed the house and lived on the proceeds of the demesne farms.

Later, in 1896, the house was opened as a Brothers Novitiate School. The boys and some of the teachers at the school told of having seen a singularly shapeless purple figure walk down the stairs and pause for a moment in front of the glass case which lay on a table in the hall. This case contained a braided-leather whip with a malachite handle. Many said that, after the figure passed out of the front door, they heard the sound of horses hoofs and carriage wheels on the gravel drive. This apparition was not a daily occurrence, however.

In 1937 I paid a visit to Shallardstown. As I walked up the curving driveway on a biting cold February afternoon (the house is closed these days, except for a month or two during the summer), the long frontage of the house looked forlorn and neglected. All about the place there was an awareness. The blank windows seemed to watch my advance. I looked over my shoulder once or twice as I approached the door. No, there was no one about, though I seemed not to be alone.

A large, red-faced woman, who told me she was the caretaker and had been notified by the estate agent in Clogheen to expect me, showed me over the lower rooms of the house. Like all long-closed houses, in the dead of winter, it was arctic cold. I asked the woman, a Mrs. McArtagh, if she had ever seen the ghost of Princess Orloff. "Well, sir, I have and I haven't, ye might rightly say. Ye see, I don't live IN the house. I've me own bit av a place, ferninst." She flung her hand backwards. "I have heard foot-steps on the stairs, miny's the time. And twice I saw a strange class av figure climbin' the stairs, near the top. It may ha' been only shada, maybe not." An icicle was slowly forming on the end of her nose. She slapped it off and continued, "The divil's own hand is in that glass box on the table, surely. Half the time I find the lid open, always after four o'clock in the afternoon."

I walked over to the table. The lid was closed now. Glancing at my watch, I saw it was just a few minutes past four. Opening the lid of the box I grasped the richly green malachite handle of the Orloff whip. I was startled to find that, in this bitterly cold room, the stone shaft of the whip was as warm as if it had just been held, for a long time, in Princess Orloff's gloved hand.

Place de la Reine Hippique

Ballymagullagh

COUNTY WATERFORD

TAN-TAN
REINE HIPPIQUE
JR

Place de la Reine Hippique

ON EVERY COUNT, BALLYMAGULLAGH IS AN attractive house. To stay there is a pleasure to roll under one's tongue in happy memory long after leaving. Built originally as a fort commanding the farthest reaches of Tramore Bay, it was never used as such, but fell into disuse when Oliver Cromwell withdrew his troops from County Waterford and the South Counties after the Battle of Mount Mellary, in the pass of the Knockmealdown Mountains.

Neglected for a decade, in 1801 Ballymagullagh was wakened suddenly from its drowsing by a contractor from Cork named Moreland, who set about reconditioning the old walled drilling yard, the walls of which were so thick they contained rooms of fair size, intended for officers of the Waterford Dragoons. Moreland tore down walls separating the officers' rooms and added at one end, facing Tramore Bay, a charmingly spacious Regency house. Moreland had a mind to open a school for boys at the old fort. All went well for a time, and the place was nearly in readiness, when word got about the county that Moreland intended to open a Protestant school. So loud was the outcry that the plan fell through. Hard on the heels of this stroke of ill-luck, a smile spread across the devious countenance of Dame Fortune. Moreland was able to recoup.

Among the men returning to Ireland from France and the Napoleonic Wars at this time was a Captain Dermott Costigan. Wounded in the groin by a musket ball which no amount of probing would dislodge without grave results, Costigan now planned to secure a country demesne near his cousins, who bore the same name as his own. These kinsmen lived at Lantarra House, overlooking Tramore Bay, in County Waterford, the mildness of whose climate vastly appealed to a retired soldier seeking rest and sea air.

The Captain seemed well supplied with money, and, to the extreme dash of his person, added the interest attached to a man who had served for two years as aide-de-camp to the Iron Duke. It was not the title, Duke of Wellington, that rang grandly in Irish ears, for, no matter what titles the British bestowed on the victor of Waterloo,

129

the Irish remembered only that he was born Lord Arthur Wellesley, in a tall brick house in Upper Merrion street in the city of Dublin-on-the-Liffey.

Captain Costigan drove out from Lantarra House one spring morning. He saw Ballymagullagh crouching like some amiable watchdog on a spur of the Mulltanagh Hills. Cool shadows from rustling green oaks cast pleasantly upon its whitewashed walls. The Captain sighed with content, won completely at a glance.

The day Captain Costigan first saw Ballymagullagh I dare say it had no ghost of any description. It has a ghost now. One of the most winning I have ever known, a ghost thoroughly in keeping with the tradition of the house, the tradition of great happiness.

A well-known writer told me one day, and we discussing ghosts in houses all over the world, how greatly interested she was in all things pertaining to ghostly manifestations. After we had talked for a while, she said, "Ghosts only appear in houses which have known great happiness, or great misery." How right she is. The benison of great happiness is given to few in this world, and so it is the ghosts of dreadful events we encounter more often.

Captain Costigan, it is said, bought Ballymagullagh on sight. Two years later, when the halcyon days of rest were beginning to weary him, he married a Miss Darcy from the County Wexford. After a few months on the Continent, they returned and settled down to enjoy the many delights of living offered at Ballymagullagh, among them raising a family.

At this juncture, a little diversion into the fusing of Norman-Irish families will clear the air. Neither Costigan nor Darcy were originally of Gaelic stock. Both families were Norman and came to the South Counties in the train of Strongbow the Invader. In Counties Wexford, Waterford, Limerick, and Clare, many Norman families settled, and there the names of Norman knights still persist. Some have changed in spelling and pronunciation down the years; for example, Baron Keating of Moorstown Castle, County Waterford. This name appears on a twelfth-century roster of barons as deKêtinge. Darcy is d'Arcy, Costigan appears as deKastaigne, Dumesnile is now Dumineely, d'Haute is now pronounced Doughty.

It may have been this Norman-French background which prompted Dermott Costigan to spend as much time as possible in Paris or watering places along the Côte d'Azur. Six children were born to Anna and Dermott Costigan. They were named, alternately, Irish and French names. The four boys were Dermott, Jacques, Patrick, and René; the girls were Brigid and Monique.

Every summer the Costigan family—that is, the little Costigans—spent three months in Brittany. Anna wisely spaced her accouchements a few years apart, giving her two or three fairly free years between. When Monique, the youngest, was born, Dermott was seventeen. Patrick and René were twins.

At first, when the children were babies, Anna and Dermott would accompany children and nurses to St. Lauric, a few miles from Mont St. Michel, where there were both forest and sand—long stretches of brilliant, golden sand where one could wade out incredibly far, then climb up on dark red and blue fishing boats. One adventure always ended in the wildest excitement. Dermott would play Saint George and the Dragon, the dragon being a giant lobster which thrashed about in the most terrifying manner in a basket of wet ropes that hung along the side of one of the boats. Brigid always complained, as if she had not got her money's worth, that the dragon did not spout forth tongues of red flame. But that could not be helped. Brigid always wanted the earth.

Once the children were settled for an enchanted summer, Anna and Dermott would whisk off to Deauville, Nice, and Paris. In September, on the return journey to Ireland, a few gay days were always spent in Paris. There the little Costigans were treated to the Cirque, the Petit Guignol in the Champs Elyseés, and ices and cakes at Rumpelmayer's. The last day of their visit to Paris was almost more than the Costigan children could bear, and afforded conversation which lasted far into the night for weeks after. On that day they all took long naps in the afternoon, because they were allowed to stay up until half past ten o'clock. After an early dinner, the entire family started: Mrs. Burnley, the nurse, Mary and Bridie Callahan, her two strapping helpers, young Dermott leading the way, with René, Brigid, Patrick, Jacques (later joined by Monique) forming a phalanx around him. Anna and the Captain followed, smiling broadly at their great possessions. Quite an entourage. All climbed into three bursting fiacres and were driven towards the Boulevard. Presently they swung into the bustling Place Clichy, then a sudden turn to the left and they had arrived.

It was a tiny, brightly lighted square, hardly bigger than Captain Costigan's pocket handkerchief. In the center was a tent of pink and green canvas, a little the worse for wind and weather, but still handsome. Most wonderful of all to the assembled Costigan children was the sign, a cutout piece of board, shaped like a wide ribbon blowing in the breeze. The sign was painted a shrill yellow and inscribed, with many a flourish and curlicue:

"Place de la Reine Hippique"
Soeurs et Frères de' Kastaigne
Propriétaires

To the Costigan children this lurid sign remained throughout their lives a spell-binder. When they had returned to Ballymagullagh after their debut, so to speak, as *propriètaires* of a French circus, the very mention of it caused their eyes to roll so far back in their heads, "with the pure wonder of it," that distracted Mrs. Burnley would shout, "Glory be to Mary, if ye're not careful yer eyes'll get stuck in yer skulls. I'll have to lead the lot of ye around be a halter. Now come off it." She would then belt the first one handy. No amount of belts, however, could shake their faith that they were the luckiest children in the world. It all came about in this manner.

Late one afternoon when young Dermott was six, Jacques three, and Brigid one year old, Captain Costigan had been hurrying along the Place Clichy. As he turned into a short cut to the Rue Garon, he had been startled by hearing the sound of frenzied sobbing. Stopping short in his tracks, he looked hastily around. He saw that he was in some sort of cul-de-sac. At one side of the street was a carousel in front of a three-sided tent of pink and green stripes. Sitting on an upturned stool, the kind used in a trained-dog act, was a woman, rather fat, extremely disheveled, and evidently in the very depths of woe. Dermott Costigan, like any other man, hated to mix with anything of this kind which did not concern him. On the other hand, if help was needed, he would do what he could. Approaching the woman, Dermott lifted his hat and asked what was wrong. A perfect torrent of sobs, accompanied by violent rocking to and fro, was his answer. He was about to turn away and continue on his errand, suspecting, since this was Paris, that it was some domestic upheaval which he would be wise to avoid. As he hesitated, a young girl appeared in a doorway of the house behind the tent. Actually it made a fourth wall.

Slowly wiping her hands on a cloth, she said, "Monsieur, it is good of you, but there is nothing anyone can do. That is my mother. She weeps because this morning we discovered my father had decamped in the night, with our dog trainer, Mlle. Du Carte, and all my mother's savings. Well, there it is. We are beggars. Now we wait for a man to arrive who will give us"—she shrugged—"what he will for all this." She spoke with the guttural *r* of the Paris slums.

The girl spread her hands in a wide arc. It included the tent and the carousel with its six plunging horses—fat, dappled horses with amber and blue glass eyes and vari-colored hemp tails. The carved hoofs were shod with gilt metal shoes. The woman roused, gazed lovingly at the painted sign, then dropped her head to her knees again in an abandonment of grief.

"You see, Monsieur?" said the girl. "That is what hurts my mother most. When she was young, she was very beautiful. Around the corner in the Place Clichy she was regarded very highly. Queen of Haut Ecole, they called her. My father met her when she had an act with six horses, three black, three white. She wore a trailing black habit and a tricorn with white plumes. He was ringmaster for whatever equine acts came to the Cirque D'Hiver. She traveled with the Cirque Valévar from Lyons. My father fell in love with her. He called her his Circus Queen. They were married. For years they toured their own circus, up and down France, even Belgium. I was born in Bruges. That is when the sign was painted, when I was born. A present to my mother. Later my father broke his hip. Then, as we circus people say, we "planted" here. It is not much. To her it is everything. You understand, Monsieur?"

Dermott looked for a few minutes at the blistered sign, "Place de la Reine Hippique." He was a man of quick decisions; that is one reason he had been the Iron Duke's favorite aide-de-camp. Now he made one of his quickest. He noticed the girl watching an approaching individual, dragging one foot along the pavement of the malodorous Rue Garon. A seedy old fellow he looked, bearing all the earmarks of the classic Paris junkman. Captain Costigan said, "I will buy your circus, lock, stock, and barrel. Understand, I am buying it for my children. You and your mother can continue to run it and keep the profits. Here is two thousand francs to bind the bargain.I will pay anything within reason. Later I will return. I am in a hurry now." Lifting his beaver hat, Captain Costigan left two gaping women staring after him as he turned the corner into the Rue Garon.

That evening, Dermott returned to the Place de la Reine Hippique. Already a sense of change for the better hovered in the evening dusk. Margot and Mme. Didier were busy cleaning up the disorder caused by the departure the night before of Aristide Didier and Mlle. Du Carte. Margot confided privately to Captain Costigan, "I am glad he has gone. A bad hat, that one, but maman loved him—you know women." Before the Captain left to return to his hotel, another sum of money changed hands, there was a little drink of cognac all round, for *bonne chance,* and the circus now belonged to six Irish children by the name of Costigan.

Each year when the Costigan children left St. Lauric in Brittany tó return to Ireland, they stopped in Paris for two days. The same rapturous procedure, now become a ritual, was repeated. First they attended the Cirque Hippique in the Place Clichy, which they called "Grand Cirque" to distinguish it, in their later highly colored descriptions, from their own "Petit Cirque," then a visit to the Petit Guignol, and Rumpelmayer's.

Margot Didier was a fine manager. The carousel was spic and span with fresh paint. The music box played three tunes, rather strident, a bit jumpy, but very popular. They were "Belle Vivandière," a rousing march, "Valse Libérté," a trifle slow the children agreed, and the smashing "Gallop." In Ireland, in succeeding years, this rather meager repertoire was supplemented by "The Minstrel Boy," "The Low-Backed Car," and an English music hall ballad, "Where Did You Get That Hat?"

Of course the tales told by the children about their ownership of a real circus, when they returned to Ballymagullagh, were a nine-day wonder in the countryside. A carousel, a trick dog (getting old and stiff, but no matter), a wonderful clown (played for all it was worth by Margot), and a monkey to collect coins in his red fez were all enthusiastically described. The monkey had been a late addition, a present from a sailor, an admirer of Margot's.

When an envious Darcy cousin suggested that the circus be brought to Ireland and set up in the old drill yard at Ballymagullagh, Patrick, the spokesman, proceeded to tell how the circus was managed. While it actually belonged to the assorted Costigans, Mme. Didier and Margot kept the show running. It was their living.

In 1845, the year young Dermott was twenty years old, he spent the summer in France on a walking tour with two friends through the Ardennes and the magnificent mountains of Haute Savoie. At Langoville, in the Ardennes, Dermott and his friends stayed for a few days at Chateau Fouard-de Trennière. With Irish suddenness he fell in love with the granddaughter of the house, Mlle. Clotilde Beauharnaise, whose cousin had married the lovely Creole, Josephine, later Empress of France. When Dermott returned to Ballymagullagh in September he announced to his father and mother his intention of marrying Mlle. Beauharnaise before Christmas.

Dermott Costigan and Clotilde Beauharnaise were married on Christmas Day in the beautiful Church of St. Germaine L'Auxerrois in Paris. The entire family Costigan braved the fiendish winter channel crossing to be present. In the throng breaking eagerly forward to wish *bon voyage* and *bonne chance* to Dermott and his bride were Mme. Rosanne Didier and a rather buxom Margot, married these five years to the tobacconist at the corner of the Rue Garon.

Before Captain Costigan left Paris after Dermott's wedding, he visited Mme. Didier in the Place de la Reine Hippique. He had a plan which he spread before her. It was this.

Now that she was quite alone with the circus (Margot having left when she married), the Captain felt that the small patronage, which, she admitted, grew alarmingly less each year, hardly warranted her continuing. Just keeping the circus alive was too much for her. Let him settle a sum of money on her which would insure her every comfort as long as she lived. He would buy a small property for her. She always said she liked Poissy. What little was left of the circus, he suggested, sell to the still-hovering junk man in the Rue Garon—all except the carousel, of course. That would be crated and sent to Ballymagullagh for future generations of little Costigans to enjoy as much as his children had, these many years. Monique was only five years old; she would love it.

Mme. Didier agreed with alacrity and all was settled. The morning the carters came to crate the carousel, Dermott turned into the small Place which for thirty years had housed the circus of Mme. Didier. A strange sight met his eyes. In almost the same position that he had first seen her years ago sat Mme. Didier, sobbing as if her heart would break. She was sitting sidesaddle on Tan-Tan, one of the eternally prancing horses of the carousel, her arms encircling his neck, her tears mingled with his ratty red mane.

Dermott hesitated; he hated breaking in on so poignant a farewell scene. Mme. Didier heard him and looked up: "Oh Monsieur, you must think me a great fool. It breaks my heart a little to say good-bye to all my little horses. I've known them all my married life. But this is silly." She slipped from Tan-Tan's dappled back, smoothing her stiff black skirts. "Monsieur, we proceed," she said. As the last crate was being nailed shut, Mme. Didier walked over to where the yellow sign was leaning against the brick wall of the house. She regarded it for a moment; then, smiling warmly, she slipped it in the crate. "Mlle. Brigid would never forgive me if the famous sign were missing when the crates are unpacked. It is her pride, as it once was mine." The last nail was driven home. The six little horses, very snug in their wrappings, set out on the journey to Ballymagullagh.

When the crates containing various parts of the painted carousel arrived at Ballymagullagh, the Costigans had not yet arrived home. The Darcys of Lantarra House were christening a new twig, freshly sprouted on the flourishing Franco-Irish family tree of Darcy. As many members of the clans Darcy, Costigan, and Blannor as could possibly assemble at Lantarra were enjoying its hospitality.

Nails were drawn from the crates arranged for unpacking in the court known as The Parade Ground at Ballymagullagh. The Costigans returned so late in the evening that the actual unpacking of the circus had to be put off until next morning dawned, cool, crisp, and clear. The children were out of their beds by cockcrow; nevertheless, it took the entire day to join together properly the many intricate parts of the machinery which made the painted horses spin round in slow and stately fashion, rising and falling in the movement of the gallop.

To say that the Cirque Hippique was a nine-day wonder to neighbors of the Costigans and the entire surrounding countryside puts it mildly. All day long the wheels of the machinery were grinding out action and music, with scarcely a "stop out" for meals. Stableboys, grooms, household servants, and friends and neighbors with their guests from country houses in the vicinity trooped up and down the steep stairs leading to the big playroom over the parade barracks entrance.

The mechanical music box, functioning in false pretense behind the CALLIOPE

135

boldly painted in gold, blared forth its French and Irish tunes. For the first few days, lemonade, ginger beer, and sweet cakes were generously served to all comers, heightening the circus atmosphere. Days took on the semblance of one long party. The Costigan children, in the dual role of proprietors and hosts, were in raptures.

In about a month, however, interest waned to some extent. Captain and Mrs. Costigan drew deep sighs of relief. There had been times during the past weeks when Captain Costigan harbored thoughts of somehow spiking the cogs and wheels, or hoisting an OUT OF ORDER sign, just long enough to get a few days' rest.

Then, as in all things of this kind, the first sharp edge of novelty dulled. The circus ceased to occupy every waking and most sleeping moments of the Costigan children's lives.

The weather was splendid. It called the children out of doors in a voice too magic to go unheeded. Riding and fishing, ever favorites with the children, were resumed with ardor. Late in the afternoon, when a bountiful tea was brought to the nursery, or on dark rainy days, the Reine Hippique came into her own again. The horses reared and plunged. The music shrilled. The children, leaning out at perilous angles to spear brass rings, yelled in frenzy when they scored, and called forth many "Glory be to Gods" from Mrs. Burnley.

The years passed. Succeeding generations of growing Costigans enjoyed the carousel. Constant rough usage took its toll. The once gaily-dappled horses lost a flashing eye, or a hoof. The cleverly placed leather ears, once so attentively pricked, drooped now, or hung by a thread to the carved skull. Tails were nearly nonexistent. Once-bright harness was mended with all sorts of substitutes. Most noticeably dilapidated of all was the musical calliope. When the pronged metal cylinders were put on the shaft and the crank was turned, a threnody issued forth, funereal and cracked. It played its allotted time, then subsided into a moan.

It may have been this subsiding moan, heard when someone was tinkering with the mechanism, that started the rumors. Word was spread about that the Reine Hippique haunted the carousel which had been her wedding present.

In any case, around 1880, servants and members of the Costigan family living at Ballymagullagh began to circulate stories of waking in the night and hearing the strident notes of the "Gallop" and "Belle Vivandière." Some said they had gone to the playroom to investigate, but, as they opened the door, the music stopped, dying away in moans which seemed to be mingled with the sound of sobbing. The carousel, they said, had only just been in motion, for the horses' manes still fluttered, and the dust caused by the spinning had not yet settled.

During the summer of 1900, a Darcy cousin, Moira, aged nineteen, was staying at Ballymagullagh for her first "long skirt and hair up" party. Having dressed early, she wandered, while it was still twilight, along the corridor outside the playroom. Hearing a voice speaking in French behind the closed door, she opened it a crack. She saw, standing in front of the horse named Tan-Tan (who had always been the favorite of Mme. Didier in the long-gone days in Paris) a figure of a large woman dressed in a circus costume of yellow and pink, thickly sewn with spangles which winked and glittered in the fading light. The woman seemed intent on feeding the wooden horses, crooning words of endearment, while gently stroking their carved necks.

As the Darcy cousin uttered a startled "Oh," the figure suddenly turned towards her. An angry look crossed her face, as if she were mortally disturbed. Slashing the air impatiently with a small whip she carried, she disappeared down the back stairs. As the figure of the woman passed through the doorway at the top of the stairs, Moira noticed the dusty sign hanging by frayed ribbons above the door, "Place de la Reine Hippique."

As every one knows, cats are very susceptible to a ghostly presence. Cats have been known to feel, and apparently see, a ghost in manifestation when a human being in the same room sees and feels nothing extraordinary.

A cat will crouch, its fur rising, each hair standing on end. Spitting and yowling, it will glare at a fixed spot, then suddenly dash from the room.

One night in 1922 a nurse to the Oranmore children, then living at Ballymagullagh, was walking across the playroom towards the back stairs, intent on giving supper to a large blue Persian cat she carried in her arms. It was still daylight, and the nurse noticed that the carousel seemed to be slowly coming to a stop, as if someone had just been riding on it. She knew the children were securely tucked in bed at the far end of the house. Surely no one else would be playing on the rather battered contraption. As this crossed her mind, she felt the blue Persian stiffen in her arms. His claws dug into her flesh. Spitting and clawing, he leaped from her hold, to disappear like a flash down the corridor. She waited for a few moments. No one appeared. All was silence. As she turned to go downstairs, she felt a contact as if someone was standing close beside her, and distinctly felt a hand gently stroke the red welt on her forearm where the cat had dug her.

And so the stories continue. Some people tell, each in his own way, of having seen a gaudily dressed woman, sparkling in spangles, sitting on one of the horses or walking beside the carousel as if she were holding small children in the plunging saddles for ten sous a ride.

Visitors at Ballymagullagh, as well as occupants of the house, tell of being wakened at night by tinkling music. Many people have heard high, light laughter, the laughter of pleasure, as well as infrequent sobbing.

I last visited Ballymagullagh in August, 1939. I saw or heard nothing of the Reine Hippique. The carousel, more than a little derelict, occupies its accustomed place in the barracks playroom. The only children at Ballymagullagh were two Costigan babies. The nurses held them in saddles that were bursting at the seams. But the gentle motion of the dingy horses evoked delighted chuckles from the babies, as it has done from countless little Costigans before them.

Nurse Rolly Callahan, who has brought up three generations of small Costigans, with now and then a Darcy thrown in for good measure, told me what she thought about it all. "Yes, sir," said Rolly, "ye'd be hearing about the French circus woman now? She died lonely, I'm thinkin', on her bit of farm. She's happier now than then. She keeps busy be all accounts, mending a bridle here, tightening a bolt or screw there. Sure that carousel would niver have lasted this long while with all those wild childer climbing on it, if she'd not tended it. The screech of that music box is a cross to bear, surely, but I've lived to ignore it."

The Bloody Stones
of Kerrigan's Keep

Moycullan

CONNAUGHT

LIAM
KING OF
MARIA KENNAN
FATHER.

The Bloody Stones
of Kerrigan's Keep

MY FIRST GLIMPSE OF KERRIGAN'S KEEP WAS from the sea and was appropriately dramatic. It was on a late October evening, an hour before sunset. Hags Head Light, on its jutting rock, flickered palely to westward, but my eyes regarded the sheer cliffs with disfavor, for it seemed that at any moment we might run aground on the ridge of saw-toothed rocks which rimmed the coast for hundreds of yards, a sort of devil's barricade which had spiked more ill-starred ships than I cared to think about at this time.

Inland rose gaunt hills, a drab ocher-brown in color. One of them stood out prominently, higher than any in the surrounding landscape. A small lough, choppy now with angry little waves, ran in under the lee of this hill. A dark tangle of trees crowned its top, and in the fading light I was not quite sure whether or not I saw a pair of stone towers rise from among these trees.

At that moment the captain of the little coastal steamer on which I was making this journey from Cobh to Ballyvaughn came up behind me. "Ye look a trifle uneasy. Don't fear, we'll ride 'er out all right. That's Liscannor Lough, and behind it on the hill is the terrible old house ye're looking for."

The steamer dropped anchor presently. There was only one other passenger, besides myself, who was bound for Ballyvaughn. This man was a commercial traveler, with a number of sample cases. I let him go first, over the side, and down the rope ladder. Then I made the "descent perilous" of the swaying ladder. It bucked and writhed the like of a king python in his death throes, but, soaked to the skin, I made it.

Waiting for us below the ladder, a largish curragh manned by two fisherboys stood by. As I was rowed away from the side of the chunky, black hulk of the *Queen of Galway*, the evening star shone out suddenly, bright and clear. A good omen, I thought, for my visit to the dreadful precincts of Kerrigan's Keep.

Arriving at the quayside wharf, which forms a sort of rim to the waterfront of

Ballyvaughn, I was no time at all getting settled in a fine front room at Mrs. Anna Grogan's Mariner Hotel. My room was smothered in red plush furniture, three sizes too big for it. Two wide windows looking out over the harbor gave to the room the effect of being on the deck of a ship. With all this red plush about, it might be the bridal suite. Lashings of steaming hot water soon arrived in big brass canisters, and a tageen of well-aged whisky was handed discreetly in at my door. An unseen voice said, "A sip, sir, on the house like. I'm to say yer supper will be ready the minute next to the one when you are."

A few minutes later I went down to the parlor of the hotel, where I was informed my supper had been laid. A grand meal it was, too—simple food, beautifully cooked, which I find makes all the difference. Thick slabs of "green" ham (a Connaught specialty—fresh-killed pork, roasted), flaky potatoes baked in their jackets, sharp tomato pickles, and, to finish off, a blackberry-rum tart. I went to my room, after a little talk with Mrs. Grogan as to the best way to get to Kerrigan's Keep next day. In the morning, I looked out the window and saw a day of variable weather. Ragged clouds tore across a feeble sun. Most of the disturbance, I noted, was in the upper air, for the sea was scarcely disturbed at all.

About noon I approached the deserted, fire-scarred mass of stone that is Kerrigan's Keep. Suddenly come upon out of the light mist that lay across the hilltop, the ruined old fortress was emotionally impressive. The broken and charred battlements against the racing clouds still held an illusion of strength and terror—a secret sort of terror, I thought that first day when I saw this fortress of the Kerrigan-Dartry's; and I still think, in retrospect, that there is no other feudal house on earth with so forbidding a demeanor.

I stood for a long time viewing the house from the end of a grassy, rutted cart track. The color alone is very different from most ancient Irish castles. The mass is splotched in pale, leprous gray-green, combined with brown and black smoke stain. At intervals, all over the surface of the massive walls, huge purple boulders are set in, often to box a window mullion of flint.

The variable morning had taken a change for the worse. Heavy black storm heads were gathering in the east. As I peered through a crosshatching of bare branches, the castle—in fact, the whole landscape—took on a sinister quality of unreality, an Italian wash drawing in chiaroscuro, the black masses sharply defined against the white. I had the curious impression that I was looking at the dwelling place of Morgan-le-Fay.

All is so quiet about the hilltop that it is hard to credit the stories of a raging force of massacred people who forever strive for revenge within the sealed room of Kerrigan's Keep. And the stark, empty eyes of slit windows tell you nothing. Deserted by man these hundred years, the Keep cradles the four winds and sends them howling among its battlements.

There are many interesting features to study in this castle besides its frightening ghosts. In both the towers which spring from either end of the Keep there are double staircases. Two men may ascend and descend the staircases at the same time, yet never see or hear the other. A solid stone wall six feet thick divides the steps in the center from ground to battlement. In the now roofless Great Hall there are four vast fireplaces.

A stone screen placed directly behind the raised stone dais is built in the form of arches. The pillars supporting these arches are so thick that each contains a secret room. These rooms, ten in number, are roughly eight feet square, large enough to hold five or six men-at-arms. When a visitor was entertained at the Kerrigan's table, these unseen guards watched through chinks in the stones—chinks that were invisible to anyone in the lighted room. It is fairly safe to assume that, on the night of the massacre of the O'Downy and his men, these hideaways were fully manned by the villainous gallowglasses in Kerrigan's pay. It is the shrieks of Ordlin O'Downy and his followers as they were set upon and murdered behind barred doors that still curdle the blood of night walkers on the road below the Keep.

In the year 1360, Roe Kerrigan, chief of the tribe bearing his name, had warred so continuously and to so little avail with the Black O'Flaherty of Menlo that, like many another west country chieftain, the Kerrigan at last gave up the fight. Assembling his decimated followers and packing his household gear, the battered old warrior struck off south along the Atlantic coast. He wished to build a stronghold in fresh territory and start a new life.

A bare hilltop near Moycullan, in Connaught, caught his eye. It had the advantage of overlooking all the countryside in the vicinity, and, at the foot of the hill, a convenient lough, small but deep, ran inland from the sea. Roe Kerrigan went no farther. On this barren hilltop he built a towering fortress, a mighty keep that no man alive could breach. It took ten years to build, and was a wonder to all who beheld its strength. It came to be a scourge as well.

For fifty years comparative quiet reigned at Kerrigan's Keep, as the place was called. Then Roe's son, Anair, married a Dartry from the kingdom of Leinster. Marra Dartry was a bold, ambitious woman who sought power and cared not how she gained it. From the battlements of her new castle, Marra Kerrigan viewed the rich lands that lay about her on three sides. Her acquisitive eye first came to rest on the castle of

MARRA KERRIGAN.
KERRIGAN'S - KEEP.

Liam O'Conahey, whose demesne, comprising many prosperous farms, marched with Kerrigan land on the south boundary. It did not take Marra long to lay her plans.

One night Kerrigan men, heavily armed and led by no less a person than Marra Kerrigan herself, crept by stealth across the walls of the O'Conahey demesne. All who contested her way were put to death by fire and the sword, for Marra was tasting power, and she would not be brooked. This was only the beginning. The garrison at Castle O'Conahey, made up mostly of farmers, was soon reduced. O'Conahey was slain and his men that survived were taken in bondage.

And so it went. Farm after farm was despoiled by Kerrigan men-at-arms. Driven by an insatiable lust for power, Marra attacked and overwhelmed a score of castles, many of which were feebly defended because of rumors of her strength. She waged her pillaging as far south as Ballylongford, in Limerick.

After a few years, during which Marra sorted her gains and reared a family, the banner of the Kerrigans was again on the march. This banner, displaying a stalking leopard, had brought so many landholders to their knees as soon as they sighted it that Marra expected the west country to yield to her demands at once. But this time, as a start to her campaign in the west, she picked the wrong man. When Ordlin O'Downy was attacked at his Castle Kelso, he put up such a stiff fight that the infamous Marra Kerrigan from Moycullan retired to her keep minus most of her men. She licked her wounds and nursed her pride in silence. But it was an ominous silence, and boded no good for the O'Downy.

One fair spring morning, when the mind of a woman should have been put to better use than being bent on despoiling the rich green countryside, Marra Kerrigan rode out across the drawbridge of her frowning keep. She bestrode a great roan stallion and was in full armor. Under the cuirass of her body armor she wore a full-skirted, white-wool surcoat. Her raven-black hair was hidden under a small, uncrested helm. She was armored for fighting, not for show. Marra Kerrigan was again bound for Castle Kelso on the Lough Rea, near Killreekill. She bit her under lip and thought to herself, "The O'Downy's game is up."

Marra rode eagerly to battle, secure in her strength. Five thousand men bore arms behind her, one thousand horse and four thousand foot soldiers. These men had been masterfully trained by Marra. She divided them into groups—javelin, battle-ax, and the lethal longbow. A gossoon of twelve rode at Marra's right stirrup as her standard bearer. The boy had difficulty in keeping aloft the Kerrigan banner, an orange leopard, spotted in crimson. A strong sea wind kept it streaming above the heads of the leading horsemen.

It has been rightly said that there is nothing so terrible as an army with banners, an approaching army of destruction, arrogant in its might. One can evoke the picture of this cavalcade. It must have sent the pulses of all beholders leaping in awe and terror.

Years of brooding over her defeat at the hands of the O'Downy, whom Marra considered a poor adversary, had caused her blood to turn to bile. Her one object now was to destroy everything in her path—farmsteads, livestock, castles, men, all. She would lay waste the west country. In this way, and this way only, could she re-establish her reputation of a ruthless conqueror.

Hearing of the approach of Marra Kerrigan and a formidable army, Ordlin O'Downy sent messengers far and wide to arouse the farmers and the chiefs of tribes. Swift messengers ranged the countryside rallying the inhabitants. The very thought of the blazing banner displaying a spotted leopard against the sky and the implacable Marra Kerrigan riding under it strengthened their resolve. They would crush this menace, once and for all.

The O'Downy chose a morning of light ground mist for his attack. He reasoned that Marra was in a countryside strange to her, trappy and deceitful at best. A wild, windswept bog lay on all sides of Marra's encampment, a wasteland, crosshatched by narrow, twisty streams. The O'Downy was at a loss to understand the reason why an astute campaigner the like of Marra Kerrigan would choose a spot so open to enemy attack as the Bog of Bealaclugga. Once in it, there was no way out but ahead.

The truth was that Marra had left the finding of a suitable place for encampment to one of her sons who was her second in command. Young Ailor Kerrigan had in turn told an aide to find a spot, free from ambush. In the darkness of night, when the army had come upon the fringes of the bog, the aide, tired and hungry, had chosen the first piece of treeless ground he had come upon, to the eternal undoing of Marra Kerrigan and her plans for conquest.

The Battle of Bealaclugga Bog is an epic. It still rings in the annals of Irish history. Surprised in the eerie dawn, Marra's half-awakened men stumbled and ran amuck. On a small rise directly in front of the tent of Marra Kerrigan appeared Ordlin O'Downy under his banner of a white heron in full flight on a grass-green ground. A bugle sounded brassily across the bog, and immediately small groups of men rode into Marra's camp. Slashing to the right and left, these warriors were only half seen in the clinging mist. But their impact was deadly. They came, it seemed to the Kerrigan men, from every side. Men and armor seemed to rise from the soggy ground. They rained from heaven itself. Bright banners tangled with spears and swords.

These banners showed that many chiefs of the west had joined the O'Downy: O'Harra, a purple lion on a red ground; O'Boylan, the device of a sapling larch tree;

MacCarrick, a mailed fist, grasping a flaming arrow; O'Malley, a golden watchtower. Other banners came forward as well, the banners of lesser chiefs: McDuvan, O'Hagan, O'Conran, and the youngest chieftain of them all, the stripling O'Mahoney Mor.

The ferocity of the ensuing battle knew no bounds. As the sun broke through the mist at high noon, the proud army of Marra Kerrigan lay slaughtered, half drowned in the bog, or choking to death in the runnels of slimy water that ran deep down in the black muck. The fury of encounter died away. A hush traveled over the littered field. Even the shrieks and moans of the dying ceased. There was a doom abroad. The body of Marra Kerrigan had been found. Trampled, and all but unrecognizable from blood and smoke, she lay behind her shield in the charred ruin of her tent. Near by lay her severed right arm, cut off cleanly at the shoulder. Clutched tightly in the stiff hand was the bronze-hafted sword of the Tribe Kerrigan. When the body of Marra Kerrigan was lifted and placed upon her shield to be sent back to Moycullan, the O'Downy saw four words written in blood on the hem of her white homespun surcoat.

As she lay dying, with the battle still raging all around her, she watched as two of her sons, Ailor and Brodon, were slain defending her. Marra had then traced in her own blood four words which were to travel down the years like thunder. In these four words, her last will, Marra spoke a doom worse than her own:

AVENGE ME—NEVER CEASE

The O'Downy lifted Marra's left hand from the ground. The index finger was stained to its base with her dried blood.

The years passed. Marra Kerrigan's third son, Dulin, now ruled at the Keep. Outwardly a mild-mannered man, Dulin was too much his mother's son ever to forget the words traced in her blood on the hem of the ragged surcoat which always hung behind his chair in the Great Hall.

No longer was the banner bearing a spotted leopard used by the Kerrigan as his sole device. This was now used as a pennon, or banneret. From the top of a spear pole now floated a square of white cloth. In letters red as blood were written the four words: AVENGE ME—NEVER CEASE. Like his mother, during the years he had suckled at her breast, Dulin bided his time.

There came a day when Dulin heard that Ordlin O'Downy, now an old man close on ninety years of age, was journeying by litter, accompanied by a small retinue of men-at-arms and a few women of his household, to Inchiquin, near Moycullan. A daughter of the O'Downy had married the chief of the Barony of Inchiquin, and, this journey being arduous at the O'Downy's great age, it was planned that he should remain with his daughter for the few years left him on earth.

When his litter train was accosted at the crossing of Liscannor Bridge at the foot of Kerrigan Rock, the O'Downy was not unduly alarmed. Who would trouble now to harm an old man like himself? Wars between the tribes O'Downy and Kerrigan were over and done with these many years, and, by himself at least, forgotten. But in his great age a clouded memory caused him to forget the words written on the hem of Marra Kerrigan's body garment. Whatever he may have forgot, the Kerrigan never did.

A captain of the garrison in the Keep acted as ambassador for his master. He told the O'Downy that the hospitality of the castle was offered him and his retinue. Unseasonable floods had torn away the bridges between there and Inchiquin, and the roads were death traps. Word would be sent by messenger to Lady Inchiquin at Castle Arvagh to expect her father when the bridges had been repaired. This all seemed plausible and friendly enough. The O'Downy thanked the captain, and the litter train mounted the steep road, cut into the living rock, which led to the towering portcullis of Kerrigan's Keep.

On the second night of the O'Downy's forced visit at the castle, a message was brought to him in the chamber he occupied in one of the towers. The Kerrigan wished his honored guest and all the members of his retinue to join him in a banquet which he had ordered to be spread in the Great Hall. It was the birthday of his eldest son, Cullen. The boy had reached his majority this day. Tumblers, jugglers, and a strange class of mountebank from Spain would entertain them.

The O'Downy summoned his followers, who, all told, men and women, numbered close to one hundred. He bade the men lay aside their armor. They were to carry only small side arms. This was a festivity, and small children would be present. There was nothing to fear. It may well be imagined that the men-at-arms were not so sure. However, they complied with their old chieftain's wish. The entrance of the O'Downy and his retinue into the Great Hall was received with outward good will by the assembled Tribe Kerrigan. He was seated at the right hand of Dulin Kerrigan, who throughout the meal paid high honor to the old warrior and threw his friendship, like a protecting cloak, over the stooped shoulders of the O'Downy.

When the O'Downy had taken his seat, he might have noticed the bloody symbol of undying hate which hung in its accustomed place, high on the wall above the Kerrigan's chair. But the rheumy old eyes of O'Downy failed to see it. To him all was well, as it should be in the house of a friendly chieftain. But O'Downy's men had seen it, every one of them. They were afeared and weighted down with a great dread.

The banquet proceeded. The food was a wonder to behold as well as to taste: huge

THE O'DOWNY
'KERRIGAN'S KEEP'

pink salmon, from out the River Finn in Donegal; spiced flesh of the wild boar, roasted before their very eyes; and the sugared fruits and mounds of clotted cream from Kerry cows delighted the Kerrigan children. Then came the jugglers, who tossed balls of fire into the air and caught them with their bare hands. The tumblers leaped upon each other's shoulders, then onto the shoulders of a man standing ten paces away. The mountebanks in streamers of brilliant colors danced comically and pantomimed a miracle play.

Everyone seemed very intent on the entertainment, and there was little movement in the hall. Once the man-at-arms standing behind the O'Downy's chair thought he heard movement within the stone pillar just behind him. Perhaps, he thought, it was one of the wolf hounds rubbing his rough coat against the stones. These hounds were slinking about the hall and rummaging in the corners for bones.

As it was nearing midnight, the mountebanks withdrew, followed by the female members of the Kerrigan household, the children, and Dulin's son Cullen. The O'Downy rose shakily from the table, about to follow the others who had left. His old bones cried for rest. He would leave the younger men to their drinking. As he turned towards the door leading to the staircase in the tower, it was banged shut, and he heard the sound of iron bars falling into place. A clamor, sudden and horrible, broke forth in the Great Hall. The solid-looking stone pillars seemed to split apart, and fully armed gallowglasses rushed out. All carried double-handed battle swords.

The massacre that took place that night in the Great Hall of Kerrigan's Keep wiped out every man and woman of the hundred-odd souls who had come in the train of Ordlin O'Downy. Through all this terrible blood-letting, Dulin sat hunched in his carved chair. He sat as a man hewn of rock. The only sign that he saw what took place was the continuous mumbling of his lips. Over and over he repeated the same words: "Avenge me—never cease." "Avenge me—never cease"; a monstrous litany, as much a part of him as the pumping of his heart. In such a manner was Marra Kerrigan's last wish fulfilled by her son.

Behind the Great Hall the Kerrigan had started to build a vast room. It was tall and narrow and had no windows with the exception of small slits in the walls high up under the eaves. This room was inside the walls of the inner keep or bailey. It may have been intended originally as a sort of muniment room or museum for arms of war. Floored, walled, and roofed in massive blocks of cut stone, its intended use will forever remain a mystery. Being built on a much lower level than the hall, a long flight of stone steps curves down from a door in the narrow corridor off the Great Hall. No matter what its intended use was, the infamous use to which it was put on the day after the massacre was part of one of the most hideous acts of revenge that it is possible to conceive.

Another unsolved mystery is why the Kerrigan resorted to such rash haste in disposing of the hundred bodies of his victims. Perhaps Lord Inchiquin got wind of the outrage in some manner, perhaps the Kerrigan heard he was riding towards the Keep to investigate. Who knows?

In any case, the stones of the floor in the unfinished room were hurriedly pried up, pits were dug, and the bodies of O'Downy and his followers were pitched in, with less ceremony than is accorded a flock of sheep who have died from a plague.

The floor stones were replaced. The empty, echoing room was sealed up. To anyone standing in the Great Hall, there was no sign that a graveyard room existed.

There comes a long blank now in the history of Kerrigan's Keep. Then, in 1600, one hears of a member of the family, one Connard Kerrigan, to whom the estate reverted in default of a direct heir. This man, by all accounts, was interested in architecture. It was he who put up the Renaissance doorway in the wall of the Keep, where, in Marra Kerrigan's time, the portcullis yawned. The irony of this Renaissance doorway is that Connard was the first man to charge headlong through it, after encountering the Bloody Stones. Heedless, in his raving state, Connard plunged straight over the cliff into the Lough of Liscannor below. After a few more unfortunates had run screaming through this classic doorway, the natives in the surrounding villages started calling it "Madman's Door."

After Connard, came a Dartry descendant, in 1730. This man cared only for books and shut himself away in one of the towers. One day he came across an old, mildewed document pertaining to the Kerrigan-O'Downy feud and which must have contained some reference to the graveyard room. Curiosity overcame Michael Dartry. He engaged a workman who was a newcomer in the locality and a scoffer to boot. The workman set about removing the stones which sealed the door leading from the Great Hall to the strange, vacant room. The man removed the stones one by one, setting each carefully aside in case the door had to be sealed up again. Then he started down the stairs into the dark chamber. A roaring noise and a crashing as if a hundred stones were hurled against the wall reverberated through the castle.

When the man had crawled back up the stairs, only to die just inside the Great Hall, he was found to have marks of bloody hands all over his body. He had been beaten almost to a pulp, and the marks of great flat stones could also be traced on his battered flesh. Because the workman died almost immediately, it was never learned what he had seen in the haunted room. When someone more brave than the rest peered down into the void below the stairs, every stone was in place as it had always been since the day Dulin Kerrigan's men had tamped them down on top of the O'Downy dead. It was the year after this occurrence that a devasting fire swept through the living quarters of the castle. Michael Dartry was burned in his bed.

In 1802, Fitz-Allen Dartry inherited the Keep from his uncle, Michael Dartry's son. But Fitz-Allen was a sportsman and wanted none of the grim feudal barracks with the bloodiest history on record written all over it. However, he liked the demesne which lay around it. He forthwith built himself a house designed for him by a young Dublin architect, a simple, friendly house where he could entertain his friends, ask the local hunt to meet, and live without fear of a murderous revenge overtaking him unawares. He called the house Kerrigan's Acre. A mile away one could see the old gray Keep bulking large on its hilltop.

A few months after Fitz-Allen Dartry established himself in his new house, the hunting season opened. Kerrigan's Acre was filled to overflowing with guests, all keen on the sport of fox-hunting. Among the guests was a young Britisher, an officer in the Coldstream Guards. His name was Hambelton. The night after his arrival, someone brought up the subject of the frightful doings in the sealed room at the Keep. Hambelton not only laughed at, but derided, the whole story. He declared he would go down the fatal stairs into the room, look about him, and, when he returned, prove for all time that the ghost-haunting was all an old wives' tale and arrant poppycock. When someone mentioned the case of the workman who had unsealed the door of the Great Hall for Michael Dartry and had been smashed to a jelly when he went down into the stone room, Hambelton had an explanation ready. In his opinion the stones could easily have fallen from the roof, jarred loose when the stones sealing the door were pried apart.

Next day a number of the Kerrigan hunting party rode over to the Keep. Hambelton climbed up the blackened steps of the west tower. From the battlements he looked down onto the roof of the stone room. Not a piece was out of line, nor had one been displaced since Dulin Kerrigan had caused it to be dovetailed into place over three hundred years before.

Hambelton stuck to his theory that a simple explanation would be forthcoming once he was allowed to penetrate into the farthest and darkest corners of the stone room. He added, "I promise you my findings will have nothing to do with feudal vengeance or supernatural phenomena." And so it was all arranged.

Next day at sunset a group of six men gathered in the Great Hall of Kerrigan's Keep. The door was breached by crowbars wielded by two of Fitz-Allen's laborers. When the stones were removed, a dark rectangle gaped in the wall. A fetid odor, as of carrion long unburied, rose up in gusts from the dark room below. The men in the hall covered their faces. This reek of death made them retch. Wrapping a cloth around his mouth and nostrils, Hambelton made ready. Lighting a little pit lamp, such as is used by coal miners, he turned and waved gaily to his friends. Silently they watched the young guardsman start down the stairs to the noisome room.

For a few minutes the motionless watchers heard nothing but the sound of Hambelton's footsteps receding on the stairs. Then a most appalling noise rose in waves from below—a low rumble of moans, then inarticulate voices, gabbling, as if smothered under earth and stones, a hundred voices of the murdered crying for vengeance. Next came the deafening clamor of stones being hurled against the wall. Some seemed to crash together in mid-air, for sparks flew in at the door. There seemed to be one concentrated volley of stones, followed by a silence one could cut with a knife. The watchers in the hall ran towards the breached door and looked down. All was in darkness, for the pit lamp lay flattened on the stones. What they did see was the cruelly mangled body of Hambelton lying halfway up the stairs. He still lived, for his hands groped feebly towards the lighted door.

Hambelton lived for ten days after his gruesome experience. He suffered unbelievable agony until the end. Nearly every bone in his body was broken, and huge purplish welts covered him. It was as if each stone had left its imprint on his skin. Only the amazing vitality of his strong heart enabled him to talk at all. This is his story.

As he started down the long curving flight of stone stairs, he sprayed the ray of light from his pit lamp along the walls and floor of the stone room. Halfway down the stairs, he saw what appeared to be the stones of the floor heaving, undulating, as an oily swell rolling in from the outer sea. He tried to cry out, to call the attention of his friends above, but all sound froze in his throat. Then the stones seemed to rise up on end. Eyes, eyes, eyes, blazing eyes, everywhere, were leveled balefully at him. Great skeleton hands with earth-stained rags still clinging to the bones lifted from the ground. Each hand held a flat stone which seemed to drip with blood. As the fearful cries rose in volume, these waving hands hurled the stones at him. A veritable wall of flying rocks seemed to strike him. With the odious stench of the grave cloths overwhelming him, he knew no more.

After Hambelton died, the room was sealed up again, a tomb in which no stone in the floor was found out of place.

In 1924, an odd-appearing individual arrived at Kerrigan's Acre. He gave his name as Dr. Santley. At this time Mrs. Tancred Kerrigan-Dartry lived at The Acre. On being admitted to her drawing room, Dr. Santley produced a rather soiled visiting card which appeared to be his professional card as well. Accepting the bit of pasteboard rather gingerly, Mrs. Kerrigan-Dartry read: "Dr. Arno Santley. Magician. Prophycist. Exorcist. All Ghostly Apparitions Expelled Forever. Fee Nominal. Partly Street. Galway."

The lady thought to herself, "A very flamboyant and ambitious array of words." She told Dr. Santley she did not require his services in any form. The Keep, she added, no longer bothered the family, nor anyone else. There had been no recurrence of ghostly incidents since the Hambelton tragedy in the day of her ancestor, Fitz-Allen Dartry. The infamous stone room, and the horror it contained, was stoutly sealed. Fire had made the castle untenable; in any case, the sooner it fell into complete ruin, the better.

Dr. Santley persisted. He argued that to exorcise the famous Bloody Stone Ghosts would be a great feather in his cap and would add enormously to his prestige as an exorcist. He would do it without charge.

Mrs. Kerrigan-Dartry finally gave in to "the little clown," as she called him. She even said he might have a laborer to remove a few stones from the sealed doorway, enough for the doctor to enter the room. More than that she could not do. Dr. Santley was overjoyed and returned to Galway to fetch his paraphernalia.

A week later, Dr. Santley appeared at the Keep alone. He carried a small black bag and in his hand was a long metal rod tipped with a gilded metal cross.

He waited in the great hall of the Keep while the workman from The Acre removed four or five of the big stones, just enough for the doctor to crawl through on his hands and knees, which, he said, was all he wanted. The workman, who was not at all interested in "such shenanigans," opened the front door and settled himself for a smoke. Dr. Santley gathered the various articles he needed, grasped the rod with the gilt cross firmly in his right hand, and crawled through the aperture in the wall.

Meanwhile the workman drew pungent smoke from his cobeen pipe and thoughtfully regarded the "Madman's Door" towering above him. Suddenly a wild discord resounded through the empty house—a low roar, then the crashing of stone against stone. While the bewildered workman was puzzling what to do, a figure covered with blood came crawling through the hole in the wall. As he reached the great hall, he staggered to his feet and started to run crazily across the room. The workman had a glimpse of the doctor's face, the sight of which scared him out of his wits. It was surely the face of one demented, eyes starting from their sockets, drools of slaver hanging from the mouth. Out the door he sped blindly, making for the sheer drop of the cliff over which two unfortunates had already lost their lives. The workman was galvanized suddenly to life and followed him on the double. Almost at the brink of the cliff, he caught up with the crazed man and hauled him back to safety.

Shortly after this, Dr. Arno Santley was committed to the Asylum of St. John of God's, near Dublin, a retreat for the hopelessly insane.

Badminton in Bloomers

Shireen House

COUNTY WATERFORD

Badminton In Bloomers

THE O'HAGGERTYS OF SHIREEN HOUSE, IN County Waterford, have always aroused more than mild curiosity in the minds of their neighbors and in the countryside for miles around. A touch of eccentricity manifests itself in some member or members of each succeeding generation. For the most part, however, the unconventional touch has never caused any great alarm as to the sanity of an O'Haggerty.

Life was never dull, surely, in the vicinity of Shireen House, with such little tricks as Jarrock O'Haggerty, returning from the Tullamore Horse Fair, lighting Farmer Grogan's hayricks on a cold, dark night, "to light my path on this death-trap road, and warm my hands," he said.

This little diversion was paid for instanter, and the matter forgotten by an abundantly overpaid Grogan. When Elzira O'Haggerty, the heroically molded mother of Jarrock, while on a visit to Paris, calmly took a velvet manteau off a wax model in the "Reine de Bretagne," modiste, in the rue St. Honoré, the hue and cry was loud and strong. Madame of course paid and had only taken it, she said, to see if it looked as well in the daylight as in the gaslit fitting room. That she had walked nearly two blocks swathed in folds of purloined ruby velvet did not signify. These constant shenanigans were simply evidence that the O'Haggertys, male and female, played a whim to the hilt, whenever or wherever it might manifest itself. They were naturals, no matter what the cost.

In 1859, twin daughters were born to Morvin and Lotta O'Haggerty of Shireen House. One might add, with never a fear of understatement, that on the summer morning when the O'Haggerty twins let out their first duet bellow, the dam burst. Certainly Shireen House was never to know a quiet moment again until the death of these outrageous twins sixty years later, a fortnight apart. Even after death they were ever on the alert. A more unquiet pair of corpses has seldom been buried.

Lotta O'Haggerty never in all her life, and she lived until the twins were in their late twenties, knew quite what to make of them, much less how to control their "freeness," remarkable even for an O'Haggerty. Lotta was a flutterer; she fluttered through life, always upset by the behavior of her resourceful daughters.

The babies were christened, in identical Carrickmacross lace robes, Fiona (the elder by five minutes) and Rena. The christening was bedlam. It set a key on which Miss Fiona and Miss Rena patterned their lives.

Mary Moriarity, the cook, who brooded away her life in the dark kitchen of Shireen House, preparing a superb meal when the spirit moved her—but a scandalous and inedible one most days—always referred to the twins as "thim two." This phrase was the like of an accolade in reverse. It designated, to the satisfaction of the entire countryside, in two scathing words, the disapproval in which the Misses O'Haggerty lived and had their being.

Life for "thim two" progressed. They were the despair of nurses, and later, when a governess was brought over from Vienna, she spent most of her time in tears and rages. Fräulein Lisa returned to Vienna after a month at Shireen House, feeling that perhaps "she had not the call to teach the young."

From then out, Mamma said, "Just let it ride. They can learn all that's necessary by watching me," which on the face of it was small guarantee as to how they would turn out. No one was kept long in doubt.

One hot, airless day when the twins were sixteen, Fiona and Rena wandered about the gardens, listless and snapping at one another. A day as humid and devitalizing as this one is very rare in County Waterford of the cool breezes. They did not know how to combat it. To lie down and rest was unthinkable. They visited the kennels—no, the puppies, tumbling against their shins, were hot. They visited the stables—empty. The hunters were out at grass, and old Micky Barrow, the head stable groom, usually a monument of wit, was dour and dispirited with the "great tragedy of this scaldin' weather athwart me." Very low in their minds, the twins approached the rose garden. At the far end, the terraces shelved away to a stretch of green lawn with a circular lily pool in the exact middle.

To the sun-drenched eyes of Fiona and Rena the limpid water looked cool and inviting. They sauntered up to the rim. Inspecting it closely, Fiona said, "It looks slimy."

Rena, always practical, replied, "Yes, but wet."

It took no time at all for the girls to divest themselves of the comparatively few clothes they were wearing. Naked as jay birds, they joined hands and stepped gingerly into the pool. Fiona was only too right. It was slimy—down she went on her bottom, dragging Rena with her. The floor of the pool was ankle deep in mud, and when they opened their eyes they were aghast to see the very great-grandfather of all bullfrogs sitting on Fiona's knee. No banshee, no Old Woman of Gonn, not all the far-collected

Dread Women of Moher ever let out such spine-shattering screeches as did the floundering Fiona and Rena.

Out they leaped, their discarded clothes and the proprieties never entering their minds as they streaked across the yard in front of the stables, to the joy of a couple of spalpeen lads and the rheumy-eyed Micky Barrow.

On they sped, Undine in duplicate. Trailing muck and lily pads in their wake, they made for the shelter of the yew alley leading to the kitchen wing. Mary Moriarity had just emerged from her stifling kitchen to sit in the shade of a mulberry tree close to the well, hoping to catch any stray breeze that might rise. The only breeze she found was caused by the flying figures of "thim two" hurtling past her on the double, down the area steps, through the kitchen door, up the back stairs to their bedroom, where they flung themselves, winded, on the bed.

Clainy, the "all girl," slopping a mop bucket down the scullery steps, found Mary Moriarity in a state bordering on apoplexy. Grabbing a pot lid, Clainy fanned the large red face of the hysterical Mary. A small swig of whisky from an apron pocket quickly brought her round. "Glory be to God!" shouted Mary. "If this little shindig isn't the black end of the road! Thim two prancing past, not a stitch on here nor there, and they young ladies grown. Sure those gaums at the stable gate'll know where ivery pound of flesh lays on the pair of thim. Ochone, the wide world don't hold the like av thim two."

As year after year unfolded, this little bathing party and its record-breaking dash through the garden at Shireen was cast into limbo. Each succeeding escapade of the twins shone out bright, clear, and exasperating for a few days, then was completely overshadowed by a new "charade," as fond, foolish Lotta always called it. In her bewildered outlook on life, Lotta O'Haggerty called everything she didn't understand a "charade."

At nineteen, the twins were as wild and crafty as sandpipers on Bray Strand. They could not read or write. Conversation was carried on, even across the dining-room table, in loud bursts of shouting that would have embarrassed a bargee. When Morvin O'Haggerty, mortified beyond endurance, reproached his wife for her footling attitude towards the girls, she would moan, hold her head, and cry, "I just don't know what to do. It's a terrible cruel cross to bear, and me far from well." Morvin would fling his hands to heaven, stamp out, and all would go on as usual at Shireen House. Catch-as-catch-can-as-can-be.

One morning at breakfast when the family was assembled over morning tea, Morvin O'Haggerty threw a bombshell. It was thrown with gusto, but proved a dud. With a flourish, he announced the grand but rather dangerous idea that he intended to marry the girls off—had in fact picked the husbands. "Why not?" he sputtered, his mouth full of toast. "Can't feed you forever, you know. You're fine, strapping fillies, no flightier than any other gels."

Neither Fiona nor Rena was strapping. They were tall and, for such rapacious feeders, astonishingly slender. Both were rather long in the tooth, their light-blue eyes were small and too close together, and they were between sandy-fair and redheaded. "Nondescript" described them exactly.

Precisely what processes of gray matter went on under the sandy-red frizzes of the Misses O'Haggerty was anybody's guess. For, blatantly talkative between themselves, they were deeply secretive, even taciturn, when other people were about. Fiona and Rena O'Haggerty lived largely in a world of their own imagining. It was a strangely personal world, bounded by the four walls of the Shireen demesne. Today it would be called surrealistic.

The idea of marriage was greeted by the two it most concerned with shouts of derision. They wanted none of it and said so. "No, papa," said Fiona, the spokesman, "Rena and I don't want to marry, ever. We just want to go on as we are. Why, we'd never have any fun if we married two strangers and left Shireen." The case rested, and, as far as anyone knows, the subject was never referred to again.

On their twentieth birthday, Great-Aunt Gormanston arrived to spend the festivities at Shireen. She brought the girls a tandem velocipede, remarking, "All the girls in London have velocipedes. It's very smart, the newest fad. You must dress properly when you ride it. I'll see to that, too."

She produced a fashion paper from London, *The Ladies Mode*. Fiona and Rena pored for hours over a fascinating picture of a dashing young girl of about their own age standing in a wooded park. She held grimly to the handle bars of a tricycle. What caused thrills of delight to chase each other up and down the spines of the twins was her costume—bloomers! For a long time they had wanted to appear in breeches, to be no longer slaves to hoops and pantalets which were forever falling down, tripping them, and caking stiff with mud. Once they had mentioned this, in one of their rare confidences, to Clainy, the "all girl," who, blenching with horror ("What would the priest say?"), had promptly told Mary Moriarity. The twins weathered this storm, but had never mentioned it again. Now, with Great-Aunt Gormanston at the helm, and she brooking no interference with her wishes, they could kick off the shackles of hoops.

The costume was chosen and patterns of stuffs were ordered sent from Tyson's in Grafton Street, Dublin. Wispy, mouselike little Miss McIvery, the itinerant seamstress from Ballydavan, was summoned. Under the authoritative and watchful eye of Great-Aunt Gormanston, Fiona and Rena O'Haggerty were transformed from creatures of roundabout crinolines to bean-pole Amazons whose finished appearance was a catastrophe.

From head to foot, the outlay consisted of a bright-green straw boater worn at an angle over the eyes and up behind. Only a skewerlike pin managed to anchor it on the famous O'Haggerty topknot of frizzes. A puff-sleeved jacket of Scottish tartan displayed the McKenzie colors. (A remote paternal grandmother had been a McKenzie of Cudollock Castle; this choosing of her clan tartan was by way of tribute.)

The bloomers were, as the Great Condé said of Impregnability, "a thing apart." They were immense, in every nuance of the word. Belling out like a galleon in full sail, they cut sharply in at the hips, padded to show a richly curving behind, which, in a state of nature, neither of the Misses O'Haggerty possessed. These remarkable garments terminated just below the knee with a rosette composed of shamrocks and thistles cut cleverly from brilliant felt. They resembled nothing on earth so much as giant penwipers.

Heavy stockings of roundabout stripes, alternating purple and green to pick up the tartan colors, encased pipestem legs devoid of padding at the calves. Either Miss McIvery had given up the idea of so much padding lest the finished products become unwieldy, or, more likely, the padding gave out. High-laced boots of rich russet cordovan were finished at the top front in tassels of purple silk. Thus completed. the outfits were, in very truth, as the fashion paper said, "A country costume of highest elegance, and comfort, for the sport of cycling."

Nothing in all their lives had thrilled or touched the twins so deeply as did these costumes in all their splendor and the final emancipation that they signified. Forthwith, they adopted them as a uniform.

Their first public appearance was indeed a shocker. The day the costumes were finished was a day of cold, steady downpour. Fiona and Rena, with the aid of Miss McIvery, were pulled and hauled into their "bloomer suits," as they were forever after called by divers persons. "Thim two in those bloomer suits are the world's disgrace," Mary Moriarity had said in flaying scorn. From then on different inflections of the voice proclaimed the feelings of the speaker.

Fully arrayed, arms encircling each other's waists, the girls strolled into the drawing room just as Clainy Ryan brought in the tea barrow. Mrs. O'Haggerty, pale and sniffling from a head cold, reclined on a chaise longue in front of the fire. In her favorite role, she was enjoying ill-health, swathed in an elaborate but rather frowzy Parisian wrapper. Across from her sat the village priest, Father Faley, and his Gothic carving of a sister, Miss Constantia Faley

Each stoutly puffing on one of their father's cheroots, the twins came to a halt on the hearthrug. The effect on their audience was devastating. From Miss Constantia's rigid hand dropped one of the best Beleek teacups, shattering to atoms on the stone hearth. Father Faley swallowed a whole cup of scalding tea the wrong way, and collapsed in a violent fit of coughing. Mrs. O'Haggerty let out a low moan, but, more or less used to such entrances by her outlandish daughters, said sweetly, "Very original, girls. What charade is this?" Met by stony stares from the twins, she added hastily, "Go ask Clainy to give you tea in the study."

Clainy, meanwhile, was practically sliding down the back stairs to report the latest trick of "thim two" to the ever-waiting ear of Mary Moriarity.

Next day dawned fine and brisk, and the velocipede was brought out from the garden house, where Micky had oiled it. Down the long ash-tree drive peddled Fiona and Rena. As they peddled, they sang, in raucous unison, "The Widow with a Breast of Snow," a forbidden favorite taught them by one of the few boys they had ever made friends with, Timmy the Rake, a half-gypsy stable boy once employed at Shireen stables, but dismissed because of complaints from the entire female household staff, including Mary Moriarity, who had probably never been molested at all.

Turning out of the gate of the demesne, they speeded up a bit along the highroad leading into Ballydavan. Rena said, "Why are these things called bloomers?"

Fiona replied, "Named after a woman, I believe—my collar's tight."

What the villagers in Ballydavan thought of the Misses O'Haggerty of Shireen House, as they skimmed through the one long street, is not recorded. Rumblings of disapproval, however, reached the itching ear of Mary Moriarity. She expounded to Micky, "Jimsey Ronan got the fright of his life when his horse reared and upset the cart, full of crates of fowls for Dublin, burying Jimsey underneath. It was the like of the poor animal catching sight of thim two that made him stampede." Mary heaved a long sigh. "Sure no one in this part of Ireland ever clapped eyes on one av thim Divil's velocipedes before—I don't know where thim two 'ull end. They'll be draped with the sin of murder yet."

The years waxed and waned, and with them the escapades of the O'Haggerty girls grew more diverse, but never diminished. Marriage appeared forever out of the question. Any man in his right senses ran like a scalded cat at the very name of Fiona and Rena O'Haggerty.

The year the girls were twenty-seven they set Shireen House ablaze; not intentionally, of course, for they were not vicious, whatever else. Their mother, lying ill in a front chamber one late autumn afternoon, complained bitterly, when her tea tray appeared, that the house was cold as a vault. An icy wind swept through her room every time the door opened. She must have warmth. Fiona and Rena, in their bloomer suits, now threadbare from constant usage, were passing her chamber. They heard her say to Clainy, "Do you hear me, I want a roaring fire." She got it.

Walking slowly across the park in front of the house, scuffling leaves and eating sharply-sweet rose hawes. Fiona mused, "Mama must be warm, she's not well!" On the twins walked. Before them spread a sea of dried ox grass, ruddy and crisp in the autumn sunset. Rummaging through a little alligator-skin knapsack, which she always carried at her side for just such an emergency, Fiona found a box of Swedish matches, little sticks of wax tipped with bright orange sulphur. Calmly she struck one. Flinging it far away into the ox grass, she struck another. By this time, Rena was busily helping her, and a ring of swirling yellow flame sprang up all around them. Not realizing that they had practically lighted their mother's pyre, the girls started back towards the house, hoping that "Mama would soon be warm enough."

The flames, fanned by a light twilight wind, leaped from hedgerow to thorn-apple-bordered bohireen and across fields of ox grass like forked lightning. Straight up to the front steps of Shireen House they roared. Billows of thick smoke encircled the house and hid it from view. Every man, woman, and child old enough to carry water or to beat out flaming grasses with water-soaked sackings worked for two hours to save Shireen. Gardeners and stablemen from Clonorgan Castle, a mile away, arrived as soon as smoke was seen. Aided by them, and the heaven-sent shower which succeeded the sunset, the fire was at last reduced. But not before the pearly white façade was blackened, the like of a baudeen's heart.

For a while after this affair, the twins were watched more closely than they had ever been before. An indigent cousin of Lotta's from Cork, a spinster called Emeline Ponty, was fetched. Ostensibly a guest, she followed Fiona and Rena about so openly that even they, living in another world, were not long in perceiving that they were being spied upon. Furious, having always been as free as hawks, they set about making life such a hell of small but constant death traps for Miss Ponty that she fled back to Cork at the end of three weeks.

Mary Moriarity expressed her relief loudly as the carriage wheels bearing Miss Ponty away from Shireen turned out of the gates, en route to Cork. "Sure, the day I set me two eyes on the beaky face av 'er, the like av a molting crow, I said to meself, 'With her added to the weight av thim two loonys, life won't be worth sustaining.'"

Stories told of the ta-ta-ra-ra caused in the countryside by the goings on of the Misses O'Haggerty during the years would fill a book. Villagers in Ballydavan and Garryvoe tell legion tales as flamboyant and incredible as if one were peering with Alice through the looking glass.

It appears the Misses O'Haggerty, once they had put their legs into comfortable breeches, never wore skirts again. In due time the original masterpiece, "A country costume of highest elegance," was tossed, perforce, into the rag bag. Others followed, more or less lurid, concocted by Fiona, with the help of aging little Miss McIvery, more wraithlike with the years.

In the fashionable world-at-large, hoops were superseded by the bustle. Save for one instance only, the changes of fashion left Fiona and Rena cold. It is told that "for Mama's funeral," which occurred when the girls were in their twenty-ninth year, they wanted to appear in black bustles. Bolts of inky-black cloth were sent to Shireen from Dublin. Miss McIvery, practically on her own deathbed by this time, obliged. Sweeping skirts, enormously bustled, were draped on Fiona's and Rena's incredibly thin figures. As yards of crepe "weepers" were being tied over the black scoop bonnets of the twins, Micky Barrow came in to say that the frozen ground had melted in the sudden thaw to such a mess that mud and slush were near knee deep. Fiona called Clainy. "Fetch us the hip boots we wear when we fish, will you?" Tucking the considerable yardage of mourning skirts into the tops of their hip boots, with bustles jutting out behind, the Misses O'Haggerty clumped forth to the graveside. Rather like a pair of deformed Elizabethan gallants, they must have looked, striding along. Appearing ridiculous was nothing new to Fiona and Rena, nor were they ever remotely conscious that people for a moment thought they were.

It was when they took up the exhilarating game of badminton that life at Shireen House became one long series of accidents, owing to the sisters' passion for playing the game smack in the middle of the entrance drive leading to the portico of the house. They would rush down the alley of ash trees at all hours of the day and stretch their net between two trees.

Dressed in bloomers and tight-fitting jerseys of yellow or scarlet, or sometimes, as one may see in a rather blurred old daguerreotype at Shireen House, in black bowlers, swathed in spotted veils, the twins would play, wildly, as if pursued by Furies (the way they did everything), a series of games of badminton. As quickly as their ardor waxed, it waned. Throwing themselves onto the cool turf, they would shout with laughter, or sing. Suddenly they would stroll away to the stables or go boating on the river, forgetting completely the badminton net stretched across the driveway.

One dark night, Doctor Dancey, hurriedly called from Garryvoe by Morvin O'Haggerty to ease his wracking chest pains, drove his little cob along the drive at a smart pace. Neither horse nor driver noticed the net drawn tightly across their path. The sharp impact so startled the cob that he became frenzied and ran away across the park, splintering the gig on the first stone wall he encountered.

Even the twins themselves suffered. Returning on their dilapidated old velocipede one evening of long shadows from tea at Clonorgan Castle, they ran smack into the net. Fiona, on the front seat of the tandem, sustained a broken nose, and Rena suffered cuts and bruises. Next day Micky was ordered to fold the net away in its box in the garden house. Badminton was never mentioned at Shireen House again. Many years later the ghostly game was seen.

On a soft summer evening, in her sixtieth year, Fiona O'Haggerty died of a heart attack. She lay as if sleeping, in a vast flounced bed in her bright-pink chamber overlooking the park, the same one occupied by her mother the day of the Big Blaze. A fortnight later, Rena, who had grown terribly frail and listless during the last year, cried herself into her grave, utterly lost in her deep, black grief.

For the past five years a series of deaths had struck like a plague at the supports of Shireen House, supports very necessary to continuance of the fairy-tale existence of the sisters O'Haggerty.

First, that staunch supporter, Great-Aunt Gormanston, died at the supreme age of ninety-six. One cold morning Morvin O'Haggerty's chest pains overwhelmed him. Mary Moriarity had died, as the result of a fall, soon after Lotta O'Haggerty; and that perfect example of perpetual motion, Clainy Ryan, an old, mumbling woman, served out to the last her apprenticeship of "all girl." A passel of younger, more fractious servants now lived *in* Shireen House, but not *of* it.

The precarious finances left by their father bothered his daughters not at all. A lawyer in Dublin fought, bled, and all but died in the losing game of trying to keep Shireen over their heads and food in their mouths. The O'Haggerty exchequer sank woefully low in funds. When it seemed imperative that Shireen House be sold and the ancient twins commited to the religious retreat of the Sisters of Eternal Solicitude at Clondalkin, Fiona and Rena elected to take matters into their own hands; almost it seemed they sensed what was in store for them. They stepped "Through the Looking Glass" permanently.

When lawyers and bailiffs climbed the stairs of Shireen House to the second floor, where the bedchambers opened one into the other, strange sights met their eyes.

A veritable carnival of color, brilliant and jumbled as a kaleidoscope, appeared. Pots of paint with brushes still standing in them stood in rows along the baseboards. It appeared that whenever Fiona or Rena felt the urge, she grabbed a brush, loaded it with crimson, violet, orange, or green paint, and swept a wide swathe of color across whichever wall was nearest. Crosshatchings of violently contrasted color sang on every wall.

In one room which had been used, apparently, by little gray Miss McIvery were stacked, clear to the ceiling, decades of issues of French and English fashion papers, *L'Art de la Mode, La Mode Nouvelle, Godey's Lady's Book, London Fashion Album,* and *Costume Royal*. Thousands of fashion-plate figures had been expertly cut out and, in the manner of *découpage,* pasted on the walls. Brilliant throngs of simpering mannequins strolled through these bright pastures.

In another room, a maypole occupied the center of the floor. Hundreds of dusty, tatered ribbons hung limply from a crown of paper flowers.

Still another room was all but impassable because of fishing tackle, nets, poles, boxes of flies, enormous baiting hooks, such as are used off the Aran Islands, not in the quiet River Lee, surely, and fishing tongs, which hung from the ceiling or were piled in corners. A strong stench of stale fish pervaded this room like a lethal gas.

Perhaps the most fantastic of all was a large room at the back of the house, a room always reserved for Great-Aunt Gormanston during her frequent visits. In this room, hung from the ceiling, were dozens of pairs of bloomers of all patterns. Tam-o-shanters, bowlers, top hats garlanded with veils, straw boaters, and water-proof capes and caps. The dreary habiliments of mourning with outcropping bustles, which had been worn by Fiona and Rena at all family funerals, hung in a corner. The room was a Valhalla of moths; as the door was opened they fluttered like myriad golden motes in the slanting shafts of sun. It was a curious world, surely, behind the white walls of Shireen House; a world in which two women who never grew up dashed hand in hand through the middle-mist that is neither fact nor fantasy.

Fiona and Rena O'Haggerty, of Shireen House, County Waterford, aged sixty years, spinsters of this parish, were buried, according to their last wish, in a double coffin. They were dressed in identical bloomer suits of white silk, especially made for this occasion many years before by the spindly fingers of Miss McIvery.

Shireen House remained shuttered for a few years, for in 1890 the Land Rent Riots were abroad in the land and houses the size of Shireen did not change owners easily. Finally, an Irishwoman named Trevalton, widow of a rich Cornish shipbuilder, leased the house. Although she had heard of the repeated visits of the "batty O'Haggerty girls," as they were called in the countryside, she scoffed at the idea as a lot of nonsense.

Mrs. Trevalton, a rather ponderous lady, took up residence early in the summer. Her household consisted of herself, three sons, ranging from six years to fifteen, two daughters, both small, and a staff of English and Cornish servants.

The widow Trevalton's tenantage lasted precisely one year. The servants complained bitterly of tricks played upon them in the night. At first Danny Trevalton, the eldest boy, was blamed, as it proved, falsely. Then, one by one, the servants left. Richard, the second Trevalton boy, aged twelve, was riding his bicycle late one evening along the driveway, returning home to a late tea. He was startled by an apparition of two giddy women in bloomers who ran out into the middle of the drive, leaping up and down, arms outstretched, apparently batting a shuttlecock. So sudden was their appearance and so demented that Richard ran into one of the ash trees beside the drive and broke his collarbone.

Then began a series of mishaps. Mrs. Trevalton, returning from the garden, was entering the study through an open French window when she saw a figure of a woman in full fishing kit, even to a net to ward off gnats, tied over a wide-brimmed hat. She called out, "What is this? Who are you?" The figure disappeared, as a violent blow on Mrs. Trevalton's cheek sent her reeling. Later, a garden boy found a fishing pole of old design just outside the study window.

A visitor from England was wakened one night by raucous laughter and wild singing. She was sleeping in the chamber that had been occupied by Fiona and Rena before Lotta O'Haggerty died. Rising and throwing on a dressing gown, the woman went to the hall and opened the door. Silhoueted against the Palladian window at the end of the hall stood two tall, thin figures, holding hands. They wore bloomers and were rocking back and forth in paroxysms of laughter. As she watched, the figures seemed to fade through the window.

One evening, a delivery boy from Cappoquin was driving his cart up the driveway towards the house. Suddenly his horse shied and reared, snorting, to his hind legs. As the boy sawed wildly on the reins, he saw, dancing along the drive in front of him, two tall old women. Slung across their shoulders and hanging in a loop between them, they carried what looked like a badminton net, very much in need of repair. As they skipped off among the trees, shrill laughter died away through the ash branches.

Later that night, when the puzzled boy recounted his story in the pub at Cappoquin, one old man, enjoying the peaty smoke of a black cobeen pipe, nodded his head. "Sure, now, and that'd be the two Miss O'Haggertys. A great pair they were entirely, the like of little childer grown old and tall. Arragh, they haunt the place now, just as they did in life."

The Phantom Portrait

Drinshallon Park

COUNTY CORK

The Phantom Portrait

PATRICK DUNTARRAN SLOWLY CLIMBED THE hill, which fell away behind him in undulating pastures as he approached its wooded crest. There, a crescent-shaped swath had been cut out of the dense oak and beech wood. In the center of this clearing stood his tall, graceful house, Drinshallon.

Patrick had walked the four miles across country, over the hills from Ballincurrig, by way of Garryvoe and Castle Cloyne. Often he took this path, for it led him past the farm where he was born. (Old Sir Patrick, the squireen, his father, had elected to live at Ballybandon Farm within sight of the slowly rising walls of Drinshallon.) All the happy memories of his boyhood stemmed from there.

The house had not been finished and ready for occupancy until young Patrick was a man grown. He remembered playing, with his brother Regan, up and down the windy, roofless corridors and huge empty shells of rooms for years before sufficient money could be found by the sporting squireen to complete the house as it had been originally planned.

Many times, he remembered, he and Regan had glued an eye to the door of his father's office at the farm, when the "counting man" had arrived from Cork. On his father's desk stood rows of calfskin bags filled with clinking sovereigns. These golden beauties were the rents from docks and warehouses in the teeming seaport of Cork. When they ran to their mother with the grand news that "the rents have arrived," she would smile and wink at them. "Now we can proceed with the building of this great house, perhaps. Who knows, we may be able to enjoy it before we die."

But it was a long, tiresome wait, surely. Somehow, after each opulent visit of the "counting man," it always seemed that the next day there was classic racing at Kenmare—Good Luck Kenmare, it was called—or Mallow Course, or perhaps trappy Tramore, where the heartbreaking jumps were known to man and horse alike as "Paradise and Purgatory." If you got clean over, you were in Paradise; if not, you were damn well in Purgatory. Squireen Sir Patrick would fill the pockets of his plum-colored greatcoat with fistfuls of the minted gold. Off he'd go to one race meeting or

173

another. When he returned that night, the next day, or three days distant, his pockets would be bone empty. He would laugh, a great roar in his throat, then slap the sides of his coat. "Sure there's luck for ye. Me pockets as empty as a Protestant's promise." Long-suffering Lady Duntarran would roll her eyes to heaven, cross herself, heave a long sigh, and resign herself to the fact that no more work would be done on Drinshallon for months.

At last, after twenty-odd years in the building, Sir Patrick Duntarran marched himself and his family through the soaring portals of his fine new house. He called it Drinshallon Park.

The house stands today looking away across the farm-dotted valley much as it did when it was finally completed in 1766. On long summer evenings, the light and dark of shadow from beech and oak form a lacelike pattern across its classic façade. Drinshallon is a pleasant house. It wears well with the years. Even its ghost brings a smile to the lips, for one feels that poetic justice triumphed when Anna-Mary Fernold eventually had her way, even though she had to die to achieve it. But as Anna-Mary herself would say, and she smiling up at you through long lashes, "No matter."

Anna-Mary Fernold was fourteen years old the day she came to Drinshallon Park. She thought it a fine way to spend her birthday, bowling along the highway from Cobh to Garryvoe in the mail coach. From her vantage point on the front seat beside the driver, high above the dappled gray backs of the four coach horses, she eagerly scanned the smiling, overly green countryside of County Cork. At the "Bran and Barley" in Garryvoe she was to get down. A gig from Drinshallon would meet her there. After a cup of strong, peat-smoked tea, she would continue her journey to her Cousin Patrick's house.

All she had ever known were the wild, blue distances of her native Connemara. Vastly different was this almost tropical abundance of flower and leaf, spread out on either hand as far as she could see. She even remembered hearing travelers from the south of Ireland call Connemara "bleak." It used to raise her dander when she heard it. Now she saw what they meant.

As Anna-Mary sat over her tea in the tavern in Garryvoe, she mused upon the last weeks of her life. A veritable maelstrom they had been, seeming doubly so after the long, quiet years of her childhood, locked within the circling arm of the Partry Mountains, the reaches of the wind-riffled water of Lough Mask, and gorse-strewn bog and pasture. Until today, she had never been farther afield from her own hearthplace than rackety little Toormakeady or Leenane to buy tweeds and homespun, straight off the looms, for winter clothing.

Her life since she could remember had a pattern of days that to many might have seemed monotony itself, but to Anna-Mary it was all she asked for. She was out early in the luminous dawns on the broad breast of Lough Mask, fishing with her father. Sleepily, she would lie in the bottom of the curragh through the hot noons. At night she sprang into activity. The long, brilliant twilights of the west country made eating out-of-doors very pleasant when weather permitted, and Anna-Mary prepared the day's catch of tender lake trout and pike on sizzling iron grill plates over a hot peat fire.

After her tenth birthday, she had not been able to spend as much time on the lough with her father and his guests as she wished, for her mother had caught a fever of the lungs, and her increasing invalidism needed Anna-Mary's constant care. The mists and drifting fogs around Corly Lodge had proved too much for Mrs. Fernold, the sister of Patrick Duntarran's mother.

About the time of Anna-Mary's birth, Jasper Fernold had turned his small house near Ballintober, on the far north reach of the lough, into a hotel for fishing enthusiasts. The sporting gentry always filled to overflowing the confines of the small stone house, yet her father never admitted, even to her, that he ran this fishing hotel for gain. He was too proud for that. He would announce to Anna-Mary and her mother, "I expect two cronies from Waterford tonight. Hope to get a bit of fishing." They would nod their heads. Her mother would say "How pleasant for you, Jasper, to see your old friends. But isn't the house full to bursting now?" This little comedy continued regularly through the years. They had managed very well.

Suddenly, Fate had struck the family Fernold a sharp, a mortal blow. The father was drowned in a treacherous squall on the lough. It had blown up in the flick of an eyelid. The boat had capsized. In pitching out, Jasper had cracked his skull. A group of rod boys who were cleaning reels in the boathouse witnessed the accident, tortured by not being able to help in time. Later, they brought his body home and laid him on a brown denim couch in the taproom. From this time out, affairs at Corly Lodge took a speedy downward turn.

In a few weeks Anna-Mary's mother died. Corly Lodge went to satisfy creditors of the friendly, improvident Jasper Fernold.

In desperation, Anna-Mary wrote to her only relative in Ireland to whom she could turn in her extremity—Cousin Patrick Duntarran. When Anna-Mary was a small child, Patrick often came to Corly Lodge on a fishing holiday. They had become firm friends. He told her the way she cooked his catch of trout, served with parsley butter, was "ambrosia." She did not know what that was, but believed it something very fine, the way he *mmmmmm*'d and smacked his lips.

Patrick's first wife had died in childbirth, the baby dying as well. He had come to the Lough Mask, with its sparkling air and water, to rest and orient his mind. Long walks with Anna-Mary through the bohireens and purple-bronze gorse had restored him. When he left to return to Drinshallon, he felt that perhaps life was not over for him, after all.

As he turned to wave good-by to his young cousin at the water steps, he said, "Come one day to Drinshallon. I will show you from a hill back of my house the grandest sight in Ireland, the Knockmealdown Mountains."

Here she was. Her task now was to fit smoothly into life at Drinshallon. The new mistress, Patrick's second wife, was an heiress from Dublin. She had heard her mother say, on hearing of the marriage, "Honoria Dunphy, very grand indeed, or so *she* thinks."

Anna-Mary stood in front of the fan-lighted door of Drinshallon just as lights of countless tapers were beginning to wink from windows over which curtains had not yet been drawn. A footman ushered her into a softly lighted drawing room. In front of the fire sat a woman. Anna-Mary curtsied to Lady Duntarran, who sat far back in the shadows of a claret-colored brocade wing chair. She was slowly sipping tea from a fragile porcelain cup. Lady Duntarran nodded, but did not speak. Slowly she appraised Anna-Mary. Anna-Mary appraised Lady Duntarran. Each did not like what she saw.

Ever after, when she shut herself in her room, trying to force down the storm of tears which sprang to the back of her eyes twenty times a day, Anna-Mary would vividly remember her first encounter with Honoria Duntarran.

Inclined to overplumpness, Lady Duntarran managed to restrain her opulent bosom within rigid stays. However, these stays pushed so much flesh up under Honoria's chin that her neck seemed short to the point of deformity. A gown of plum-and-green-striped taffeta swirled in great billows about her feet. Her soft, pink hand caressed a small tortoise-shell kitten who tumbled about on the Aubusson rug and played with the fringes of a white China crepe shawl which was thrown over the back of the chair.

Honoria's light-brown hair was unconfined by ribbons or flowers. Piled high on her head, it was a welter of puffs and finger curls. Lady Duntarran stirred in her appraisal. To herself she said, "A country creature. A bold eye. Proud. That will not do in my house. I'll take her down."

Anna-Mary thought, "Selfish, lazy, and a glutton. I don't like her, and never will."

It was very soon apparent to Anna-Mary that her life at Drinshallon had been carefully mapped out by Lady Duntarran, who saw her as just another servant in her already amply staffed household. The baby Patrick, not yet two years old, was given over to Anna-Mary to amuse. Never having had a brother or sister of her own, she did this with the greatest pleasure, for she loved him deeply. From breakfast to late at night it was Lady Duntarran's petulant, affected voice that called, "Anna-Mary, fetch my China shawl," or, "Anna-Mary, quiet the baby, instantly. I cannot abide his howling." Little by little, Anna-Mary adjusted herself to Honoria's erratic ways. She answered the numerous summons automatically, and let them in no way disturb her.

When taking long walks over the hills, as she so often did, she would meet Patrick returning from Ballybandon Farm, or Castle Hyde, near Fermoy, where his sister lived. They would walk together for a way. Patrick, who seemed fine-drawn and quiet these days, would smile and say, "I'm sorry, my dear cousin. I had not planned it this way. But Honoria, as you well know, is such a devil if crossed, I let her have her own way. Weak of me, I admit, and as you see I spend more and more time at Castle Hyde. If you want to leave Drinshallon, I shall understand. I'll provide for you. You know that."

After three years of life amidst the tumult and shouting at Drinshallon, caused by Lady Duntarran, who was waxing into a first-class virago, Anna-Mary found that, except in direct encounter, she minded Honoria not at all. Little Patrick, growing fast, and Cousin Patrick were her friends. Life could be endured, even mightly enjoyed, at Drinshallon, because the house itself was so friendly.

Honoria, however, complained bitterly that the house was filthy and the furnishings out of date. She imported a new lot of servants from Dublin. They drank heavily, skeltered over their work, and made a brothel of the attics. After a few weeks, Honoria packed the whole unsavory crew back to Dublin. The lovely, mellow brocades and damasks, brought by old Sir Patrick from Italy, remained at the tall windows. Honoria found herself carrying her second child. She quieted perceptibly after this knowledge. Life at Drinshallon became markedly more pleasant.

One day in early April, Anna-Mary came into the house from a long walk. The day was a pure wonder—what the Italians mean when they say of a mimosa-laden day in spring, *primavera assoluta*. She had taken the dogs for a run down the hill road past the gaunt ruins of Kilbraden Castle, burned by maurauding Red Eva McMurrough in one of her marches across Cork in 1180. While Anna-Mary drank in the splendid view across the flower-strewn valley, the terriers carried on their demented burrowing under the huge stones of the castle keep. Badgers and foxes had for centuries honeycombed the place with their earths. The dogs never tired in their efforts to find quarry. They played a losing game, for the earths extended for hundreds of yards, emptying into the sand pits along the river. Calling to the frustrated terriers, Anna-Mary continued across the bridge which arched the River Bride. Like a ribbon of blue enamel it lay, so stilly reflecting the rain-washed sky.

Crossing the lower meadow, where a few mares with their spring foals scampered away at her approach, she mounted the hill in front of the house. The entire rise, moving upward in terraces, was spread with primroses, poet's narcissus, jonquils, and daffodils, bending their heads to the light breeze that swept the ridge.

Regarding the brilliant yellow flowers shimmering in the sun, Anna-Mary thought of the rainy afternoon a few weeks before when she had been sitting in the window embrasure in the "Venetian Room," a kind of state chamber on the second floor of Drinshallon. The quiet of this room attracted her. She often slipped away from the strident commands of Lady Duntarran to read or embroider in the white and silver shadows of the room. Looking closely at an oval pane of pale amber glass set midway in the window casement, she saw for the first time a scratched kind of writing on the glass. Someone, sometime, had roughly etched, probably with a diamond ring, this line. *And Phoebus strews the shattered sun, to gild an Irish spring.* With great flourish it was signed *Desmond K.* A date was also added—*April, 1770.* It must have been just such a day as this which prompted the unknown Desmond K. to inscribe the window pane. Later, when she asked Patrick, he said he knew no Desmond K. and had never heard anything about him. Besides, Patrick had been in Italy in the year 1770.

Anna-Mary took the dogs around to the kennels and came into the house by the garden door. Just then Patrick came slowly down the circular stairs and, stopping at the front door, he turned. Smiling lazily at Anna-Mary through narrow eyes, he said, "Cousin, how would you like to have your portrait painted?" Picking up a crop from the hall table, he continued, "Thomas Hudson from Dublin has just finished painting Lady Mountrath. She's been staying with my sister Barbara at Castle Hyde. He comes here as soon as he has painted Barbara. He's devilish good at the conversation piece, which is all the rage now in Dublin. I plan to have Honoria, you, little Pat and myself sitting on the east terrace. Perhaps we can have one or two of the dogs as well."

Anna-Mary held her breath in pure delight. It was a magical idea. "Its grand, entirely, Patrick. Do you suppose I could hold little Pat? Or would Honoria want to do that?"

Patrick shook his head and replied, "Who knows what Honoria will do? Wait till the time comes, I suggest. Meanwhile, get yourself a fine dress for the picture. Something yellow, like those primroses in your hand. With your black hair and blue eyes, it's your best color."

A month later, one morning at breakfast, Honoria said airily, "My gown for the portrait arrives from London today. It's from the Court Manteau Makers in St. James Street. I sent Parlow in to fetch it off the Bristol Packet." Turning to Patrick she continued, "I hope you have chosen something dark in color, that will set off my rose and silver dress. Have you?" Patrick looked up from a letter he was reading. "I shall stand in the background in a dark green coat. It is Anna-Mary in a fine new gown of primrose yellow who will set you off by contrast. The picture will have color."

There was a resounding silence. Slowly Honoria put down her teacup. For a space of minutes she looked searchingly, first at Anna-Mary, then at her husband. Coldly, on a rising inflection, Honoria said to Anna-Mary, "What ever gave you the idea you are to be included in a conversation piece of the Duntarrans? Most certainly you are not." Her voice rose hysterically: "I'll not have a cluttered canvas. There are only three in this family—yet. And, pray, where did you get a primrose-yellow gown?"

Patrick, reddening in embarrassment, started to protest. Anna-Mary stopped him and rose quietly from the table. As she passed Honoria, she paused for a moment in front of her. "You are right. There is no reason for me to be painted with the Duntarrans. Please believe that I never asked to be. As to the dress," she shrugged, "no matter."

Quickly she went out of the room.

Many admirers of Thomas Hudson regard his portrait of Diana, Countess of Mountrath, which hangs as one of a loan collection at the National Gallery, Leinster House, Dublin, as his finest picture. It is beautifully painted. The quality of rich textures is masterfully handled—silvery taffetas and Irish point lace flounces, strong in design, delicate in detail. In his subject, actually a rather plain woman, Hudson has caught a swift intelligence in the hazel eyes. The witty and candid Mrs. Delany wrote of Lady Mountrath, "Her forbearance is proverbial, her fortitude formidable." It is all there in the portrait. Hudson was not prolific, not a whirlwind of performance like his contemporary, Sir Joshua Reynolds, who painted so many of the Irish. But he left, in the few signed portraits and conversation pieces, today in private collections, a brilliant company of human documents of the epoch. Of such is his painting of the family of Sir Patrick Duntarran, Bt.

Grouped on the white stone east terrace at Drinshallon, under the branches of a beech, are three figures. The arrangement is delightful. The placing of the figure of the baby boy gives great animation and fluid line to the composition. The boy wears a white satin suit with knee breeches. At his hip swings an absurdly small dress sword. He stands on his mother's knee. His arm is flung upwards, his hand resting in the palm of his father's right hand. The smiling boy, little more than a baby, is a gallant and a beau of the period, in miniature. The tall figure of Sir Patrick stands behind him, a little in shadow. Wearing a coat of laurel-green velvet, his left hand rests lightly against a column supporting a wing of the Palladian window to the drawing room.

The portraits of Sir Patrick and little Pat are agreeable and painted with authority.

The portrait of Lady Duntarran is revealing to the point of embarrassment. The flesh, while delicate in color, looks flabby and unwell. It is an exposé of a showy, conceited, ineffectual woman in a blatantly pink gown. She is painted so slickly as to be repellent.

The picture on the whole is immensely decorative, and amazingly subtle. One instantly falls under the charm of the man and the little boy. Of the woman, you feel, as your eyes are compelled to turn back for one last look, "I wouldn't trust her as far as I can throw this house."

As far as I have been able to trace, Anna-Mary Fernold left Drinshallon shortly after the portrait was painted. In her diary, now in possession of a descendant, she tells of having seen the picture hung in the same place it now occupies. Her comments on it are few. She "dotes" on little Pat, she "admires vastly the style of Mr. Hudson," but she says little else.

Two years after she left Drinshallon to live in Galway Old City, as governess to children of the Burkes, she married one Tynan Driscoll, barrister. One might now say that Anna-Mary Fernold Driscoll fades from this picture. In doing so she from time to time illumines another.

Anna-Mary Driscoll is reported to have died in Dublin in 1801. The first time she was seen to appear in the portrait painted by Thomas Hudson of the Duntarran family, hanging in the morning room at Drinshallon Park, was in the winter of 1820.

A manservant entered the room at dusk one evening. It had been cold and blowy since dawn. He noticed that the fire he had so carefully tended all day had died on the hearth, and a window leading out onto the terrace was open and banging in the wind. Closing the window and drawing the curtains, the man lighted a squill from the few coals left smoldering in the fire place. He turned to light the candles in a candelabrum standing on a table near the door to the hall. The candles lighted, he looked around the room to see if all was in order before he sent a boy to rekindle the fire.

Glancing at the familiar portrait, his eyes nearly dropped from his head. There had never been more than three figures within that frame, surely. He had seen the picture nearly every day of his life for six years. Standing beside Sir Patrick in the painting was a fourth figure, a black-haired young woman. She wore a yellow gown and seemed to be looking down at the little boy in front of her, who stood on his mother's knee. The servant ran from the room in search of Sir Patrick, who was an old man now. He found him in the study and told him what he had seen. Sir Patrick went quickly to the morning room. As he stood in the doorway, Sir Patrick trembled at what he saw. It was Anna-Mary, whom he had loved, and never told her. She seemed to know he was in the room, for she smiled softly at little Pat, and touched his curls. As suddenly as she had appeared, Anna-Mary faded from the portrait. There was a rustle of silk; the curtains of the terrace window parted; the window opened and banged to and fro. For a long time, Sir Patrick gazed at the spot in the portrait where Anna-Mary had appeared. Then he went back to the study.

Later, in a letter to his sister, Lady Hyde, who now lived in Paris, Patrick described what had occurred. He wrote, "It is impossible for me to tell you how lovely Anna-Mary looked, or the tender expression in her eyes as she touched the baby's hair. In the drab clothes which Honoria decreed she should wear, one seldom realized the beauty, the beauty that comes from Connemara, that was Anna-Mary's. The thing which impressed me most in all this unusual appearance was how rightly Anna-Mary fitted into the picture, just as I had planned she should. She completed the composition, but, Lord, how she showed up Honoria." In two other letters to his sister in Paris Patrick mentions having seen the apparition in the portrait.

Sir Patrick Duntarran died in his eighty-sixth year, and there are no further references to ghostly visitations at Drinshallon until 1899, when a Mrs. Carew, a tenant at the time, went into the morning room, where her daughter, aged eighteen, was lying on a sofa convalescing from a long illness. She found the girl nervous and curiously aware that there had been someone in the room for the past half-hour. She lay with her back to the wall on which the portrait hung, so she could not see that a clear yellow radiance slowly suffused the painting on the right-hand side.

Mrs. Carew saw it and, hesitating to mention something which she was afraid would upset her daughter, she rang for a servant to help her move the girl to another room. As she went to the door to call, when no answer to the bell was forthcoming, her daughter turned on the couch and saw the gently smiling face of Anna-Mary gazing at her. Instead of being alarmed, the girl took a great fancy to the "Smiling Ghost," as she always called it.

Many times afterwards Anna-Mary appeared for a brief time to the sick girl. The procedure was always the same. About five o'clock in the afternoon, as twilight was descending, there would be a rustle of silk petticoats. The window on the terrace would open and the curtains would part. A slow, pale, yellow light would appear and glow for a few minutes. From this would materialize the clearly drawn face and figure of Anna-Mary. She never stayed long, and no one ever saw her enter or leave the room. Yet one could feel her presence and see the window open and the curtains part. The ghost of Anna-Mary never closed the window after herself, nor did she ever rearrange the curtains across the windows.

The next year Mrs. Carew gave up the house, and it remained untenanted for a number of years. In 1917 a member of the original family again went to live at Drinshallon. He had married a Miss Darragh, of County Limerick, and splendid entertainments were given in the house.

One night, just before a large dinner party, one of the guests went into the morning room to retrieve her knitting bag. She fumbled around in the dark, trying to find an electric light switch. Unable to find the switch, the woman was about to leave when she noticed a radiance in the room. It seemed to come from a large, framed picture on the wall opposite the door. As she watched, she clearly saw the lovely figure of a young woman in yellow standing beside the tall figure of Sir Patrick Duntarran. The girl in yellow looked straight at her, smiled, and pointed to an overstuffed chair by the window. Crammed into the space between the arms and back of the chair was the lost knitting bag.

In all the stories I have heard of people suddenly seeing Anna-Mary materialize in the portrait, she is so winning a person that no one becomes alarmed. Everyone agrees that it would take more than a pretentious shrew like Honoria Dunphy to keep her out of a portrait in which she really belongs..

The Ghostly Catch

Drumnacrogha
The Castle of the Scald

C O U N T Y   S L I G O

DRUMNACROGHA, COUNTY SLIGO

The Ghostly Catch

NEVER IS DRUMNACROGHA SO IMPRESSIVE, its dramatic impact so startling as on a brilliant moonlight night. A still night it should be as well, although I have also seen it impressive when a murderous gale was driving in from the gray Atlantic and lifting the combers so high they dashed their life out halfway to heaven, or so it seemed. During such storms, the gaunt old pile shudders and growls at the sea gnawing at its foundations, and the sea roars back, "I'll topple you one of these days."

Drumnacrogha jeers in answer, "So you have said for longer than I can remember. I defy you." And so it goes.

But on a soft, moonlight night, when the sea runs stilly in little white caps, then does this monumental old house come into its own. For then the story of wonder and dread which Drumnacrogha holds cradled in its arms comes to life. It breathes and takes shape, and all men watch and fear.

Many names are given to this ancient house, standing sheer, untouched by tree or latticed flower. Murmurous black ivy clings fitfully to the half-ruined tower of the keep, which rises a little to the side of the strong, high ramp on which the whitewashed house stands. "Drumnacrogha," the old ones call it, for Drumna was a sea queen from out of Gaelic lore. "Crogha" may derive from the old Sligo term for "lone." "The Lone Sea Queen" has a very Gaelic ring, surely.

"The Castle of the Scald," others call it. The fishermen around Inishcrona and Killileg say that the devil scalds the water for his tea in the churning whirlpool at the foot of the escarpment.

Around the walls of Drumnacrogha forever hangs the banner of power. Out of the mists of time march an army of stories and legends telling of the caves and dungeons used by roving pirates and local tyrants, such as the dreaded Black O'Flaherty of Castle Blake in County Galway, who at one time or another held all the coast of Sligo, Donegal, and Galway in bondage, even as far as Antrim and its nine glens.

Who built Drumnacrogha Keep is not known. When the original towers and bailey were recorded, and that only sketchily, the O'Doon fought marauding pirates to hold the castle for their own, though legend tells us the O'Doon acquired it by force themselves, from whom no one seems to know. Tenure of coastal and border castles was short, at best, in Ireland in the year 900, which is when we first hear of Drumnacrogha as a fortress.

What man builds he can destroy. Sometimes he is aided considerably by the elements. Neither man nor the elements have completely destroyed Drumnacrogha, and both have put their minds to it for centuries. True, the old bailey is useless except as a windbreak for sheltering livestock. Only one of the old towers survives, but the core of this stronghold vaunts its impregnability to all comers. Great deeds have blazoned its walls, and many an infamous story is handed down, by word of mouth, of happenings within its towering walls. Of all the secrets guarded by the old house, and they are many, it is the fabulous story of the Ghostly Catch which captures and holds my imagination.

No one knows when the first manifestation of the Ghostly Catch was seen, churning the dark Atlantic waters at the foot of the serried rock on which Drumnacrogha stands. Some say it happened on a calm, moonlight night in 1600 or thereabouts. Others tell of hearing their grandfathers say the catch of ghostly fish happened hundreds of years before that.

As the whole picture of the occurrence never alters appreciably, the actual time does not matter. The reason for the appearance of the phenomenon, which always includes a raging battle of the elements wind, rain, and sea, is not clear, nor is the reason why it should happen at precisely this spot. The coast line of Ireland is three hundred miles long. Many ancient castles guard its headlands, and the Dread Women of Moher, who are most hideously linked with these thousands of ghostly·fish, are supposed to inhabit and haunt the Cliffs of Moher at Hags Head in County Clare, many miles down the coast. Perhaps it gives zest to the appetites of these Dread Women, who fly a long way for their bloody banquet.

The Dread Women of Moher play a vastly important part in the annals of Gaelic legend. Many is the black, windy night, and myself a small boy, when I ran as if all the furies of hell were on my heels, hoping to gain the shelter of a house before they got me. For the Dread Women are the Harpies of Greece, those frightful winged monsters "with perpetual hunger pale." They are the Lokii, Norse harbingers of discord and disease. They are the Tiri, ghouls of Persian lore. The Dread Women of Moher forbode destruction.

However we wish to interpret these creatures, the fact remains that their appearance is without warning. Prefaced by a night of shimmering moon and stars, a whistling whirlwind comes suddenly, like a wolf upon the fold. Black clouds pile high, the sea mounts, thunder and forked lightning split the sky. The Dread Women shriek. The play is on.

Wind sweeping in from the Atlantic often drives these storms across the island and into the English Channel within twenty-four hours. It has been put on record that storms of unheard-of violence continued unabated for three days and nights, until the entire Atlantic coast, from Bantry Bay in the south to Inishtrall at the northmost tip of Donegal, was a welter and a scourge of battered corpses and foundered ships, a royal banquet for the ravenous Women of Moher, to be sure.

One wonders if these Gaelic Harpies were not out in full cry the night in May, 1588, when the Spanish Armada was wrecked on the Galway coast. From the journal of one survivor, Don Francesco de Cuellar, comes this excerpt:

> My hand holds a quill for the first time in many weeks. The galleon San Pedro, which I commanded, was set upon by high winds, such as no man has ever seen, I vow. Waves tossing to the mastheads brought down the rigging. All night this hell prevailed. Great schools of white fish, giants in size, hurled past us in the wake of the shoal swell. The screaming of huge flocks of birds resembling cormorants, as they attacked the fish, was hideous. So strident were the cries of these birds as they tortured the slapping fish, they were heard above the wrack of the storm.

This appears to be the only reference to the Ghostly Catch recorded by a foreigner who actually suffered from the visitation.

Many times when I have been in Sligo I have gone down on to the sands at Killileg. A clutch of thatched and lime-washed coteens hugs the salt-rimmed rocks near Drumnacrogha. So slippery are these kelp-strewn rocks that one must keep a wary eye peeled; many is the broken leg scored up by these timeless stones. Sitting on an overturned curragh, watching old and young fishermen mend iodine-yellowed nets, or manipulate kelpies, the long, swath-like rakes by which these harvesters of the sea gifts bring in the huge bundles of kelp one sees drying on the rocks, I gather stories of the Ghostly Catch first hand. Sometimes a man whose son went out in a trawler, or in his own curragh, one mild, moonlight night, and never came home, is reluctant to talk.

From a smiling, swarthy fisherwoman, the raven-haired Spanish type, who sported the most magnificent mustache I ever beheld on human lip, I learned what might be called an annotation on the margin of this legend. Her fragment of news led me straight to the one man in Ireland who had witnessed the Ghostly Catch with a vengeance and who could tell me of his experience. He was also familiar with the history of a number of other old houses along the west coast.

The woman flung me a smile as wide as the Gap of Dunloe as I approached the spot where she was "treading down" a mountainous pile of kelp, which was the morning yield from an abundant sea. I asked her if she could add anything to what I already knew of the legend of the Ghostly Catch.

"I could," she said, "but I'll not, and don't mistake me, sir. It's not rough I'd be. It's only the way ye should hear it told much better than meself. Why don't ye go to Mr. Coney? He writes the history of all Ireland, I'm told. He's away now at Drogheda, but he's often at Castle Clogher with the Moriaritys. Sure he's great cause to remember the Catch. The sea nearly drowned him the night. He'd the dread on 'im fer a week, and he still drags his foot from a fish bone drove clean through it."

That was all I needed. In a cloud of sand I was off to Drogheda. There I located Mr. Coney at the house of a famous Gaelic scholar, Sir Teague Gorland, who very kindly asked me to stay and take supper with them. Sir Teague proved, in the long run, as much of a chronicler of legends as his friend Coney, and I am immensely indebted to him for the story of "The Bridal Barge of Aran Roe."

After a substantial high tea of wonderful Drogheda bannocks and a salad of spicy cress, fresh from the icy brook behind the house, mixed with sorrel, and the whole doused with mustard cream, a grand dish of the County Meath, Mr. Coney said, "To-night I'll give you a rough idea of the magnitude of the legend of the Women of Moher and how they are concerned with the Ghostly Catch on the beach at Drumnacrogha. It is a monstrous tale, and I suggest we return to Killileg tomorrow. I want to be on the spot when I tell you what I saw."

Mr. Coney's Story

One day early in August, 1926, I journeyed from my house overlooking Killiney Strand, just outside Dublin. I was on my way to visit a friend of my university days, one Shamas O'Murrough, whose family hailed from County Kilkenny. For five years or more Shamas and his family had lived at Drumnacrogha, an ancient house dominating the coast line for miles, at Killileg, in County Sligo. In all Ireland probably no more romantic house exists than The Castle of the Scald, to give it only one of its many names. Drumnacrogha, however, is the name most widely used, save by the native fisherfolk.

Centuries ago, when Drumnacrogha was built, it was a vast and draughty keep, quartering men and horses. At one time the O'Malley stormed its walls and, though they never reduced the castle, effected some sort of compromise with the O'Doon, who had held it for many years. Both O'Doon and O'Malley battled the Menlo O'Flahertys from within its walls. Once—the date is not clear—some of the Clanricarde lived there, and it was during their stay that the Palladian façade was erected. One of the interesting things about the house is the fact that quoin stones and Palladian windows and detail show only on the front of the house and one side—that facing the North Atlantic.

Apparently the high, broad causeway which lifted the bulk of the house above the fury of the Atlantic rollers was walled up and whitewashed with lime and white sand mixture about 1741, as nearly as anyone knows. This towering ramp, with a rake of twenty feet, is equivalent to a six-story building, and within its thick walls are countless rooms and winding passages. Whatever may go on in the white rooms of Drumnacrogha itself, this labyrinth has a separate life of its own. Shamas told me that when he took possession, the house had not been lived in for nineteen years. It was in a state of incredible violation. Tinkers and drunken fishermen had fouled the high, beautifully proportioned rooms. Gulls and rooks used the wide terrace, which stretches full across the front and along one side, for battleground and nesting place. Muck and refuse of all kinds clogged the entrances to ramp and house alike. But Shamas was not disheartened. He loved the wild beauty of Drumnacrogha, and he knew that the old house would respond to kindly usage. Drumnacrogha was built to flourish. Under his hand, it did.

After Shamas had pulled order out of chaos, life at Drumnacrogha assumed a regular routine for all concerned. Shamas wrote two of his best novels at a big table in the morning room with the tall windows, which occupies a corner on the second floor, facing Killileg. From this room spreads a seascape of incomparable beauty, made unique by the constant panoply of clouds on the horizon. After receiving Shamas' letter asking me to spend July and as much of August as I could at Drumnacrogha, I put my affairs in order and set out.

I had heard, of course, as everyone in Ireland has, the story of the Ghostly Catch at the ancient Castle of the Scald. I confess to hoping I would be so fortunate as to witness it, being mightily interested in such phenomena. Little did I think I would not only behold this manifestation to the hilt, but would, so to speak, become part of it, to the unhappy extent that I would for all my life bear a scar caused by it, a very irritating scar, let me tell you, amounting almost to being crippled.

On the first night after my arrival, those present were Shamas, Margaret, his wife, Sheila, aged fourteen, his daughter by a former marriage, and his small son Conard, aged five, Margaret Murrough's boy. There were no guests but myself, although three or four friends were expected within a few days. The night was perfection, the heavens fairly blazing with stars. The starshine on the gently rolling sea laid a shifting, spangled film across its surface.

After we had had coffee, and the youngsters had been packed off, grudgingly, to bed, we settled down to talk. I first asked Shamas if he had seen any evidence of the Ghostly Catch. He replied, "Not so far, and, as you know, we have been actually living in the house five years. It took a goodish part of a year to retrieve it from the pigsty I found. We lived at Killileg in a cottage meanwhile. Of course, there have been some whopping storms—quite a lot, in fact—and I dare say the Dread Women of Moher have been in full cry in the midst of them. But I cannot say we have seen anything that might be called a ghostly visitation. Old Maury Beedy, who brings in firewood and shines the family plate, when it gets any attention at all, says the door to the stairs leading from the beach to the passages in the ramp cannot be kept shut, no matter what, and the rain comes in and wets his stacks of firewood. But then, that may very well be an alibi for chancy Master Maury."

Margaret spoke up, "There is a bit more than that. As you know, some of the fishermen who live on the edge of Killileg store their nets and kelp swaths in those small rooms in the ramp. They've always done it, but two or three times I've seen these hardy customers run out of the ramp at night without their nets, then stand off on the road to the village, fingering their chins and shaking their heads. I asked that big, strapping strongeen of a Flathery what had happened the night before, when I'd looked down from the terrace and seen him streak out the ramp door and across the beach, hell for leather. He came all over confused and said, 'Faith, ma'am, those damned old Harpies are at it again, writhin' me nets into a tangle. They're about ready for a wild old shindig again. I know the signs.'"

How right he was, though we didn't believe it then. A nightcap was drunk all round, and we went up the wide, dark stairs to bed.

A few days later, August 10, to be exact, I walked along the beach towards Drumnacrogha, after depositing a letter in the bright red post box at the shop of Mrs. Mag Binney, at Inishcrona, three miles down to the west. It had been rather more of a pull than I had bargained for, and, the day being hot and sunny, I sat for a while in the cool shadow of the door, in the wall of the ramp which led up the stone stairs to the old cellars and cubbies that honeycombed the place like a rabbit warren. This was the door that refused to stay barred at night, according to Maury Beedy. After I had cooled off a bit from my walk, I examined the frame of the door and the old rusted iron latch. A greasy leather thong and a bent iron hook hung at the side of the latch.

I remember thinking, just for fun, I'll use them all. Drawing the door shut, I fastened latch and thong and pushed the hook into its stout eye.

Turning, I started up the partially lit stone stairs which wound up in a half spiral. Directly I had turned my back, the door was wrenched open by a force that not only ripped latch, thong, and hook completely out of the sockets, but damned near ripped the heavy oak door off its hinges. It banged back against the stone embrasure and hung crazily on one bent hinge. I rushed down the stairs and out on the beach. Not a human being was in sight, and a sheer wall was behind me. I waited, peering up and down, thinking to myself that not so much as a rock higher than two feet offered a hiding place for half a mile. Well, this was odd, and no mistake. I seemed to see the gnarled claw of one of the Women of Moher in this. I began to believe that the strongeen, in his fear at the mangling of his nets, was right.

I took Shamas aside later and told him what I had seen. We went down to the door together, and, as we were examining the latch and broken hinge, there was a startling sound above us in the vaulted reaches of the ramp. We were both knocked off our feet by a rush of wings, as some gigantic bird streaked past us out into the sunlight with a sort of snarling, unhuman cry. We stared at each other, too mystified to speak. Presently Shamas wiped his brow with the back of his hand. "Well, I'll be damned, and in broad daylight, too," he said.

Shamas and I agreed not to say anything to Margaret for the time being. If a manifestation were due, she would know about it soon enough. Dinner passed quietly as usual. We sat on the terrace. The night was warm and utterly still. Two or three times I noticed Shamas leave the wicker deck chair where he was lying, walk along the terrace, and stare into the heavens. Margaret noticed it too, eventually. "Shamas, what are you so restless about? Isn't the book going to suit you? Have some more coffee."

When he came back to his chair, he said, "The book's all right. I was just wondering if perhaps this dead calm at sea and the heaviness in the air mayn't mean a storm. We haven't had an Atlantic Particular in months."

Before we said our good nights, I too had a look around. All seemed normally quiet, but the trawlers were not venturing out, I noticed. There were no dancing lights on the horizon. Evidently the fishermen, as well as ourselves, felt uneasy.

I had sunk into deep slumber as soon as I touched the bed, tired out from my walk to Inishcrona along the sand, and, as I sat suddenly bolt upright in bed, I couldn't collect my thoughts. What was that rumbling, I wondered, far too loud and sustained for thunder? Collecting myself, I leaped out of bed and grabbed a dressing gown off a chair, scuffed into slippers, and went to the window. The room assigned to me at

Drumnacrogha was on the corner of the third floor, directly over the morning room where Shamas did his writing. The third floor was not the top one; there were still two tiers of attics. From two sides I had an uninterrupted view of Killileg Strand, the first rise of the Danrea Mountains, little more than hills at this point of land, and the immensity of the North Atlantic.

If I live to be a million, I will never forget the sight that held me riveted to the spot. What had been a calm, star-powered sky with a high-riding moon only a few hours before was now a furious welter of indigo blue, purple, and black clouds rolling in across the sea, landwards, with demoniac speed. They seemed to smother the world, slashed and lit by the fires of Beltane, which are green, purple, and red all at once. The sea was calm but brooding in a terrifying and ominous way, and oily as a snake. I suddenly realized it was as hot as the Sahara, and so far the wind that was racking those thunder clouds was not apparent on shore. Then came the most horrifying sound I ever heard, and God forbid I ever hear it again—far, far off, the unhuman cries of a host, moving shoreward, demented in its anger, or was it hunger, or lust?

Now the sea had begun to rise, and a great swell surged inshore, but the surface retained the thick oily scum I had seen before. As I gazed fascinated by this spectacle of combustion of the elements, the Dread descended. It was, I realized, more felt than seen. The tremendous whirring sound as of thousands of wings grew in volume. The nightmare cries rose in intensity and mingled with the storm wind. There was a crescendo of mingled sounds, and then, sharply, silence—the silence of doom. As I ran from the room from which I had watched, I paused at the stairhead. Margaret hurried past me, on her way to the nursery. I called out to her, asking where Shamas was. My voice boomed in the dreadful silence. Margaret pointed down the stairwell. Three steps at a time I ran down the stairs and out onto the terrace. Shamas had pulled on some sort of clothing and was intently watching something far out to sea. I followed the direction in which he pointed, and a sight that even now as I think of it makes the hackles rise on my neck rooted me to the spot.

At first it seemed to be a vast, clammy, white monster fighting for its life a half mile off shore. Then I became conscious that the heaving surface of this shivering mass was made up of myriads of separate entities, each in turn convulsed in torment. "Salmon," yelled Shamas. "By all that's holy, and God knows this isn't, whopping great Achill salmon, and by the million. Look, Larry, they are so thick there's not a drop of water between them."

I did look, and put up my hand to dash away the sweat that was running into my eyes. "It's a multitude, Shamas," I yelled back at him. "It's all the salmon in the world. Mother of God, what's going to happen now?"

The curious silence was pierced then by the rustling sound of trillions of scales and fins grinding together. I confess to having been weak in the knees, and looked around for a place to sit down. Before I had located such a place, I was brought up sharply by the major part of this grisly show. Out of the livid clouds, with such deadening impact that the corpse-white, glutinous mass of fish bodies sank beneath the surface, came dark, winged shapes. Streaming out behind them, tangling together, were rags or dank feathers. Were these birds? Were they Harpies? Like a flash, I realized that they were the Dread Women of Moher feeding upon the Ghostly Catch at Drumnacrogha. This was hell as I imagine it.

The whole viscid mass was by now being devoured by these ravenous, insatiable bird fiends; no cries now, only the tearing of flesh and the grinding wash of sea on sand, with tatters of wet flesh dropping back on the writhing surface of the water.

Shamas called out, "Look, a boat, nearly swamped, being forced on the rocks at the causeway." We both raced down the steps towards the boat. In this short time the picture had changed. Gorged on their feast of sea salmon, the Women of Moher had disappeared in the clouds.

The sea was less oily, a dark gray green, and there was only a gentle swell. As the drifting boat, a tiny curragh, bumped onto the rocks, we waded out and hauled it in, for we had seen a man in the stern who looked knocked out. When we had placed him flat on the sand, we realized it was too late to do anything for him. His body was contorted into a strange shape, arms over his head, and knees doubled up under his chin. We had a hard time straightening him out. But it was the look in his eyes that froze our blood, as his had been frozen by what he had seen—bright blue eyes literally hanging out of his head with terror.

Leaving Shamas with the body of the husky young Killileg fisherman (we learned about him later) I started down to the water's edge to see if I could save anything of fishing gear from the smashed curragh. All had been washed overboard. I was turning round to rejoin Shamas when my foot slipped on the treacherous rocks. I was still barefoot, for, ever since I had leaped from bed, there had not been a moment to think of clothes other than the robe I had thrown on. Losing my balance, I plunged into a blowhole deep as the eternal pit, and let out a howl as the most agonizing pain I had ever felt shot up my leg. There, lying in the wash of sea, among the slimy green kelp, was the carcass of a huge salmon, shreds of gnawed, red flesh still dangling from the bones. One razor-sharp bone had stabbed straight through the fleshy part of my right foot, between ball and toes. So, you see, I will bear to the last day I live a mark of the Ghostly Catch.

Next morning a proper Atlantic Particular broke. A nor'easter howled. Mountainous waves ran up the strand in front of the house and shattered in magnificent showers of foam against the centuries-old bulwark of the stone ramp. But it was a clean storm, such as anyone living on a spur of rock jutting into the North Atlantic expects. Save for a few mewing gulls wheeling against the wind, no sign of life was apparent. Killileg and Inishcrona had bedded down until the storm passed. A tramper was wrecked a few miles down the coast, driven inland to break its back on the rocks of Ballyconeely.

With my foot bandaged by Margaret in an expert manner, I was propped up, as comfortably as possible under the circumstances, on a sofa in the drawing room. The doctor from Inishcrona had found a tendon severed, so I knew I was in for a seige of inactivity. Along about midmorning, Maury Beedy tramped in bearing an armful of firewood. I asked him what the village people had been up to during the horror of last night. Maury hunched his shoulders. "The idintical thing, yer honor, they do be always doing, when Daghda's daughters are about. Hanging back in the dark rooms of their coteens. Some on their knees, like meself. No man with half a wit would be abroad when them streelers is scourging the world."

I remembered, then, that during the height of the visitation I had looked down from the terrace towards the village. Not a face was to be seen. The storm blew itself out in a blaze of glory with another show of Fires of Beltane, and impressive rolls of thunder to heighten the drama. Beltane Fire is a magnificent spectacle at any time, and I have seen it over the Mourne Mountains on a fair, soft night. But then there is no dread in the waving fingers of light.

It took the old vaults and passages in the ramp a week to quiet down. Rustlings, murmurs, and half-human chatterings were heard at intervals, day and night. One of the village net boys found two or three half-eaten Achill salmon wedged in crevasses in the stone. Yes, it took a long time to expel the reek and the refuse left behind by the Ghostly Catch at Drumnacrogha.

I stayed on with Shamas and Margaret until the end of September. Then, my foot healed as well as it ever would be, I set off for Dublin. I made a detour in my journey, however, and spent a few hours with Sir Teague Gorland. Settled at ease in his library with a glass of incomparable 1805 brandy in my hand, I asked him to tell me what the story was that caused all the row between Harpies and salmon.

Sir Teague smiled. He said, "I could have told you when you were here in July, but thought it better to wait until you had seen the show. Well, now that you have seen it in no uncertain manner, here it is." Sir Teague took a long pull at a clay Shalla pipe from Antrim, and continued:

"Naturally, this is only conjecture, make of it what you will. When Daghda, the father of all the ancient Gaelic gods, was up to his neck in sin, he purged himself of all these sins by wringing himself dry into the Atlantic at the spot where Drumnacrogha now stands. Resuming shape again, and feeling very fit, free of all his nagging sins, he made off, abandoning them. A great howling and cursing took place, and, being hungry, the sins swooped down and devoured a school of huge Achill salmon who happened to be swimming in the vicinity. Later, replete with this banquet, they flew off down the coast to the high, stark Cliffs of Moher. These creatures, half woman, half beaked bird, reside among the crags of the rocky headlands of Moher, a kind of demoniacal realm. A word chosen by the Greeks for just such a kingdom is 'Pandemonium.' It sets a seal on this noxious retreat.

"Legend and 'the old ones' say this realm lies between the Cliffs of Moher and Hags Head. Sometimes for months, even years, these dreadful creatures lie fallow. Then, usually on a calm summer night, they strike. At this season of the year, huge and tender salmon spawn in the deep waters around Achill Island and Sligo Rock. First comes the banquet in which they gorge themselves. Then follows a raging storm, a kind of witches' lullaby to regale them as they sink into stupor. It would appear that at some time one of the creatures, a sort of queen perhaps, made her home inside the walls of the ramp at Drumnacrogha. Some say she is still there. It may have been this queen's handmaiden, entering the ramp to acquaint her with the approaching salmon catch, who nearly split the door asunder and knocked both you and Shamas clean off your feet. Old Drumnacrogha knows many mournful secrets, but she's not telling."

The Cerements on the Stairs

Portaranmore

COUNTY LIMERICK

The Cerements on the Stairs

"So comes a reckoning when the banquet's o'er,
The dreadful reckoning, and men smile no more."

ON A FROSTY MORNING IN JANUARY, 1788, Brian Montalan O'Hanaray lifted his black, curly head unwillingly from his pillow. Damnation, it was scarcely dawn, and the rising bell gone fifteen minutes ago. "Well, here goes." Out of bed he leaped.

To Brian it seemed a winter day, the same as any other winter day, a bit more frosty and dismal, perhaps, but had he even dreamed what this day would bring to him, he would have done well to lie in his bed, and die there.

Brian Montalan O'Hanaray was the only son of Lady Caroline O'Hanaray. Lady Caroline was the daughter of the Marquis of Montalan, an Irish peer. She had married dashing, improvident Captain Brian O'Hanaray of the Irish Guards and regretted it from the moment she turned round from the altar. But Lady Caroline had kept a stiff upper lip, and a wide smile on her generous mouth. No one had ever suspected just how revolted she had been at the antics indulged in by the pleasure-loving captain. Women adored him, and he was far from reticent in rewarding their adoration.

Being a Catholic, Lady Caroline could not divorce him, so she took her young son to Rapallo, where they lived quietly for years. When the boy Brian was sixteen, Lady Caroline received word that her husband was dead in India. She returned to England and put Brian in a good tutoring school near Oxford. Later he entered Magdalen College. Brian was just down from Magdalen when his mother died and he inherited a small annuity. This money, windfall though it was, would not go far to further the grandiose ideas which were forever looming large behind the retinas of Brian O'Hanaray's flashing blue eyes. There was more of the captain's arrogance and vanity in Brian than his mother would ever admit, even to herself. Plus the unstable O'Hanaray taint, there was the flamboyance of his grandfather, the Marquis of Montalan, who had lived at Castle Montalan, in County Clare, in a manner which rivaled the Dazzling Desmonds in splendor, even when he had to sell the family portraits and plate to keep at bay the hordes of creditors which washed in and out his scroll-iron gates, the like of the tides of ocean.

So, as the state of his affairs became acute, Brian availed himself of a job tutoring at his old school near Oxford. He had the Irish trait of always hoping that the next sunrise would "slit the bag of Fortuna, and spill gold at his feet." This side of his nature came from his optimistic mother, whose sporting outlook on life in general had stood her in good stead for years.

But Brian did not know that his Fortuna was twins. His great-aunts, the Ladies Mary and Clara Lantry, sisters of the late Marquis of Montalan, lived at the castle in County Clare. They lived an existence so remote from the world, even in 1788, that many persons did not know they were still alive. Indeed, they hung suspended in time for nearly a year; so tenuous was their hold on life that it seemed almost not to be. One day Lady Mary made too quick a move. She died for it. Turning her head to see what had come over sister Mary, Lady Clara breathed no more. In one gentle swoop, the twins Fortuna slit the bag of gold, which spilled out in a glittering torrent at the feet of the eager Brian O'Hanaray.

On the January morning when Brian leaped so reluctantly from a warm bed, he dressed hastily and went in to commons for his breakfast. Beside his plate lay a long, white overlap document having a very legal aspect. As Brian slit the red wax seal, the Old Woman of Gonn must have flown howling past the busy commons-room window. The banshees must have wailed their throats raw in the dank glens of Antrim. For what Brian read in the legal foldover was a portent of a doom such as is visited on few humans. Yet, oddly, the reading of his letter at this time was monstrously pleasant to a long-patient Brian O'Hanaray.

The document read:

BABCOCK, CARLEW AND BABCOCK, SOLICITORS

LINCOLN'S INN FIELDS

LONDON

January 14, 1788

Honored Sir:

Word of great moment to yourself has just been received by ourselves. We therefore beg you to pay a visit to our above address, at your earliest convenience, and oblige,

Your obedient,

St. John Babcock.

As Brian O'Hanaray stood on the deck of the bouncing little mail packet crossing the Irish Sea, he was still quivering with excitement. It had been a week now since his trip to Lincoln's Inn Fields. The "word of great moment" had most certainly been that. On the death of his twin great-aunts, a month past, he had inherited Castle Montalan, in the County Clare, and a very considerable fortune in land holdings, rent rolls, and minted gold. It seemed, so Mr. St. John Babcock had told him, that for all their quiet way of life, the Ladies Mary and Clara Lantry had been actual sharks where the multiplying of their money was concerned. From the small fortune left them by their extravagant father, they had, by wise investment in London housing shares and the lucrative East India trade, built one of the largest fortunes in Ireland. They had left it all to Brian.

The packet churned into Cobh Harbor. Brian O'Hanaray stepped onto the soil of his mother's country for the first time in his life.

Alone at dinner in the castle that night, Brian mused on his future. Ancestral or not, he would never live at Montalan. As it was entailed, he could not sell it, but even if he shut the place, the rents from the tenantry and the revenues from the prosperous farms within his demesne were huge. What he wanted, and now what he wanted he could have, was a big, showy place in the Palladian taste, like Clontarra Park, the great white stone house he had passed on his way from Cork. He must drive about the countryside in the coming weeks and pick just the right spot. He must make a name for himself in the county. Brian yawned and stretched his long, supple frame. He was tired. It had been a busy, exciting day. As he walked up the stairs to his bedroom, he did not feel lonely in the least, for he was accompanied on either side by a huge boarhound, shaggy of coat, lean flanked, and extraordinarily adoring of eye.

For the next few days, Brian stopped quietly at the castle. All this ease and grandeur was too new and far too exciting to leave until he had assured himself he was not dreaming. There was much exploring to be done, as well, for the demesne of Montalan was wide spreading, composing some seventy thousand odd acres. It was, in fact, the richest estate in the South of Ireland, save only that of the Desmonds of Kinsale.

The stables interested Brian vastly, for, while he had never owned a horse in his life, he had learned to ride in Italy. An Irish stud groom, on the podesta of a Contessa Fazziani, an Irish woman from Bantry, in Cork, married to an Italian sportsman, had taught young Brian to ride, to jump a good stone wall, and had even contrived to erect an Irish bank, a stone wall topped with turf. Brian had broken his shoulder the first time he had ridden at this gut-tearing obstacle.

But "No matter," as old Patsy Pattorla had said, "Faith an ye'll break ivery bone in yer carcass, before yer through, if ye spend yer life wid harses, but who wouldn't, yer honor, sir?"

Brian, through a haze of pain, agreed, in part. "I know that's the way most Irish-men feel, but I'm not all out in favor of it," he replied. From that day, he detected a slight coolness in Patsy's attitude towards him. Brian thought that, to reinstate himself in Patsy's good graces, he would send to Rapallo for him. Patsy should come to Ireland and take charge of Brian's breeding stables, when he had established them. That is, if old Patsy Pattorla was still alive.

The kennels were formidable, for Lady Mary Lantry had bred Irish wolf and boar hounds. The Kinhalla strain, brought from the wild glens of Antrim, were magnifi-cent, powerful animals. Brian would carry on with these hounds, as well as with the horses.

The gardens, which had been gentler Lady Clara's domain, did not move Brian to any great extent. Flowers, if showy, had their uses, of course, to build up a picture of luxurious living. He would procure expert gardeners for his outdoor gardens and conservatories.

What awed and fascinated Brian most of all at Castle Montalan was Mrs. Man-gasereen, a woman most surely out of fable. Her story, which she loved nothing better than to tell to a listener, the like of the new master, who was "fresh fields," having never heard it before, was this.

She was born Kilda Tannforly, and her father was one of the Scotch-Irish ship builders who maintained a calking yard on the Island of Mull, off the coast of Scot-land. He was a dour, hard-tempered man who had taken a second wife much younger than himself. High-spirited Kilda Tannforly could not stomach the highfalutin man-ner of her new stepmother, nor the fancies she indulged in with the good-looking young men working at the Tannforly Yards.

Kilda knew that life at Yards House was riding for a fall, and no mistake. She wanted to be quit of the place before this occurred. One night, Kilda bribed one of the boat boys to sail her across to Ireland.

There is a "pocket" in the "temperamental journey" of the flashing-eyed Kilda after her landing in Ireland. She never refers to the few months that elapsed before she turned up at Castle Montalan, and no one has the temerity to ask. It is a closed page in the "Book of Kilda."

Later, Kilda took two rooms in a small hotel at Kilkee, which was the market town nearest to Carrigaholt, where Castle Montalan was situated, on the rocky headland. Miss Tannforly sent out cards to the ladies of the neighboring gentry saying that she would be pleased to receive their patronage. She was a seamstress of the first order. It was not long before Miss Tannforly was swamped with work, far more than one pair of hands, however nimble the fingers, could take on. After a year, Miss Tannforly packed her bags, closed her small shop, and departed for the castle on the headland. She was to be "resident seamstress" for the twin Ladies Lantry.

Common gossip in the pubs at Kilkee and Doonlicka credited her with duties at the castle far more horizontal than the art of sewing requires. However that may be, she was certainly in the good favor of Lord Montalan. In fact, she frequently accompanied him to Paris, when, alas, the Ladies Lantry were indisposed, to buy silks, laces, passementeries, and the bobbins and bobbinets required in the fashioning of ladies' frocks of the exacting period of 1750.

During one of these visits, Miss Tannforly met a handsome and masterful Syrian rug merchant. He paid ardent and very definite court to the flashing Scottish woman, who, at this time, was in the full ripeness of her thirty-five summers. They were married, and Muhafa Mangasereen took his tall bride to Constantinople, where his rug business flourished. There in a latticed house on the mysterious, whispering Bosporus she lived for a few years.

His death took place under rather strange circumstances, since, considering his reported wealth, he left his wife penniless.

Kilda then wrote to Lady Mary Lantry inquiring if the post of "seamstress extraordinary" was still open to her if she returned to Ireland. Lady Mary replied that it was, and that they were all eagerness to have her back. From that day out, she had lived at Castle Montalan more as friend and confidante to the aging ladies than as seamstress.

Although Mrs. Mangasereen was over seventy when Brian first met her, she was remarkably well preserved, and none of her faculties was in the least impaired. He forthwith engaged her as housekeeper for his as-yet-unfound house.

The twin Ladies Lantry had lived a cloistered life, driven in upon themselves, yet diffusing an atmosphere of intimacy and affection upon those who worked for them. The reverberations of an uneasy world impinged but faintly upon the uneventfulness of days at the castle.

But the day that Mrs. Mangasereen took Brian to the Dower House, or Knockaleedy Rasp, as the house was called, was the first faint hint that his future fortunes were to be cataclysmic. As Brian stood in the small fore-court and looked up at the perfect proportions of the white, Connemara stone house, for all its pleasant mien, he had a boding.

Mrs. Mangasereen told him that old Lord Montalan had reversed the order that the female members of the Lantry family should take up residence at Knockaleedy Rasp. The Dowager Marchioness and her daughters had never lived at the house, but Lord Montalan had. He had kept it as a sort of "garconnière." The "Rasp," or "cut in the rocks," led straight up from the sea, affording the house a private entrance from the water stairs. The house had been built by the Lord Montalan who was father to the twins. As a small boy he had been a page to the then-aging Duchess of Cleveland. Brought up in the midst of the profligacy of the London of that day, Carolus Lantry had been a brilliant and dissolute figure. If the walls of lovely Knockaleedy could talk, what wonders of perfumed debauchery they could unfold!

One day soon after Brian's arrival at Castle Montalan, Mrs. Mangasereen told him of a demesne that was for sale, just over the boundary to the south, the demesne of the Abbey of Portaranmore, in County Limerick. It was near a very beautiful village called St. Patrick's Well. There had been a house on the land until five years before, but it had burned to the ground, and the Conboy-Dillon family, who owned the demesne, had moved into County Cork.

There was a huge old ruin of a Cistercian abbey on the place, reported to be haunted. An old abbot with the face of a skeleton was seen to walk at night in the ruined ambulatory. On such occasions the ghostly abbot was dressed in ecclesiastical splendor, mitered, and carrying a crozier. Great pomp was observed, and he was surrounded by five or six acolytes, some swinging silver thuribles wafting clouds of incense through the night air. This pungent odor of sanctity was reported to hover in the air of the ambulatory for days after the ghostly parade.

The story in the neighborhood is that the immensely rich abbot directed that on his death he was to be buried in a niche behind the altar in his chapel. This tomb was to be walled up. Before the stones were to be mortared in place, all his worldly goods were to be piled at his feet, his miter was to be placed upon his head, his richest cope clasped across his shoulders, and a crozier placed in his hand. A curse was to be inscribed at the foot of this wall tomb. If any mortal disturbed his rest or his riches, that mortal would rue the day he was born. Brian listened with interest to Mrs. Mangasereen's story, more from his wish to see the demesne of Portaranmore than because of his credence in the ghostly visits of the abbot.

Two days later, it being fine, with a light breeze, the two drove over into County Limerick and put up for the night at the Star of Fiona Hotel, at Pallas. Next morning, in continued fine weather, they drove on to Portaranmore.

Brian was enormously taken with the rolling meadows and the winding River Felim, a tributary of the Shannon. Backing all this springy turfed countryside was the gently sloping greenness of the Slieve Felim Mountains. He found the exact spot for his house, a gentle rise a mile back from the coach road which ran between the great market town of Limerick and the harbor city of Waterford. On a crystal-clear day, as it was when Brian first saw the place, one could see the white-capped waters of the Irish Sea, thirty miles away.

After lunch, which was eaten from a basket put up by kindly Mrs. Duly at the Star of Fiona, Brian and Mrs. Mangasereen walked the half mile from where he had chosen the spot for his house to the ruins of the abbey. A romantic pile of violet-gray, lichen-covered stone it was, standing like a sleeping monument to the past glory of the Cistercian Brothers. The dark, highly burnished ivy on the walls of the ambulatory gleamed like Byzantine enamel in the bright sunshine. Withal, for so silent, un-inhabited a place, Brian seemed to sense watching eyes behind every crumbling buttress.

He walked through the pointed, empty archway where once had swung a thickly studded door. This door now lay in the grass, the twisted, rusty hinges, thick as a man's forearm, embedded in the turf. The roofless room had been the private chapel of the long-dead abbot. Thick swags of ivy now concealed one wall of the chapel. It was this wall, the caretaker said, that concealed the tomb in which the abbot was hidden. Brian noticed particularly that a number of heavy slabs of gray marble, veined in black and white, had been let into the wall and laid in front, like roughly arranged steps. These he immediately coveted for the entrance porch of his new house. Ever since he had seen the splendid demesne of Portaranmore, Brian had been determined to buy it. Already he was planning his house. The marble might even do for his carp pool.

Brian noticed some sort of lettering hacked into a long spar of flint which acted as a console at the top of the flight of crude steps. Stooping down, he scratched away the covering of ivy and lichen and disclosed two sentences in Gaelic writing. Interested, he turned to Mrs. Mangasereen and said, "I cannot read the Gaelic. Can you, or this man here?"

Mrs. Mangasereen shook her head, but the caretaker came over to where Brian stood. "Yis, sir, I can read the Gaelic, but I don't have to do it. All me life long I've known what that rune reads. And heeded it too, fer all the riches that they do be sayin' is hid ferninst." The man appeared a bit shy of reading off what the graven words said, but he scratched his head, and, looking afar off towards the sea, repeated:

> "HERE I STAND, IN THE MIDST OF TEMPTATION,
> IF MAN DISTURBS ME HE DIES IN DAMNATION."

Brian burst into gales of laughter. "Well, that's the flimsiest protection to guard a cache of plunder I ever heard of. Why in hell hasn't somebody broached the old boy's gold pile before this?" Looking around, Brian noticed that neither the caretaker nor Mrs. Mangasereen had joined in his laughter.

The old man spoke. "I'd not take it so lightly, sir, yer honor. A dead man's hand claspin' ye be the throat's a dread thing, do ye see it or do ye not."

Mrs. Mangasereen did not say a word, but her very silence, after the old man's prophecy, put a damper on the brightness of the day. The three went down the hill, and away out of that.

One year to the day after Brian had visited the demesne of Portaranmore for the first time, he stood in the cart ruts that had plowed up the turf where, later on, a smooth lawn would be cropped by Wiltshire lambs. Glowing with pride, he surveyed the rising facade of what he fully believed would be the grandest house in the County of Limerick.

The soaring purity of line and conception of the portico was like music in the soft summer air. The well-balanced wings sweeping away from either side of the main block were provided with just enough tall windows to lighten the mass of beautifully cut and fitted Athenry stone, which was handsome at any time, but truly breathtaking in the moonlight. The soft, mauve shadows he would accentuate by planting masses of black Irish yew. The portholes which pierced the space between the tall windows on the first floor and the bedroom windows above would be embellished by busts of Greek dramatists and poets, and the lovely head of a goddess or two.

The workmen promised to start on the retaining wall for the broad terrace, which was to spread for three hundred yards in front of the portico. Fifty feet wide it would be, with a pool for carp in the center. To edge this carp pool, he needed slabs of marble, like the magnificent marble lip of the carp pool at the Villa D'Este at Tivoli. He remembered it from the many times he had visited there as a small boy with his mother.

The next morning Brian called his foreman aside. He told the man he wanted him to take as many men as needed and to tear out the slabs of black and white marble at the foot of the walled-up tomb in the abbot's chapel. Seeing the stubborn look in the man's eyes as he gave this order, Brian tried to turn it into a joke. "The old boy's been dead for six hundred years. He won't be needing the slabs any more, and they are just what I want to be cut into a molding for my carp pool."

The foreman looked straight in Brian's eyes and said, "No. I refuse to obey yer order. Ye know as well as any av us that the auld abbot protects his grave be his everlastin' curse. There's not a man I could get that'd do this thing. Ye'll never live easy in yer great house if ye touch it." The man threw down the spade he was carrying and, muttering to himself walked down the hill.

Brian was furiously angry. He strode to the steps of the house, where some men were bending over the elevations for the placing of the cornices. He gave the same order to these men. He received the same reply. The curse was respected, because the last wish of the dead was fraught with disaster if ignored. Finally Brian spied a big, red-fisted fellow who was carrying a bundle of the poles used for shoring up the scaffolds. Calling to the man to stop, he told him what he had the others. This man was a stranger to the neighborhood. He didn't believe in ancient curses. Sure he would help, "your honor, sir."

As Brian and the workman stood in front of the chapel, they automatically looked up at the sky. The soft gray clouds seemed to lower; a wind sprang up and clattered through the ivy. Again Brian had the same uneasy feeling he had experienced on the first day he inspected this place with Mrs. Mangasereen—the feeling that a hundred pair of eyes were watching him balefully.

This unease was felt by the big workman as well, for all of a sudden he flung the crowbar he was brandishing, to sense its heft, onto the turf. "No sir, yer honor, I'll never do it. There's a halt on me, and an auld fear clutches me heart."

This so infuriated Brian that he lost all control. Grabbing the prizing-iron in both hands, he yelled, "Of all the lily-livered fear mongers, you Limerick men are the worst." He swung the iron, inserting its point in a crack between two stones. The stones gave a bit, and Brian heaved the iron again. At this stroke an extraordinary thing happened. The whole side of the chapel seemed to leap suddenly into life. Old masonry, long held in place by twisted ivy fronds, gave way. The whole mass came surging forward towards the surprised Brian and the cowering workman.

Both men leaped back in the nick of time, and, as they brushed the dust of dry mortar out of their eyes, a most singular and bewildering sight confronted them. Standing, swaying, in a wide, pointed niche was the panoplied skeleton of a man. On his head was a tall, spiked miter. A shredding purple and vermilion cope, heavily bossed in gold, hung crazily from the shoulder bones. A trefoiled crozier, richly jeweled, leaned out at an angle from the crook of a bony arm. Piled helter-skelter about the feet of this cadaver was every kind of altar gear—gold chalices and silver and gold reliquaries, covered with magnificent jewels which smoldered or flashed in the wavering light. The Abbot Fenir trampled for the last time on his riches.

Brian took all this in at first sight, for, as he watched, the skeleton began to topple forward. There was first the nauseating stench of corruption, let loose like a flood, then the sound of rending cloth. Old, dry cloth it sounded like, but tough, as if hating to yield from the place to which it had been bound for six hundred years. The cerements that held the clutter of disintegrating bones to a bronze spike driven into the stone wall were all that was left of the once-earthly presence of the Abbot Fenir of Portaranmore.

Brian stood rooted to the spot, alone, for the dazed workman had pulled himself together and run screaming into the woods behind the chapel. As the skeleton pulled free and crumpled onto the veined marble steps at Brian's feet, the gray cerements crumbled into particles which floated out onto the summer air, as if time itself had pulverized them into motes.

A few shreds of this cloth settled on Brian's sleeve and on his thigh. Hastily shaking them off, he turned away from the sight of whitened bones, gold chalices, and the jeweled crozier, which seemed to point at him from where it lay in the dust of the purple cope.

As Brian went quickly down the hill towards his house, he looked back once or twice at the violated chapel. He found that he was unnerved by what had taken place. Stupid to be upset. He would give the church gear to the nuns at Lisdoonvarna. They had never seen such riches in all their lives, he'd be bound. All he wanted was the rare marble, anyway. God knew he was rich enough without filching the old boy's loot. Time he was buried in a decent grave in any case.

All this bravado proved one thing, and only one—Brian Montalan O'Hanaray was mightily scared.

During the building of the Palladian house of Portaranmore, Brian lived at a small house, a kind of hunting lodge, in a wooded valley three miles from the entrance gates of his new house. Castle Montalan was too far away, he had discovered, if he was to keep an eye on his workman, who were at best a shifty lot, given to wholesale thieving. So he had rented Kiltykinee Lodge until the day he could move into Portaranmore.

The night after the strange occurrence of the falling chapel wall, Brian sat long over his port. Finally he rose from the table and went to the morning room, where Mrs. Mangasereen was sewing on new curtains destined for the great house. Brian had not told her anything of what had happened. Now he described the incident, as simply as possible, to ease his mind.

The Scottish woman sat long, silent, staring into space. Then she sighed and said, "As you know, we Scotch are born with the sixth sense. I am told that I was born with a caul. That seems to make me even more fey. I see disaster in what you did today, Brian O'Hanaray. You should have let the old dead lie. Give the gold to the nuns. The Poor Clares can make good use of it. Perhaps that may help you. But I fear that from this day out, you wear woe on your head, like a crown of thorns."

The Great House of Portaranmore was finished. It stood silhouetted in gleaming white radiance against the hyacinth rise of the Slieve Felim Mountains. The sparkling river flowed at the foot of the wide terrace. Dark yew added rich importance to the carefully considered mass. The detail in cornice and balustrade was perfection. Yet the house had not a pleasant aspect. Simple, chubby little Kiltykinee Lodge, a mile away, had a chuckling kind of charm. One hurried back to Kiltykinee after a hard day's hunting. Hot tea, leaping fires, and a tageen of the mellow whisky of the locality were synonymous with Kiltykinee and comfort.

Portaranmore was cold, precise. It lacked the lived-in touch which even brand-new houses can achieve. Castletown, I am sure, had that touch as soon as the last chimney pot was in place. Rathgannonstown had it, or so I learn from its house book, from the moment the first log was laid on the drawing-room fire, and a flying spark burned a hole in the best Aubusson carpet. Portaranmore had no heart. Brian O'Hanaray had no heart. He had an overweening pride of self and an unimpressive arrogance, with no imagination to back it up. Behind the handsome mask of Brian's face, there was precious little but a selfish craving to indulge his every whim. Fear had not yet harnessed him. Later, when Fear had buckled all the straps, cinched the girth, and leaped full-armored into the saddle, Brian O'Hanaray would wish that he had been strangled at birth by his umbilical cord.

The first dinner party given by Brian in his great new house was progressing beautifully. Fifty guests, the cream of the county, were gathered about the massive, oblong table which Brian had had made in Genoa and sent to Portaranmore. It had taken a crate as big as a coteen. Yards of the finest embroidered linen lay shimmering on its length, a gift from the Poor Clares at Lisdoonvarna, an appreciative offering to Brian, who had given them the abbot's golden treasury. He did not say where he had found it. If they ever heard from chance gossip, he would refute it as a jealous lie.

The ladies withdrew, the port went round. After an evening spent in playing bezique and the new Spanish game of chance called *Farando*, the guests not stopping in the house gathered up their winnings, or paid their losses, and departed, vowing no house in all County Limerick was so splendid, "nor so cold and forbidding," they added, as the coaches rolled along.

Brian was in the seventh heaven of his delight, rich, powerful, and very pleasing, personally, to the ladies, or so he gathered. He would make the county hum.

The footman had put out the last taper in the hall sconces. Mrs. Mangasereen, billowing, despite her age, in black and cherry taffetas, came to wish him "God's good care." Alone, Brian stood for a while in the shadowy hall, living over his first party at Portaranmore. The clock on the landing chimed the midnight hour. Brian started slowly up the stairs.

About midway up the curving steps, Brian was conscious of a sickening smell that seemed to rise from a place just in front of him on the stairs. Then, to his surprise and horror, a shapeless mass of gray garments seemed to swirl and eddy about his feet. Out of these folds of reeking cloth, a face materialized. It was the skeleton face of the Abbot Fenir, the bony skull that Brian had seen for an instant the day of the crashing wall at the abbey chapel.

Brian tried to back down the stairs. A clutching force, which he could not see, tripped him. As he fell on his face on the stairs, the wraith floated up into the darkness of the stair well. But as the terrified owner of magnificent Portaranmore put out his left hand to steady himself, he felt it covered with a burning shower. He gazed transfixed. Shards of the gray and putrid cerements clung to the back of the hand. In an agony of distaste, Brian brushed them off. They scattered and became part of the darkness which enveloped him like a black shroud. Outside, in the park, the wind soughed through the frozen branches. Brian O'Hanaray lay on the great stairs of his house, sobbing.

The next morning dawned bright and fresh. Brian lay in his bed and wondered if perhaps it could have been a ghastly dream. That face, leering. The rotten stench of the grave. Those clinging tendrils of gray cloth. Brian looked, long, at the back of his hand. No, it was smooth, brown, and healthy, as always.

The last buckle has been tongued. The cinch has been tightened to its last hole. Now Fear leaps into the saddle, Brian O'Hanaray—Fear will ride you until you drop.

One night a week or so after Brian's shattering encounter on the stairs of his new house, he wakened in the night in great pain. For a moment, before he could collect his wits, he was conscious of a burning sensation. He found he could hardly lift his left hand. It was as if it had been plunged into a blazing furnace. Brian rose from his bed and walked into a dressing room which adjoined his bedroom. He touched a squill of paper to the red heart of the banked hearth fire and lighted a few of the candles in a branched torch. Brian sat in a hooded chair beside the window. The chill dawn crept in. Finally, as the full light of morning broke over the heights of the Slieve Felim Mountains, the tortured master of Portaranmore slept.

Mrs. Mangasereen, coming in with a cup of early tea, to wish Brian "good morning and God's grace," as was her wont, found Brian asleep. She noticed his left hand, for it lay in his lap. Oddly, she thought, it was wrapped round and round with a towel wrung out of cold water.

A few months passed. Except for an occasional burning sensation, sharp and searing, on the back of his left hand, Brian was left more a prey to fear than to pain. These sharp twinges, as if a flame licked at his flesh, attacked Brian usually when someone else was with him. At his sudden exclamation and quick move as he grabbed his left hand with his right, the person or persons would immediately ask what was wrong. These questions invariably threw Brian into an embarrassed rage. He would answer angrily that it was nothing, and hastily withdraw, leaving the questioner to speculate on his increasing surliness.

Matters were brought to a head on a night after Brian had been living at Portaranmore for nearly a year. The occasional burning sensation on his hand had been the only manifestation by the implacable ghost of the Abbot Fenir. Then, the curse again struck at Brian. He had dined, as was his habit these days, alone. After a few turns up and down the terrace with Bandor and Cyclops, two of his boarhounds, he entered the house and started up the stairs to retire. At midway of the curve of the steps, the strange sensation of being hobbled, unable to put one foot before the other, assailed him. Brian put out his hand to grasp the edge of the stair tread for support. A gray mist seemed to envelope his hand, and a few fragments of the dingy cerements clung to it like sparks of fire. Somehow he freed himself and stumbled to his room. There he examined the hand closely. On the back of it, a gray spot, which burned fiercely, showed to the size of a guinea.

A few days after this last encounter on the stairs, Brian O'Hanaray left Portaranmore, bag and baggage. He went first to London, where, in the days before he had inherited his grandfather's title and estates, he had made many friends. Now the tall, reserved Marquis of Montalan, who was known to be as rich as the devil himself, and proud as Lucifer, was received by these rather rakish cronies, with open arms, for a time. Then, as curious incidents happened, these erstwhile friends dropped out of Brian's life, one by one. He had taken the precaution of always wearing a white glove on his left hand. But a spot the size of a guinea piece always burned through the glove, no matter how many times he changed to a fresh one.

After a few weeks, a desperate Brian ordered his bags packed again. He left England for the Continent. Brindle, the valet, to whom Brian had told the whole story, accompanied the piteously afflicted man. Brindle gave Brian care and understanding through all the years that he sought some kind of peace.

The Marquis of Montalan lived for a time in a secluded house in the outskirts of Vienna. Suddenly, in the night, lights were seen to spring up in all the windows. There was the sound of preparations for departure. A coach drawn by four horses was seen to leave the gates, luggage piled high in the boot.

Next, Brian appeared in Verona. He took a house by the sea. But soon he was on his way again. By this time Brian had taken to wearing a long, black cloak, cut circular. In its thick folds he could wrap his burning hand, on which he now wore a metal guard.

For ten years Brian O'Hanaray, Marquis Montalan, ranged restlessly up and down Europe. With the watchful Brindle always in attendance, Brian was seen in Rome, Madrid, Naples, St. Petersburg, Dresden, Budapest. It was in Budapest that a scene occurred which upset Brian more than anything he had experienced in his persecuted flight half across the world.

He was sitting in a small café early one evening. It was on the lovely Margaret Island, and the famous pink chestnut blossoms were like St. Gellert's Torches. Brian was reading a newspaper. Before him on the marble-topped table stood a small glass of the apricot brandy from the Lake Balatan orchards. The evening being warm, Brian had loosened his heavy, black cloak. With his mind intensely occupied by some news of Napoleon Bonaparte which he was reading, he did not notice that the metal guard he always wore over his blemished hand had slipped, and that the cloak had fallen over the back of the chair. He was startled to hear a child scream, "Mother, look. That man's hand—it is burning!" As amazed as the child, Brian looked down. A thin spiral of gray smoke was rising from the white spot on his hand.

From Budapest Brian went to Paris. He had decided to end his wanderings over the face of the earth. He was doomed. He knew it. Never more could he go about among his fellows. His plan now was to return to Ireland. He would not live at Portaranmore, however. He could never again mount those horrendous stairs. He would shut himself away, alone, except for Brindle, in the house by the sea, Knockaleedy Rasp, near Castle Montalon.

Brian stopped in Paris for a few days. The weather was superb, the crowds in the gardens of the Tuileries and in the Bois were gay and fashionable. Brian had expected this life would be part and parcel of his own. He hated to renounce it. What a terrible price he was paying for repudiating a dead abbot's wish! His youth, his great riches— all were useless. So often in his loneliness he thought of the last line of the curse, "he dies in damnation."

The second day of Brian's stay in Paris, he received a large white envelope addressed to "The Most Honorable the Marquis of Montalan." It bore a golden "N" and a crown. It was an invitation from the Empress Josephine to a soiree at the palace of the Tuileries, the following evening. A cousin of Brian's, Lady Balbriggan, lived in Paris and was a great friend of the Empress. It was she, no doubt, who had informed the palace that Brian was in Paris.

Brian was engaged in the tricky business of properly tying a lemon satin cravat, preparing to look his best at the soiree, when he heard an altercation in the small room at the entrance of his suite. In a moment, his long, sallow face very grave, Brindle came in to where Brian waited. He told him that the voice he had heard was that of a lackey from the Empress. She regretted that, in view of certain information received by her that day, it would be wise for the Marquis of Montalan not to appear at the palace that night.

The next morning Brian left Paris (and one might say the world) for Ireland.

Brian, in his despair, "went to ground" alone, except for Brindle and a woman to cook for them at Knockaleedy. He kept the kennels at Portaranmore in running order, but very rarely visited them. The finest specimens of the Kinhalla breed of boarhound were brought to him. Portaranmore was closed. But first Brian had given orders to tear down the great sweeping staircase and burn it in the ruins of the abbey chapel. Mrs. Mangasereen had died while Brian was on his long journey up and down Europe. Portaranmore, a very whited sepulcher, breasting the changes of the seasons on its terraced knoll, showed blank windows to the world.

For twenty years the miserable, pain-wracked Marquis of Montalan lived within the walls of Knockaleedy, seen by no one from the outer world. The house stands rooted beneath the waves, or so it appears from the watergate, "in the teeth of the wind, and the eye of the setting sun," as Brian wrote Lady Balbriggan in Paris. So craftily is the house placed that the Atlantic rollers, when they break, fly over it and spill their spray on the fuchsia hedges which border the garden paths above. In summer, nettle and the flaming poppy riot together in the salt-rimed flower beds. In winter, icicles hang in flashing splendor, like diamond plastrons, and when the sudden sun melts them, they crash in shimmering heaps with a noise like thunder.

The sparsely furnished rooms might well be a habitation of the dead. Old Brindle has faded with the close confinement of many years' service until he blends with the dusty carpets and hangings. He is only a remnant of a man, and occupies his days polishing the silver that will be seen by no one. Many of the rooms are in ruinous state and have been shut away. The ballroom, where once the gay ladies of Brian's grandfather's time swayed to the music of the viols and harp, now runs ankle deep in water because of a leaking roof that will never be mended.

In the very core of this dismal house sits the owner, a tall, thin, spider of a man. A jailhouse pallor spreads a patina over his flesh. He sits day after day, cherishing his loneliness and misery, as though in them he would find a grain of comfort. His left hand is bandaged so heavily that it makes a shapeless bundle across his sharply boned knees.

So, for many years sat Brian O'Hanaray, caught in a web of silence and memory, waiting for death. At last it came. Horribly.

One night in winter, Brindle had just taken Lord Montalan his evening cup of tea. Brindle then went into a room at the other end of the corridor to arrange his master's bed for the night. Brian slept on the first floor of Knockaleedy, for after he returned to Ireland, he never climbed a flight of stairs again.

A long, wailing cry shuddered through the somber house. From room to room it seemed to slap against the cornices and slide down the walls. Brindle ran as fast as his aged legs would allow and burst into the room where he had left Lord Montalan. Brian was lying in front of one of the windows facing the sea. The window was open and a gale flapped the ragged curtains. Yards of bandage were ripped from the festered hand that lay exposed to view. It was a hideous sight—red, bloated, splotched in white. As Brindle looked in loathing at the hand he had tended for so long, he saw a thin trail of gray smoke lift from it, shudder, and writhe away in the wind.

Portaranmore is now lived in by a member of the Costello family of Spain, via Galway. The family reports no untoward happenings in the house. The new staircase is adequate, but not as beautiful as the original one that was destroyed.

In the yew alleys which border the ancient ambulatory of the abbey, people say they sometimes see the procession of acolytes swinging thuribles of incense. But there is no abbot in their midst. He has not been seen since Brian O'Hanaray violated the chapel wall, where an empty niche is now surrounded by waving ivy fronds.

I talked one day with the Mother Superior at the nunnery of the Poor Clares at Lisdoonvarna. She told me that, in the many years which have passed since the abbot's hoard of gold and silver altar gear, jeweled croziers, and the like was given to the order by the Marquis of Montalan, much has been sent to the Mother Church or turned into cash for expenses. One thing, though, she agrees, is odd, and bears on this story. The gold and silver chalices which the house at Lisdoonvarna kept in its vaults, to be used only on special occasions, never need cleaning. The silver never tarnishes. I was shown a few of the chalices. They shone with an almost unearthly radiance. I was assured that they always do.

Duel with Song
and The Shattered Mirror
Belvelly Castle

———

COUNTY CORK

A LISTENING
GIRL —
BELVELLY CASTLE

Duel with Song
and *The Shattered Mirror*

ONE NIGHT IN 1930 I DROVE ALONG THE ROAD from Ballyvourney to Cork. A mile or more before one reaches the arched stone bridge which carries the highroad across the River Lee, the road runs through the thickly wooded demesne of Lord Barrymore. Emerging from the deep shadows of the overhanging trees, towering gateposts appear on the right-hand side of the road. These lichen-covered stone plinths are guarded by frighteningly realistic wild boars, crouching and defiant. The wild boar is the Barrymore device. Never have I seen this animal more startlingly displayed than in these two gray-marble carvings. Often one sees the armorial animal of a great house portrayed as an exaggerated, heraldic beast. Not so these boars; they seem to have sprung full-formed gnashing and savage, from the surrounding trees, instanter.

These particular specimens are said to have been brought from Verona, where they were carved under the watchful eye of Lord Barrymore during one of his sojourns in Italy. The date on one of the figures is 1809. A much earlier boar, crudely carved in limestone, was taken from the mud at the bottom of the River Lee at the foot of Belvelly Tower. This is the one which played so dramatic a part in the murder of Luccero Moreno, the Italo-Spanish troubadour whose lyric ghost, high in the tower of Belvelly Castle, makes midnight music on moonlight nights.

Children of the village, and they sent on errands, are fascinated by these fearsome beasts. They know them well; ride them as they would hobbyhorses, and mark them up in brands of pink and purple chalk. For luck, I saluted the marble guardians as I passed—we say in Ireland, "Give the front of your hand to your neighbor's gatepost, for you never know when you may wish to pass through it."

As my car mounted the brow of a hill, after leaving the shadows of the demesne, I saw the moon, which during most of my drive had hidden behind a black cloud bank, shining full and bright. A sharp white radiance bathed the night world. Objects the like of trees, gateposts, hedges, and towers stood out in exclamatory black. Below me spread the flat valley of the River Lee. Mirrored to its full height in the still, moon-burnished water was the tower of Belvelly Castle. Ivied and lone, it seemed enormous, dominating the surrounding landscape even more dramatically at night than by day.

So still was the night that I heard soft voices somewhere, far up the river. A fox barked at the moon, and so sharp was the impact of sound that it seemed like a pistol shot on the horizon. The tower of Belvelly cast a long finger of shadow across the river, just as it has cast centuries of shadow across the lives of its owners, a Norman family named Hodnett.

So many stories are told of dark days and doings inside the walls of this castle that there is not room in this volume to relate them all. I will tell two. One is the story called the "Duel with Song." This duel was fought by the troubadour Luccero Moreno and a Gaelic bard called Dion the Thrush. It took place in the year 1200. The other story concerns a vain and troubled lady. It is called "The Shattered Mirror."

Belvelly, like so many very early castles in Ireland, is a single tower. I once found an old book on a stall along the Liffey Quay in Dublin. It was a sort of family log, or diary, written in exceedingly minute script. For years the writer, a woman named McIlligy, had jotted down every happening during her days. A good deal of the writing had been ruined by damp and mold, but towards the middle of the book, which was in better condition than the rest, there was one passage that interested me immensely. It concerned the "beleaguered Hodnetts" (1685), as the woman McIlligy describes them, and a siege which lasted three years, during which over half the people gathered in the tower of Belvelly starved. An inordinately vain and flirtatious daughter of the Hodnett, occupying the castle at the time, caused a Clon Rockenby of Kinsale to fall madly in love with her. When she found he no longer interested her, and sent him packing, he was not having it that way. Calling a great company of men-at-arms, he besieged Belvelly. The siege dragged on and on for three years. In the nick of time, when Belvelly and all left alive in it, including the capricious lady, were nearly reduced, a boy standing at the top of the tower shot an arrow from a longbow. It struck Clon Rockenby in the cheek. He died cursing all within the tower; with an added, extra curse for the Lady Margaret Hodnett. Whatever the other members of her family suffered is not related. For the rest of her life, however, Margaret was persecuted by the curse. She, at the last, went mad.

The covering of this McIlligy log, apart from what writing I could decipher, makes the book unique. Bound in black horsehide, it is tied with braided leather thongs. A huge letter "M" is burned into the hide on both covers. The sign of Satan's hoof is imprinted like a thumbmark in brown smudge (which may easily be blood) on the top corner of each parchment page.

I asked an authority on such matters as the curious bindings of old books what he made of this device, the recurrence of the satanic hoof. Perplexed, he said, "It might be a personal monogram, a sign for the Black Mass, or, as was often done in the Middle Ages in Europe, an imprint used by someone who has avowed his soul to Satan and is proud of it."

The sight of Belvelly Castle kindled my interest all over again. I decided that next day while I was in Cork I would lunch with a man who could give me all the fine points and high lights of the curiously involved legends of that house.

The river was high that night. Almost a small, shallow lake spread over the meadows on three sides of the castle. As the Irish countryman says, "A small class of flood, to green the turf only." Reluctant to leave the hushed beauty of this night, I walked over to sit for a while longer on the bridge coping. Sitting half in the shadow of the stone pillars at the end of the bridge were two young women. So still were they that I had not noticed them before. They sat motionless, each with her hands idling in her lap. One girl had thrown her shawl back from her shoulders, and, I noticed, she stared with rapt intensity away across the river to the window near the water gate of Belvelly, the room where Luccero Moreno is said to have been imprisoned. The bosom of the other woman was covered by only a thin white bodice, and its rapid rise and fall denoted she was holding in check a strong emotion. Both women were completely oblivious to me and, it seemed, to each other. I got into my car and headed for Cork, more determined than ever to find out what drew such silent devotion from the simple country people in Belvelly Village.

Next morning I telephoned Thomas Caley, who knows more than most other living men about hauntings, ghost-layings, and general "goings on," as he describes them, of the world beyond the grave. He lunched with me at the excellent Victoria Hotel, famous the world over for its Charles II silver service and its Limerick bacon omelets. After regaling ourselves with a generous omelet apiece, we strolled to a bench on the Parade overlooking the River Lee. During the long, golden afternoon Thomas told me the stories of "Duel with Song" and "The Shattered Mirror."

"So they're at it again," he said, when I told him of the two girls waiting and listening at the bridge. "Those bewitched women of Belvelly, streaking the roads at night, sitting till the dawn, waiting and hoping to hear the voice of murdered and long, long dead Moreno. It's strange the hold those siren songs have on men and women alike, though men won't admit it, mostly. Myself heard them many's the time, and me living as a boy and young man at Fillery, an old house, now burned, a few miles from Belvelly Castle. They are heard in the full of the moon only, and are becoming rarer and rarer. I wish I had never heard them. They put a longing on you that is hard to conquer. I nearly ran away out of Ireland a number of times after I heard them. Many young women and girls have disappeared, gone clean away from the countryside, down the years. Two that I know of drowned themselves in the river at the foot of the tower."

Duel with Song

In the year 1209, according to Caley's account of the story, a Spanish galleon was seen to be in great distress off Ballycotton Light, as the spot is known today. Beyond doubt there was a lighthouse of sorts in that early day, for it is a devious point of rock, and Cobh Harbor is just round the bend. Wallowing in a gigantic sea, the ship soon foundered. Among the handful of survivers was a handsome Spanish youth who clutched a tamboura wrapped up in a cloak. His beautiful voice, accompanied by the haunting music that he played on this instrument, soon established Luccero Moreno in the big stone houses of Cobh. A troubadour had never been seen in the south of Ireland. Galway claimed a few of Spanish and Moorish breed who had come on trading ships, but as far as is known, they soon returned to their native lands.

Irish bards were the singer-poets, sometimes itinerant, but often gifted and learned men. In the constant patronage of a king or chieftain, they were well known to the four extremities of Ireland. It was not long before an historic meeting took place between Ireland's leading bard and the troubadour, Moreno.

Dion the Thrush was the most sought-after and highest-paid bard in the country. He sang the ancient runes. He improvised at christenings, victorious returns, marriages, and deaths. No one could touch him for sweetness of voice and brilliance of improvisation. No dusty "man of the roads" was Dion. Traveling in great style, he had a horse litter, caparisoned with his colors of green and purple. A purple thrush was his device. A body-servant assisted him to change three or four times a day from one gorgeous costume to another. In short, although called "The Thrush," Dion was a popinjay.

The men retained him because he glorified their deeds and flattered them unblushingly. The women fell madly in love with him on sight. Covertly, Dion the Thrush was envied. His position seemed unassailable.

Then came Luccero Moreno. According to his story, he was the get of a Spanish troubadour and an Italian woman of position. They had met while his father was singing at the court of Pandolfo Sforza, in Milan. Luccero said that he was born in

Italy, and that therefore he sang in the Italian *romanza* style instead of in the rather harsh, dramatic, Spanish fashion.

Although not actually attached to the household of the Hodnetts of Belvelly, Dion the Thrush made it his headquarters each time he returned to Cork after his yearly journey into the west of Ireland. While Dion was absent from the Belvelly scene on one of his visits to western border castles, Luccero Moreno came under the acquisitive eye of Lady Hodnett. She heard him play upon the tamboura, accompanying his singing of poignant *romanzas*. This event took place in the castle of a distant kinsman, one Guy de Yarnelle of Burga Keep, near Balconna. Forthwith she prevailed upon her lord to ask Moreno to return with them to Belvelly as their guest.

From that moment Luccero reigned supreme at Belvelly on the River Lee. His position was "entertainer extraordinary" to the household, and cavalier to the assembled ladies. Apparently he played the field too assiduously where Lady Hodnett was concerned. She had asked for his presence in the castle, and his attentions, which should have centered on her, strayed shockingly. In a fit of pique, it was she who suggested the "duel with song," a dangerous pastime when two such unstable temperaments as Dion's and Moreno's were in the balance.

In all fairness, Luccero had not the robust delivery or the pompous technique of the court flatterer, so much in demand in the period, nor had he the knowledge of these chieftains' prowess in petty Irish wars. Dion, on the other hand, had made a life study of this grandiloquent attack. Luccero was subtle, feline, an accomplished wit. His lightness of touch and of innuendo was darting as a swallow. Withal, he was as handsome as sin.

On his arrival at Belvelly, Luccero was given a room near the water gate. Often at night, when to all appearances the castle was asleep, he would sit on the sill of a tall window in his room, looking out across the river. Nostalgically, he would sing of the delights of requited love, and the desolation of love rejected. In his voice, floating on the night winds across the river meadows, was the rise and fall of passion, the true Latin tremolo, mightily disturbing to the Irish temperament.

As his visit to Belvelly lengthened into months, singly, or in small groups, women of the countryside would gather at night on the bridge which crossed the river near the gate of the castle. They would sit on the parapet of the bridge, waiting patiently for Luccero to sing.

It was approaching winter when a thickening Dion the Thrush drew tightly the thongs of his moneybags and took himself away from the biting cold of Connemara. He had had a splendid season, singing in all the most important houses. Rich food, extravagant praise for his talents, and an ever-increasing girth made Dion more lazy than he ordinarily was, and less aware.

Wrapped in a heavy wool cloak lined with gray wolf skins, he arrived at Belvelly one evening at dusk, unannounced. Of the meeting between these two minstrels we can only surmise. One can safely wager it was stormy. Dion would instantly have sensed that Luccero was a major threat to his prestige at Belvelly and a rival for the Hodnett patronage Dion had held for so long. It took Luccero only a short breathing space to take the measure of Master Dion, as well. Moreno, crafty, imperious, tasting for the first time in many lean years the ease and plenty with which the rich Hodnetts surrounded all within the castle, was surely not going to relinquish so soft a berth without a fight.

A few days of bitterness and verbal sparring resulted. Then, at a banquet in honor of Dion's return, Lady Hodnett had an idea. She would arrange a *concours,* a tournament of song: Dion the Thrush versus Luccero Moreno, troubadour of Spain and Italy. It would take place in the Great Hall of Belvelly Castle, three nights in succession, starting on a date to be set by herself. Each contender would sing three songs of his own choosing. Ballots would be cast at the end of each evening. The winner of two out of three songs, two out of three evenings, would be crowned victor and would be retained permanently at the castle. The loser would depart, since it was now evident that one roof could not long cover both Dion and Luccero.

The date was set for the first night of the "duel with song," as Dion chose to call it. He had told Hodnett, "I would fight this Spaniard, in any case, with any weapon. I choose song."

Roses from the garden along the river garlanded the walls. All was very gala. The castle party assembled. Each woman present vied with the other in richness of attire. Dion, appareled as never before, made a late and petulant entrance. Luccero, who, on the other hand, never depended on vivid or pretentious clothes to gain notice, was in a suit of black. The neck line of his surtout was cut straight across, throwing into bold relief his handsome head.

There was a hush. All waited expectantly. Luccero, a stranger guest in Ireland, was accorded the first song. He sat gracefully in the window, silhouetted against the luminous sky. Slowly strumming the tamboura, he sang of Italy and of love.

Dion stood before a great painted arras hung from floor to groined roof. He took the belligerent stance of the warrior. His eyes roved the room. In a ringing voice, this conqueror of hearts sang a rune of Oonagh the Tawny-Haired, who triumphed in love and war alike. And so it went for three nights.

After the first night of songs, the honors were given Luccero; the second night, to

Dion. On the third night there was tension in the flower-strewn hall. It was a warm night of brilliant moon. Luccero, as was his habit, sat in the tall, arched window. He sang as never before. His songs reached such heights of passionate beauty that none could deny the crown must be his. He approached the chair where Lady Hodnett sat. She placed a wreath of dark red roses on Luccero's head. In gratitude he promised to sing one more song to the company.

As he took his place in the window, the raging jealousy, which Dion had held in check until then, broke all bonds. Rushing upon the unarmed Luccero, he stabbed him in the chest. Luccero was lithe and supple; against Dion's heavy bulk, he side-stepped the lunge just enough to take the dagger thrust above the heart. Like a flash he wrested the knife from Dion's hand. Turning the wrist, in a burst of maddened strength, he forced the bellowing Dion to his knees. Driving the point downward, Luccero stabbed him in the throat. All this took only a space of seconds. Before men from the group of horrified guests could intervene, Dion the Thrush gushed his life out in torrents of blood from his ripped throat, his last words spitting curses of blood on the quivering black legs of Luccero, standing over him.

So ended in tragedy the "duel with song" at Belvelly Castle. Hodnett was infuriated at the murder of his favorite bard. He immediately imprisoned Moreno in his room beside the water gate. For days his stab wound was inflamed and pained him greatly. Since he was in disgrace with the Lord of Belvelly, no one dared do more than feed him the sparse fare he was allowed. One evening his supper was brought him by a yellow-haired young girl who had desperately loved Dion. She smiled at Luccero and seemed deeply solicitous for his comfort. That night, in agony, Luccero Moreno died, alone in his stone chamber. His food had been poisoned by the smiling, vengeful girl.

No one at Belvelly professed to know what had been done with body of Luccero Moreno after his agonized death. Two hundred years later, in the fourteenth century, a channel was being widened in the River Lee to allow larger barges to approach the water gate of the castle. Diggers in the river bed found an odd sort of stone creature, lashed round with rusted chains. Caught in the loops of this chain were fragments of a human skeleton. It was badly decayed and stained a dark green with river muck. The stone "gargoyle," as the diggers called it, was identified as a clumsily hewn image of the Barrymore wild boar. This stone finial had stood in the Great Hall of Belvelly Castle, a trophy presented to, or usurped by, a long-dead Hodnett. The bones, many think, were those of the Spanish troubadour. Heavily weighted, this disposal of his alien corpse at the bottom of the River Lee followed the custom of the times.

Through the centuries, many people have told tales of passing the tower of Belvelly Castle on a moonlight night and seeing the slim figure of a young man in black, with a pale face and smoldering, sunken eyes. He stands in the embrasure of the window next the water gate, looking up at the moon. Sometimes he brushes lightly, with long white fingers, the strings of a curious-looking musical instrument, described by various people as a guitar, mandolin, or zither. Throwing his dark head back so that the night radiance shines full on his face, he sings soft, melting songs in a strange tongue which the Irish listeners do not understand. Sometimes they stand for hours after the singing has ceased. The haunting melodies fill them with great unease.

The Shattered Mirror

The story of "The Shattered Mirror" is this. In 1685, Lady Margaret Hodnett resided at Belvelly Castle. The Hodnett fortunes were at that time at their peak. The beauty of Lady Margaret was a legend, even as far as Holland, from whence came suitors, one of whom was no less a person than a stripling of the House of Orange. She played fast and loose with the lot of them. For as fabulous as was her beauty of face and figure, her mind was a "flutter-box," to use an old Irish term. Shallow, capricious, wantonly unrestrained, she was wild as a hawk, causing trouble wherever she appeared.

When she was rounding twenty-five, she caught the erstwhile roving eye of one Clon Rockenby of Castle Haro, which stood high above the Bay of Kinsale. Rockenby was of a cadet branch of the rich and powerful Desmonds. Lady Margaret not only caught this stalwart's eye, she held it for years, to her final undoing. For a while she kept Rockenby dangling. Imperious to the hilt, she would send him packing every few months, in a fit of pique, only to recall him post haste when she was bored. He always came running.

One object of household gear prized by Lady Margaret above all others was a mirror. She had a unique collection of mirrors, mostly peace offerings from distracted lovers—French mirrors, set in gilt, adorned with cupids and roses; heavy Dutch mirrors framed in wide bands of tortoise shell, inlaid with ivory and silver; Spanish disk mirrors of polished and oiled damascened steel, large as a barrel-top, flexible as a rapier blade; mirrors from Venice, like sheets of still water in a wooded pool. One of these she hung at the foot of the stone steps leading down from the great hall to the garrison room just inside the portcullis gate. Lady Margaret passed this spot many times a day, whenever she walked abroad, or sailed upon the river. This was a vantage point. She always took a last long look at her radiant beauty as she left the castle. Her eager reflection was the first thing she saw on her return. Because of its size and clarity, this Venetian mirror was her treasure and her pride.

The day came when, recovering from a fit of boredom, Lady Margaret did not summon Rockenby, as was her wont. To her it was simplicity itself. She was tired of him. A young Frenchman, a traveler then stopping in Cork, amused her to the exclusion of all else. Many months strung out into a year. Rockenby sent messengers to Belvelly to find out the cause of this indifference. All returned with the same answer. She had torn up his messages before their eyes. At last, past enduring such treatment, Clon Rockenby rode to Belvelly Castle himself. Lady Margaret allowed him to be admitted to the castle, even ushered into the small room outside her bedchamber. She stood in the doorway as he approached, looking her loveliest. Without so much as a word of greeting, she slammed the door in his face and drove home the bolts.

To Clon this meant open warfare. The pride of the Desmonds, to say nothing of his own, had been flouted. No woman alive could treat the serious intentions of Clon Rockenby like this, and not wish she had never been born. All she had to offer was the astounding beauty of her person. Very well, he would humble that beauty to the dust, carrying the rest of the Hodnett tribe with her.

This slamming of doors had taken place in the late summer. Realizing that further entreaty was futile, Rockenby resolved on a plan, a plan very much in keeping with the era.

Clon Rockenby rode back to Castle Haro. Here he called his captains of men-at-arms together. In a few days, Clon, with two thousand men, set out for Castle Desmond, near Baltara. He knew that his uncle, head of the Fighting Desmonds, would help him. He gave Clon a further thousand men. It was not to be open warfare, just a siege to starve this upstart Hodnett woman into submission. It irked Clon to think that, treacherous and foolish as he knew Margaret Hodnett to be, he loved her extravagantly. There it was.

Winter came down the valley of the Lee with harsh, wet winds. Cold gusts of sleet blew in from the sea. Even in County Cork, where winters are mild, cold from two quarters boded a bad winter.

The standing of the siege took all at Belvelly Castle by surprise. They had not even thought to lay in provisions for the winter. Hodnett still trusted to baggage trains coming in weekly from Cork. Clon deployed his men to harass these provision routes. He aimed to let just enough food filter through to keep alive the family and garrison of a few hundred men at Belvelly, hoping by this method to reduce the strength of their arms to a negligible point and to break the will of Lady Margaret.

One year passed. The second winter set in soft as summer. Clon allowed no harvest to be reaped by Belvelly farmers, lest they try to smuggle in grain to their overlord at the castle. The plight within the walls of Belvelly was rapidly becoming desperate. Why Margaret's father allowed this state of affairs to drag on, no one knows. Why he did not force her to accept Clon Rockenby and lift this shameful siege is a mystery. Every once in a while a small group of men from the castle garrison would wheel out on half-starved horses and make a feeble sortie. Presently, after a few men were killed on both sides, they would gallop back under the portcullis. A few times Clon saw a wan, hungry-looking Lady Margaret walking on the battlements. She made no sign she ever saw him.

The third winter of siege set in wild and bitterly cold. By this time Rockenby himself was mortally tired of this stagnant state of affairs. He called his captains and bade them completely cut all supply lines. Within a fortnight a white flag waved fitfully from a spear-point in the grill above the portcullis.

Clon called two captains. They approached the silent tower. A dreadful sight met their eyes. Bodies of men starved to skeletons lay in oddly distorted heaps. The stench of unburied dead made them retch. Entering stealthily under the arched gateway, Clon found himself in the inner court. He came face to face with Lady Margaret. Her reddened eyes looked out at him from a great desolation. She was so weak from hunger she could scarcely stand. She leaned on the arm of an old serving woman, who wept miserably. Lady Margaret stood with her back to the mirror, looking Clon full in the face. Pointing to her face she said, "Look—look what you have done." Then she turned, slowly, until, reflected in the depths of the Venetian mirror at the foot of the stairs, was a pitiful, shivering woman, the mirror which for years had given back from its shadows the face of resplendently beautiful Lady Margaret.

As Clon watched, his voice perished in his throat. He could not speak to her. Great tears slid down her face and she swayed in weakness. Clon could stand this no longer. He grasped his sword by the end of its scabbard. With the heavy hilt he destroyed in one stroke the glass and its ghastly reflection.

Lady Margaret gave a piercing shriek. Flinging up her arms, she clutched the frame of the shattered mirror. It slipped from her grasp, and she sank to the floor in a dead faint. Turning swiftly, Clon made for his camp across the river, where he gave orders to lift the siege that night and send food to the starving inmates of the tower.

On the battlements crouched the young brother of Lady Margaret. He had watched the scene in front of the mirror. After seeing his sister carried to an upper room and tended, he had rushed to the battlements, longbow across his shoulder. Carefully he fitted a bronze-tipped arrow to the thong of his bow. Oiled deer-hide thongs had strength and far reaching power. The boy took aim. The arrow, released from the bow, sped to its mark like death-laden lightning. The dagger-like tip embedded in the cheek of Clon Rockenby, just as he was crossing the bridge.

By the time his men reached Clon's side, he knew he was dying. The men lifted him in their arms and bore him to a tent. "Lift the siege—give them food," Clon said. Then his head lolled, but suddenly he stiffened and murmured, "Margaret, I curse you. May you search for mirrors all your life, and never find." Lying back in the arms of one of his captains, Clon Rockenby died, on the frozen siege-ground in front of Belvelly Castle.

It is said that Lady Margaret Hodnett only partially regained her beauty. After she recovered from the terrible effects of the long siege, her inordinate love of mirrors suffered an eclipse. At first she would not have mirrors anywhere around, probably remembering too well the frightful reflection of her face given back by the Venetian mirror the day it was shattered by Clon Rockenby. Later she had small mirrors and took them out by stealth. This was after her mind began to go. When her father died, Lady Margaret inherited Belvelly Castle. Suitors again claimed her. One learns she took lovers, but none of prominence or of lasting interest. She never married.

When her mind began to wander, it was in unaccountable ways, at first, such as attempting to dam up the River Lee, which is a public waterway. She flew into a rage when threatened with imprisonment and shut herself up, becoming a recluse. Soon her madness increased. She would wander through the rooms of Belvelly, rubbing spots on the wall. Leaning close, she would peer into these spots and preen herself as if in front of a mirror. She died in a barred room in the castle. The house passed to a distant kinsman. Later, after 1830, it was abandoned as living quarters, even by the tenant farmers who reclaimed it for a few years.

Those who have seen the ghost of Lady Margaret Hodnett disagree about her face. Some say a thick, white cloth or veil obscures it completely. Others say she has no face, only a sphere of pale luminous mist which floats, above her shoulders, where the face should be. All, however, say she walks slowly around the castle rooms, rubbing, rubbing the stones with her forearm, then bending forward as if gazing intently into a mirror. Some of the large stones in the walls of the rooms at Belvelly Castle are rubbed much smoother than others. They gleam almost as if glazed with burnished enamel. If one stoops a bit, the reflection of one's face appears, blurred slightly, as if reflected in water.

The Black O'Flaherty
of Castle Blake
River Corrib

MENLO, COUNTY GALWAY

CASTLE BLAKE, LAKES OF MENLO

The Black O'Flaherty
of Castle Blake

The years like great black oxen tread the world
And God the herdsman goads them on behind,
And I am broken by their passing feet.

Yeats

IN THE WEST OF IRELAND, THE BARE MENTION OF
the Black O'Flaherty of Menlo, in the County Galway, still evokes a shudder
of horror. The shadow of fear still stalks abroad among the simple country people
living in the "back lands of sky and bog" which stretch between the many inland
waters of this West country.

Even in Connemara, which seems to be carved from solid granite and garlanded
with swags of golden broom and rust-pink gorse, there is an echo of O'Flaherty rapine
from out the past. So alive, so immediate are these atrocious tales that the "auld ones"
use them to frighten children into obedience and to subject adults to scorn, the like
of, "Sure, ye've a low, dark way wid ye. Yer heart's as black as O'Flaherty's Keep."

The black oxen referred to in Yeats' poetic tragedy, "Countess Cathleen," were
one of the many black symbols used by the O'Flaherty as armorial devices. There
appears little that is clear-cut or comprehensive, out of the moil of O'Flaherty legend,
from which to weave a story that would be anything but episodic. The first group to
inflict their superior strength and diabolical cunning on their fellow men were the
four sons of Liam-Dem O'Flaherty. These four ruffians ruled Galway Walled City.
They gave it the name, "The City of the Tribes."

The best-known lament (and they are legion) connected with the name O'Flaherty, is this one. A countryman or woman walking along the roads in the vicinity of
Galway, Menlo, Athenry, or Moycullen (all of them were once O'Flaherty demesnes),
and perceiving a horseman approaching, would look quickly at the rider. If the rider
turned out to be an O'Flaherty, or one of their henchmen, the pedestrian would fling
himself on his knees in the ditch. Crossing himself in no uncertain manner, he would
murmur, "From the shadow of the O'Flaherty, good God deliver me."

The sprawling ruin of Castle Blake is scattered over an acre of turf and muddy

NEVIN O'FOYLE

NAMED
THE PORKER

THE DEVIOUS
BLAKE OF MENLO

cow pastures which march with one bank of the River Corrib. This mass of violet-gray stonework looms flatly against the leaden sky if seen from the battlemented gate house which flanks the road from Oughterard to Galway. If one walks to what was once the "Monks' Kitchens" and looks at the ruins of the castle, he notices a remarkable change, a sort of "now you see it, and now you don't." The stones seem to have become almost white. They gleam, softly luminous, against one of the most remarkable mountain ranges in Europe, The Twelve Pins of Connemara. These high, sharply pointed peaks are said to be twelve Connemara matrons of ancient Gaelic times. They were told to kneel in a row, their hands in supplication. In this manner they would appeal to Daghda, the father of Gaelic gods, to send rain, for the country was near destroyed by drouth. Daghda sent the rain in such torrents the women were drowned. They still kneel, their hands pointed heavenwards, and there is always a slight misty rain on the twelve tips of the mountains, no matter how fair it is elsewhere in Connemara.

The "Gatekeeper's Ghost" is an old bogey in and around Menlo. Many the adventurous-minded boy, and he in his cocky teens, bent on journeying the world with only a sixpence in his breeches, has regretted his daring in passing this lonely sentry house at night. The actual gate itself is of ninth-century stonework. There are later additions, but none later than the fourteenth century. The windows are beautifully mullioned, and the detail of carved stone masks supporting the arch is very fine; in fact, the "miniature castle" effect is arresting and probably the most photographed object in all County Galway.

The story of the gatekeeper is this. Among the small army of illegitimate children compiled by the large family of male O'Flahertys, there was one who was such a giant in stature that he could rend a red Tyrone ox limb from limb as easily as most men pluck the petals from a daisy in "she loves me, she loves me not."

Being unable to house and provide for all of these "natural" offspring, O'Flaherty Mor set this great oaf of a son to watch the toll road which passed the Castle Blake demesne. A toll was extracted from all wayfarers to help swell the already overflowing O'Flaherty coffers. If a traveler looked prosperous, he was robbed of everything he had, and usually stripped of his clothing into the bargain. If he protested, he was butchered forthwith by Arnad, the giant gatekeeper.

It finally came to such a pass that when a merchant or noble was forced to journey past the O'Flaherty demesne (in the early days, this was the only road open), he put aside his richly furred raiment and his silver-studded tabard. He would pack these in a sack and hire a boy to sneak through the woods and bogs with it and meet him a few miles the other side of the toll gate. The poorly clad and mounted traveler was only charged a toll fee by Arnad, who then let him go on his way. It became a custom in the locality that, if a man saw a friend looking seedy, he would grin and say, "God's wrath, but ye look poverty-clutched! Are ye just after passin' the O'Flaherty's gate?"

To amuse himself and, it may be imagined, to keep himself in trim, Arnad had a great clutch of rocks piled in one of the embrasures in the gate wall. A man passing would pull his forelock, cross himself, mutter the well-known "From the shadow," and walk hastily along the road, hoping to put a good distance between himself and the gigantic half-wit. Arnad would grasp one of the cannon-ball-shaped rocks, heft it carefully, and let fly at the small of the back of the unfortunate person. So many people were killed in this fashion that the roads, after years, became deserted and the toll gate was erected elsewhere. It is said that a few centuries later, in 1704, when a high stone wall fell down, nearly one hundred skeletons, of both men and women, were found packed tightly in the heavy buttresses. The backbone of every skeleton was broken in one or more places. The wall had been Arnad's gruesome cache for the victims of his sport.

As so often happens to bullies, Arnad met his match one day—more than his match, by a long way. Somehow word of Arnad's treacherous brutality reached the ears of the Mayo Burkes, who hated the lights and livers of anyone of O'Flaherty color. One day a small regiment of gallowglasses in the pay of Edmund de Burgo, who founded the Burkes and was an old man of ninety at this time, were sent into Roscommon. This little foray was to settle a score, long smoldering between de Burgo and Shamas O'Loughglinn of Ballyhaunis.

Three things the Chief de Burgo bade his gallowglasses. Pass the toll gate of the Black O'Flaherty at Castle Blake, but pay no toll. Keep a wary eye peeled for the well-known Arnad perfidy. If the O'Flaherty men should try to fight, kill them all. With these instructions well digested under their adventurous belts, the gallowglasses set out, singing and shouting.

The captain of the gallowglasses was a grand specimen of a man, standing well over six feet. He had shoulders "the like yer two arms stretched, would niver span," and his strength and litheness were prodigious. Before the company of soldiers came into sight of the gates of Castle Blake, all but Pádrig, the huge captain, deployed into a handy thicket, where they could watch all that took place and leap out at a moment's notice. Pádrig walked slowly past the toll gate. He was immediately challenged by Arnad, who demanded a large toll. Pádrig refused it, saying this was a public highway. In the resulting high words, Arnad lunged out at the big gallowglass. It was his last lunge on earth. Pádrig opened his two massive hands. When he closed them together like a vise, Arnad's neck was between them. A mighty fight resulted. The remaining gallowglasses came out of the thicket and battled with the O'Flaherty men who ran to their comrade's aid. But it was only a few O'Flaherty men against half a hundred de Burgo soldiers. The O'Flaherty group were killed to a man. Hacked and dying carcasses strewed the road in front of the toll gate.

Pádrig and Arnad swung, first one way, then the other. Both were strong men, big in themselves. At last, by a lucky twist, Pádrig broke Arnad's neck. Then, with a clean stroke of his sword, he cut off the head. A great howl of joy went up from a few boys and countrymen who had gathered to watch the grand sight. The gallowglasses tossed the ugly, black-thatched head from one to the other, playing a grisly game of handball. When they went on their way, they left the battered head where it had been kicked into the gutter by one of the onlookers.

From that night on stem the curious, fascinating stories of how Arnad returned to haunt the toll gate and the countryside. Some men say that, on windy nights, and they returning to their bit of a farm from a market fair or some other class of diversion, a hideous head, with black, bristly hair and horrid, bulging eyes will roll across the road in front of the little ass or horse, causing the creature to go wild with fright, to say nothing of himself. The head will batter back and forth from ditch to ditch, tongue lolling from the mouth. A sound of gurgling, as if a man were being choked, rises above the rushing of the wind. These men never tell what becomes of the head, for they are off and away, out of it, at the double quick.

Another form the haunting takes is the hurling of large stones, which suddenly fly through the air when no one is about. Even now, the embrasure is often found filled with stones. From such a pile, Arnad of the Tribe O'Flaherty was wont to hurl his rocks at innocent passersby in the tenth century.

I was told by a farmer living near the entrance gates of Castle Blake that he often heard the choking sound coming from a ditch, or from the top of the tower of the gate house. I asked him for his version of how the cannon-ball-shaped rocks came to be in the embrasure. He looked wary, and said, "That I'd not know fer sure, yer honor. Boys 'ull play tricks, but then it's hard work luggin' those great rocks from off the pile, ferninst. I'd be willin' to bet it was that auld Arnad, in the night. I niver seen a boy around here with that much free work in 'im."

"BLACK"
O'FLAHERTY

The Stranger Guest

Castletown

COUNTY KILDARE

The Stranger Guest

EFORE PRESENTING THE STORY OF "THE Stranger Guest," it is necessary, I feel, to give the reader a short summary of Castletown as a house. A very great house it is, architecturally supreme. Long association with the mercurial politics of Ireland, with goings and comings of the rank and fashion of two centuries, and the perfection of its appointments places Castletown at the pinnacle in a land justly famous for its country houses.

It has been said, and very rightly, that the Irish gentleman traveled the world. Returning to his native Ireland, ignoring the cities, he seated himself and his culture in the country. This I venture is only partly true, for Dublin boasts some extraordinarily handsome town houses, as do Cork and Waterford.

Little time was spent in town houses. To the country went his books, his paintings, his Italian sculpture, and his family. These houses were erected either where his lands lay, sometimes necessarily, or in some sylvan spot which caught his imagination and seemed agreeable for his house. If possible, these houses, reflected in water, were wide and generous in plan. Of all descriptive words I know, "Spacious" best describes these Irish country houses.

Today Castletown is lived in and beautifully tended by Lord and Lady Carew, whose family name is Conolly-Carew, stemming from "Speaker" Conolly, who built the house.

In the sparkling journal known as *Dublin Annals*, written by Bishop Berkeley in 1722, one reads, "Mr. Conolly is building a stone house at Castletown, in County Kildare. 142 ft. by 60 ft. & 70 ft. high. The plan is richly conceived, fitting gracefully into the surrounding wheat fields."

William Conolly was the richest man in Ireland at this time. By all accounts, and they are legion, he was a very remarkable fellow. Of pure Irish blood, Conolly was born at Ballyshannon, County Donegal, in 1660. His parents were farmers with no high connections. Where William Conolly acquired his schooling is unknown. It is a fact, however, that when barely thirty years old he was sitting in William III's first

Parliament. The origin of his vast fortune remains in doubt; he is said to have acted, when in his twenties, as agent for two elderly spinsters, who left him a considerable sum of money. Anyway, Dean Swift mentions Squire Conolly's money as something beyond reckoning.

This he augmented by a profitable law practice, acting for years as attorney to the irascible Duke of Ormond, subsequently occupying the lucrative post of Commissioner to the Irish Revenue. In 1715, Conolly was chosen, unanimously, to act as Speaker of the House, and ever afterward was spoken of, by friends and enemies alike, as "Mr. Speaker" Conolly.

In the meantime (some say on falling heir to his legacy from the two spinsters), he had acquired the Castletown demesne at Cellbridge, fifteen miles west of Dublin. This fine property had been in the Dongan family since 1130, but was forfeit because a Dongan had fought beside James II at the Boyne Water, afterwards accompanying him to France. It would appear William Conolly had the Midas touch, for when he married the daughter of Sir Albert Conyngham, she brought him a large fortune as dowry.

Mr. Speaker Conolly commissioned Sir Edward Lovett Pearce to design the great house, where he decided to establish a dynasty. Following the fashionable plan of the period, the house has immense frontage, a high central block with two long oblong blocks connected by semicircular wings, called "demilunes." Establishments were necessarily large, for Irish families are large, and hosts of servants are necessary to wait upon them and the innumerable guests whose coming and going (and staying for weeks, I may add) was a noticeable feature of Irish life. Parties were sometimes so huge that they taxed houses even as large as Castletown.

The witty and prolific chronicler of her epoch, Mrs. Delany, writes to her confidante, Mrs. Middleton, in London: "Life at Speaker Conolly's Castletown gathers momentum, although the ladies of the family are forever in childbed, or painfully near it. Parties and routs continue. Last week so many guests were asked to a hunt ball that it was only at the last minute it was discovered that there were in the house twice as many people who had been offered accommodation as the house could put up. But such a matter did not trouble our genial host. Dancing went on until five o'clock in the morning, when the ladies retired and filled all the available beds in the house. There they slept in peace until nine o'clock, when they were roused by the passage of the butler and three footmen, up and down the cold corridors, all ringing loud bells, and crying out, "Get up, girls, the boys want the beds!"

However close to childbed the ladies of Castletown hovered, according to Mrs. Delany, it was not the Speaker's wife, for she never bore him an heir, deeply to his sorrow, 'tis said. When he died, it was discovered he had left the greater part of his enormous wealth to his favorite nephew, William Conolly of Leixlip Castle. William had married, in 1733, Lady Anne Wentworth, daughter of the Earl of Stafford. Lady Anne spent a great deal of time at Castletown after her husband inherited the house, and it was she who saw the first ghost, who walked down the "stairs that were not there."

Lady Anne wrote many descriptive letters to her father; one, which bears on this story, reads in part, "Castletown is much the grandest house I have seen in Ireland. It is very lofty and deep; on either side wind, in a circular manner, colonnades of stone, supported on columns of the Ionic order. The rooms are large, light, and well proportioned, indeed they are furnished with every treasure, though inside be not entirely finished throughout, for the great staircase is not yet begun."

Mrs. Speaker Conolly was still alive when nephew William inherited Castletown —she lived on in the house until she died at the great age of ninety-four. It appears that Mrs. Conolly was pretty much of a personage in her own right, although rather obscured by the brilliant talents of her grandiose husband. Mrs. Delany leaves a vivid sketch of the old lady, who "rose always at eight, and by eleven was seated in her drawing room receiving visits until three o'clock, at which hour she punctually dined, and generally had two tables of ten to twelve people each. After dinner she sat in her gray cloth-hooded chair and napped. She was monstrously wide awake evenings, clever at business, wrote all her own letters, and until her death read a newspaper by candle-light without spectacles. She was a plain woman, a little vulgar in her manner, but abounded in generous qualities."

During the nineteenth century, the hospitality of Castletown remained proverbial in a country where hospitality acquires the status of a sacred rite. George Moore wrote a friend in England after spending a fortnight at Castletown during the tenure of "Spender" Conolly, who revived and maintained the splendor of his eighteenth-century ancestors, "I have wined and dined par excellence at the Conolly's. I venture to say that the hospitality of this splendid house is so unbounded that even in Ireland it will long be remembered."

He did not add that the strain on the family fortunes caused by this extravagant manner of living led to a major scandal in the family. "Spender" Conally embarked on an adventure which, besides the excitement it would afford him and some high-spirited friends, would, he hoped, help in recouping his sagging fortunes. The out-come of this venture landed him in an American military prison on a charge of gun-running during the war between the North and South.

Just as hospitality is the very definition of Castletown, now and ever since it was built, so it was the cause of the encounter between young Squire Thomas Conolly (son of nephew William who inherited Castletown from "Mr. Speaker") and "The Stranger Guest" in the woods near Cellbridge one cold, wet, November evening in 1767.

Squire Thomas Conolly sat far back against the plum-red rep cushions of his coach as it sped along the sun-baked road between Lucan and Cellbridge. A fine stretch of road, this, he mused, all because of his efforts, too. If he must spend so much time in Dublin, where Parliament seemed to dissolve and reconvene overnight, he would be damned if he would drive over the rutted roads that most of his friends, living in the big country houses hereabouts, endured. Why, the road he had taken last week to Milltown's house, Russborough, by way of Blessington, was nothing but a series of potholes and "break-yer-necks." Swinging through the shining village of Cellbridge, which clustered about the entrance gates to Castletown, he nodded and smiled a greeting to the many forelocks that were pulled as he passed. Strapping country women, brown from the fields, held chuckling babies up for him to see as he drove along. Monstrous pretty, these young girls who curtsied. Lucky, that's what I am, lucky, thought Thomas Conolly. He marveled a little, he always marveled, that Fortune had showered so many favors on the Ballyshannon farm boy.

The lightly built traveling coach sparkled darkly green in the summer sunshine. The four barbs, two black, two dappled gray, were harnessed vis-à-vis. The coachman, sitting high on the box, did the Conolly livery proud. It was rich claret red and primrose. Just the color red, observed the squire, of the fine French wines stored in the wine vaults at Castletown. Of a sudden, Squire Thomas awoke from his reverie. This was the spot where he always got down from the coach to walk the rest of the way, about a mile. Some days he cut out across the fields, on others he would approach the house straight up the driveway. This view of his house never failed to quicken his pulse. No matter how tired he was, fatigue and cares of state dropped from his shoulders as this picture unfolded before him.

Today in the clear, golden, late afternoon light the grandly conceived many-windowed façade of Castletown rose serenely above the fields of wheat and barley. In the east meadow, stooks of early wheat had been piled shoulder high, the slanting sun gilding them to molten, living gold. Behind the luminous sweep of stone, as delicately curved as a sickle-moon, for all its size, rose the cool jet of yew and purple-black copper beech.

As the squire paused to enjoy the loveliness of carved stone and foliage, his eye was arrested by—Demeter? Was it she? Demeter among the corn, walking towards him? It was within the realm of possibility that one might encounter the Earth God-dess on the sward of Castletown—here, surely, if anywhere on earth. And then he threw his head back and laughed, the laugh of a deeply happy man, for the figure advancing towards him, tawny garments rippling in the breeze, was his wife, Lady Louisa, still a little far off.

He waited until she should come up to him. Waiting, he recalled vividly the day three years ago when he had taken the hand of Lady Louisa Lennox. His own had trembled so, with bridegroom fright, it seemed unable to obey his will. He thought then, and he thought now, he had never seen a woman so beautifully wrought as his wife. Her sister, that touted beauty, the Duchess of Leinster, who lived at nearby Carton, was more the full-flowered, high-keyed, dashing style. Louisa had the mem-orable, haunting magic of a perfect May morning. Her color was delicate, her laugh like a hurrying brook. Yes, he decided, of the two ravishing daughters of the Duke of Richmond, it had always been Louisa he had wanted as mistress of Castletown.

As Squire Thomas and his wife mounted the wide steps of the pillared entrance, he told her of how startled he had been a few moments ago, thinking she was Demeter as she walked her shining path through the uncut wheat.

Lady Louisa laughed, and said, "Tom, if you are not careful, you too will believe you are seeing ghosts at Castletown, like your mother. She wrote in her journal, do you remember, of seeing a tall shadowy man stand on the top gallery before the staircase was built, pause for a moment against the light of the window, laugh a high-pitched, derisive laugh, and walk in a rather arrogant, mincing way down the staircase which was not there."

"Yes," said her husband thoughtfully, "I do remember. She recounted it often enough. She saw him only once. He was never seen by anyone else, though we all hoped we would sometime. She always had an uncanny feeling the man was marking Castletown for his own, the way a ghost will take possession sometimes. He seemed to have vision as well, for, according to my mother, the confident manner in which he descended a staircase which did not exist, taking the right turns and feeling the flow of shallow treads, was remarkable, considering that, when the staircase was actually built ten years later, when she was away from Castletown, its graceful, gently mount-ing sweep and two turnings is identical with the way the dark, chuckling phantom trod it."

Slowly the master and mistress of Castletown mounted the staircase and walked along the upper gallery towards the nursery.

Whenever he was at Castletown, the squire watched and deeply enjoyed the changing of the seasons. The green, undulating, and richly fertile countryside of Kildare offered all sorts of country pleasures. Walking, driving a smart cob to a high-cut gig along the bohireens and country lanes, and riding to hounds with the "Killing Kildares" and the Wicklow Hounds occupied his days. He often said, "I am the hardiest man of my time. My favorite practice of taking long walks by night, in even the most vicious weather, keeps me fit for all encounters. Like a good, all-round horse, I am immune to all weather."

It was a demented day, and he out with the Kildare Hounds, when the squire first encountered the tall, lean cadaverous "Stranger" whose oddly frightening behavior caused the damage in the dining room at Castletown. According to the traditions of the house, it was a remarkable exhibition.

On this particular morning, the meet assembled at Garanagh Cross, two miles from Cellbridge. November, a wild month in Ireland at best, never presented a worse day to a shivering world than this Thursday in 1767. Wind lashed at the writhing branches of the bare oaks and beeches. A frozen rime of water clogged the ruts in lanes and roadways, puddles left from a previous night of storm. Take-offs and landings at walls and ditches were death traps where "a man would enter purgatory in one gulp," as a farmer observed.

The field was mean; few men, lucky enough to have a roof over their heads and a warm fire to nap beside, had ventured out. A handful of hardy sportsmen milled about the Cross, half frozen already. Horses were chancy, men's tempers short. Of this little band was Squire Conolly, proud of his ability to brave all weather and enjoy it.

At last the cry, "Gone away," rang through the Garanagh Woods, and the hunt set off. They first "found" in Farmer Garry's river meadow. From then on the fox took a leaf from the wildness of the day, and traced and retraced back on himself until hounds were dizzy. The meet had been called at the Cross at eleven o'clock, but, what with one thing and another, had not got off until nearer noon. Now and again there was a hint off to the west that the day might better, but it did not hold with signs. It worsened towards midafternoon, and the cold, driving rain poured down straight as stair rods.

The hunt dissolved little by little until, as early dusk began to gather, there were no more than five or six die-hards left straggling across the plowed fields skirting Rantully Hill. Since leaving Munster Mill at a point where the Dublin Gap crossed the highroad to Portarlington, the squire had been conscious of a man riding a rangy, dun-colored horse. He seemed as fresh as if he had just entered the field and had not spent the length of a tormented day chasing a diabolical fox. The squire looked hard at the stranger, trying to remember if he had seen him before. There was something vaguely familiar, though he certainly was not one of the field when it took off from

Garanagh Cross. The newcomer was riding at a smart gallop a few feet ahead of the squire and Battle, his useful hunter, who had never put a foot wrong all day, and would reap a rich reward that night with as much hot mash as he could safely hold.

Squire Conolly turned in his saddle, raised his crop, and called out to the man, "You joined a bad hunt on a worse day. You're a stranger to this part of Kildare, I take it, or have I seen you before?"

The tall man, sitting easily in his leathers, smiled. More rightly, an odd, vulpine grin split his face, showing teeth that seemed abnormally long and yellow. The man neither nodded his head nor spoke, just smiled and pointed up the hill. As he did so, he turned his horse sharply, pointing the animal uphill for the steep climb. At the same moment, hounds set up a great hullaballoo, giving tongue to a string of notes which meant only one thing to hunting gentry—the kill.

Now, the squire was of two minds, and only the flick of an eyelid to decide whether to follow the dark stranger across a cold, deceitful-looking bog, which wound between the road and the rise of Rantully Hill, or continue on to the warmth of Castletown, which, he noted by landmarks, was only three miles away. Quickly the squire made up his mind. He would be in at the kill. A gruelling day in the wind and wet must show some sport. As he breasted the top of the hill, the squire was amazed and a bit puzzled by the picture spread before him. The stranger, an incredibly tall man in a long, gray, shad-bellied coat and a draggled gray beaver hat, spindly legs encased to the thighs in sodden, wrinkled boots, was standing with legs spread wide apart. The man held a bloody fox high above his head, seeming unaware that the hot blood ran down his front from crown of hat to the toes of his boots. He grinned again, that slit, sly grin, and offered the brush, which he snipped off as expertly as you please with his strong yellow teeth, to Squire Conolly.

The squire looked about him. Save for the dun hunter, nuzzling at a few bayberry leaves in the muck, he and the long individual in the odd gray costume were the sole occupants of the hill. That in itself was curious, for the hounds had disappeared over the brow. He would have sworn hounds had never made this kill. But that was ridiculous; it left only the tall stranger. Hounds had deserted a kill? Fantastic!

As Squire Conolly turned his horse away in disgust at the reeking sight, the man called out to him, a high, mincing voice, unpleasant, and with a strange sibilant accent, "Conolly, if you will not accept the brush, will you offer me a cup of something hot at your great house—er—Castletown?"

Now, as I have said, hospitality was a fetish with Squire Thomas Conolly. Castletown, since the day it was built, had never refused all it had to offer, to anyone. This man, however unappetizing his person and manners, had made a direct request to the owner of Castletown. No matter what repugnance he felt for the fellow, he must not refuse. Turning back, he said in as cordial a voice as he could muster, "Most certainly, sir, the pleasure is mine. I expect a few cronies to be waiting for me at Castletown. As is the custom after a hunt, there will be a bowl of hot rum toddy. Pray join us."

Jogging along at an easy pace to save his tired horse, Squire Conolly was deep in thought. Oh, well, it could do no harm. He would give the fellow all the hot toddy he could hold and find some means of sending him on his way. But where was his way? He must at least find out the stranger's name. Turning towards the man, who was riding a little behind him, the squire called out, "Sorry, but I did not catch your name when you told it to me, nor where you are stopping in the neighborhood."

With an insolent toss of his narrow, foxy head, the man continued to twirl the dripping brush between his dirty fingers. "I didn't tell you. Call me your stranger guest, for the time being, anyhow. As for where I come from, or where I go, everywhere and nowhere," he replied, and his high, whinnying laugh still sounded as the two riders passed through the gates of Castletown.

Squire Thomas rode straight up to the front entrance of his house, where a number of grooms stood shivering and walking horses of guests who had already arrived. As soon as these horses cooled a bit from their stiff run, they would be taken to the stables. The two men dismounted, threw reins to waiting grooms, and passed under the corniced doorway into the great entrance hall.

For a long time after the event which took place later in the evening, the squire remembered that, immediately he and the stranger guest had entered the high, stucco-garlanded hall of Castletown, the dark, cunning eyes of the man in bloodied gray swept up, unhesitating, to the window on the top landing of the staircase. This window had let onto the gallery before the stairs were built. Slowly, step by step it seemed, the man followed with his eyes the massive sweep of the great staircase of Castletown, which was a wonder in beauty of balance and scale to all who beheld it. A high, hissing laugh reverberated up the stair well as the man took little jig steps, which were his manner of walking, across the black and white lozenges of the marble floor.

Sounds of men's voices, mixed with the rattle of glass and china, issued from the dining room as Squire Conolly and his guest entered. The squire motioned the stranger to a chair near the fire.

A huge, smoking bowl of fragrant, hot rum was being ladled out to a group of ten or twelve friends of the squire who stood or sat about the high-ceilinged room. One or two men, early arrived, had drunk deeply of the soothing punch, and the warmth of the room, after a long, cold hunt, was causing some to settle in their high-backed chairs for a drowse. Servants were on their knees in front of some of the men, removing wet boots. As a servingman approached the chair in which lolled the stranger, he sank to one knee and grasped the boot on the right foot. Instantly the man snarled, "Get out. I'll keep my boots on. I feel drowsy as well. Don't disturb me if I take forty winks."

As Squire Conolly looked at the man, he noticed something that had escaped his usually sharp eyes before. The fellow was as hairy as a dog. Long, stiff, black hairs sprouted from his nostrils, and great curling tufts, three inches long at least, hung out of both ears. Now that his long-fingered hands had been wiped clean of the filth of the kill, they were as matted with hair as a badger's paws. This was extraordinary. Who was this boor?

Noticing that the man was by now heavily sunk in sleep, the squire motioned to one of the servants still in the room. "Remove that man's boot," he said, "and be ready, all of you. If what I think is true, this is damnable." There was a dead silence, and all eyes focused at one spot as the servant carefully drew the steaming boot away from the stranger's foot. A gasp came from each watcher, and a cry of rage and alarm from the squire. For, as the boot fell to the floor, there was revealed a remarkably hairy hoof, cloven down the center.

The stranger guest seemed oblivious to the commotion caused by this sight, for he slept on undisturbed. The squire sent a groom on a fast horse into Cellbridge, to fetch immediately the parson and the priest.

Both these men of God arrived just as the Devil—by this time it was clear to all who the stranger was—wakened from his nap. He seemed bewildered for a moment; then, realizing the situation, he leaped to his feet. One boot gone, his gait was even more jiggly than usual as he limped to the fireplace. There, spreading his arms on the mantelpiece, he stared at the assembled Cloth. The parson, a timid, worthy man of stuttering speech, turned to Squire Conolly for orders. "Exorcise the fiend," cried Squire Conolly. "Drive him out of Castletown forever, as you hope for Heaven." But the mumbling parson was too polite in his admonishments. The Devil only laughed and cut a caper, enjoying the affair hugely. Not so gentle was the priest, however. Enraged at what he saw, he adjured this devilish jackal to be gone by all the rites of exorcism. But the figure on the hearthstone only shrieked with Satanic laughter and capered the more. This was too much for the priest. In a last furious vent of anger he hurled his missal at the leering face. It missed its mark and crashed into the mirror hanging above the fireplace, cracking it from top to bottom. This attack, however, so upset the fiend that he leaped high into the air and disappeared in a cloud of yellow, sulphurous fumes. His vanishing point is a blackened crack in the creamy marble of the hearthstone, which may be seen to this day.

Castletown today is a tranquil and singularly pleasant house to visit. The descendants of the original builder dine undisturbed in the dining room where Squire Thomas Conolly encountered Beelzebub, who, in dramatically taking leave of the house, forever left his mark.

The Lady of Moyvore

Moyvore House

COUNTY MEATH

The Lady of Moyvore

A T AN AFTERNOON PARTY IN DUBLIN ONE DAY—
according to my notes it was in October, 1936—I was talking to a man
who had just bought a small house in the County Meath. Irish legend
always refers to this space of undulating, richly green meadows as The
Plains of Meath, for about it hangs the aura of two very much beset
women, Grania and Queen Maeve.

When I enquired of the man in what part of Meath his house was placed, he
replied that it was not far from Castle Trim, where Dean Swift's immortal Stella spent
many closely chaperoned years. The house, he added, was a rather smaller edition of
its grandly spacious neighbor, Moyvore. Both houses were reflected in the placid
River Boyne. Moyvore stood in a vast demesne, encircled by towering Irish oak, whilst
his small place, called Scarteen after a famous pack of hounds, was mostly paddock
and grazing for his horses. He was only five miles from the lively market town of
Moyvalley.

I found the man agreeable to talking horses and houses, and we discussed some of
the strange stories of ghosts and hauntings accredited to so many houses along the
Boyne Water.

When I told him I could remember no ghost so thoroughly engaging as the shade
of the little French comtesse at Moyvore, he agreed. Turning away from the fireplace
where we were standing, my companion motioned to a group of people talking together at the far end of the room. "You see that young man in the gray suit, the one
with black hair brushed straight back from his forehead?" he asked. "Well, he can
tell you all you want to hear about the Lady of Moyvore. His name is Gaisford, and
his mother is a direct descendant of the famous Squire of Moyvore, Ranely Fitz-
Martin, who brought the lovely Adèle de la Tour-Vérrière to his house. Ranely
Fitz-Martin was young Gaisford's great-great-grandfather."

Later in the afternoon I was introduced to Patrick Gaisford, whom I found immensely pleased by my interest in Moyvore and his favorite ancestor. When he told
me he was studying for the bench at Trinity College, I asked if he were agreeable to

253

giving me a firsthand, intimate version of a story I had heard in snatches many times, a ghost story I thought singularly moving.

Before I left the party, I asked Patrick Gaisford if he would join me at Baldoyle on the following Saturday. My big rangy, gray 'chaser, Dragonstown, was running in the fourth race, The Luttrellstown Stakes. After that we would dine at the Kildare Street Club, where one eats in the great tradition, and portraits of Rakehelly sports and Regency bucks line the walls of the dining room, in which, during the eighteenth century, resounded the wittiest conversation in Europe. It seemed the perfect setting to hear the complete story of The Lady Of Moyvore. The story, as related by Gaisford, is as follows:

One dripping, gray morning in 1791 three heavily cloaked figures were hurrying along a steep path leading down to the Channel, in the environs of Calais. A small fishing smack waited a few hundred feet offshore. Presently a rowboat containing the three muffled figures and a man sculling put out. The small boat bumped against the fishing smack as its sail was being raised; three figures climbed aboard. A few whispered words of French and a few of English floated across the misty water. A little leather pouch that clinked changed hands. The sail caught a breath of wind and turned towards the Cliffs of Dover.

The twenty-two-year-old Comtesse de la Tour-Vérrière, her aunt, Mme. de Courbonne, and a woman servant were embarking upon a new life, or so they hoped, escaping after two years of hiding in farmhouses and caves. They had managed to flee, with only the clothes they stood in, from the abattoir that Paris had become. Every day, through an iron grating high in the wall of the cellar in which they hid, they had heard the crunch of tumbril wheels on the bloody December snow, the roll of the death-warning tambour, and the shrieks of wretched victims being pushed to their knees on the guillotine, which had been set up near the comtesse's hiding place. This sustained nightmare over, the comtesse hoped to join a small colony of émigrés living near Kensington Palace in London.

For a few hours all went well. The fog was intermittent, clearing and descending again at intervals. The three women broke a loaf of bread and uncorked a liter of rather sour wine. Mme. de Courbonne, refreshed, settled herself in the stern for a nap.

In the middle of the afternoon, banks of black thunderheads came riding out of the northeast, followed by a raging wind. In the space of minutes, enormous waves were running, nearly swamping the small boat. The boatman tried desperately to keep the rudder set in a line for the Dover coast, but, alas, a mountainous wave hit the fishing boat amidships and it plunged down, down into a trough of the waves.

The boatman, Mme. de Courbonne, and the servant were never seen again, but

Adèle de la Tour-Vérrière managed to catch a wooden planking that had been across the bottom of the boat. To this she clung for hours.

The storm abated as quickly as it had come. Sun broke through the clouds. The sea gradually lessened its fury. As night came on, the comtesse was seen by a trawler beating its way to Ireland. She was taken aboard, and in two days she stepped ashore, an exhausted, water-stained figure.

Dublin was radiant in the summer sunshine. It welcomed Adèle de la Tour-Vérrière as only Dublin can.

A few French aristocrats fleeing from the Terror had come to Ireland over a period of three years. Some had relatives in County Wicklow and County Clare, where French names persist. The comtesse found friends in Dublin who asked her to stop with them. It was not long before she was earning a modest living teaching music (she was an accomplished violinist), embroidering, and sewing. People for whom she sewed said she took the tiniest stitches they had ever seen. She had, as well, a true French touch with a bonnet and ribbons and the set of a pannier. It looked as if the outrageous fortunes of Comtesse de la Tour-Vérrière had taken a turn for the better. And so they had.

To describe Adèle de la Tour-Vérrière as she was at the time of her arrival in Dublin, one must use two words which appear constantly in two chronicles of the period, Lady Clancarty's *Memoirs* and Mrs. Delany's *Journal*. The words are "exquisite" and "fragile."

Two portraits at Moyvore, one a head, the other full length, sitting, show a young woman so delicately built as to appear like a child of fourteen. Her hair, unpowdered in both pictures, is ash-gold, a nimbus of light framing her heart-shaped face. Deep violet eyes look out at you with humor and determination, which is repeated strongly in her beautifully modeled mouth. By any criterion, Adèle de la Tour-Vérrière was a most lovely woman.

Female beauty and wit were vastly appreciated in Dublin, and the bucks at balls and routs at Dublin Castle and in the big town houses in Merrion Square and St. Stephan's Green welcomed the comtesse eagerly.

One night a ball was in progress at Dublin Castle. The "rank and style" milling through the white and crystal rooms was brilliant. Most brilliant of all, many said, was Comtesse de la Tour-Vérrière. In a spreading pannier of spring-green watered silk, under a full-cut cape of cherry satin, the comtesse filled the eye.

She certainly filled the eye of a big-boned, hearty squire from the County Meath, one Ranley Fitz-Martin, who had left his horses, his dogs, and his red-faced, strapping wife at Moyvore on the Boyne Water to regale himself for a few days in Dublin.

Human relations are a puzzle as old as time. What it is in human chemistry that causes two people, as opposite as the poles,in every visible sense, to meet, to be struck by a species of forked lightning called "love," and to devote their entire lives, their every thought to each other until "death do them part" is a secret that will probably accompany the secret of the Sphinx into limbo.

Ranley Fitz-Martin met Adèle de la Tour-Vérrière on the staircase at Dublin Castle, he, just arriving, she, just leaving. He spoke to her without waiting to be presented. Receiving no rebuff, he left with her, not even bothering to present his compliments to his hosts.

For weeks, Fitz-Martin did not even think of Moyvore, much less have any urge to return. He basked as only a man deeply in love and completely bewildered by it can bask in a woman's love, to the point of completely losing his identity. Adèle de la Tour-Vérrière, a French woman, was as deeply moved as Ranley. The days in Dublin sped by.

A lovely, sunny summer was Ireland's share that year of 1791. Many excursions were taken into the Wicklow Mountains and along the sea in County Down. One day the pair had picnicked at Drogheda; after lunch, as they lay high above the sea, Ranley asked Adèle to tell him a little about her life in France before she came to Dublin. Adèle was silent a long time. Thinking her asleep, he asked her again.

"I don't like to think about it," she replied. "The days of the Terror are like slashes made by a knife across my brain. I will tell you this only, so that you will at least know who I am. I was born at Chateau des Trois-Tours, near the village of Gisors. The Chateau is between Gisors and Les Andelays, in Normandy. My grandfather's estates, from which we take our name Vérrière, are in the Ardennes.

"It was an uneventful childhood—visiting relatives at their various chateaux, learning deportment from my aunt, Mme. de Courbonne, dancing from an itinerant master, and the art of sewing from my practical grandmother. The Ardennese are very accomplished housewives. I always loved music, and the curé at Gisors had studied at Montpelier Conservatoire. I learned much from him.

"At eighteen I was sent to Versailles with Mme. de Courbonne as *dame de compagnie*. Unrest was everywhere when we arrived, Marie Antoinette was ridiculed openly, her coach stoned in the streets of Paris. No, I don't want to say any more. I arrived in Dublin, penniless and alone—now here we are."

Their idyl could not go on forever; they both knew that. Demands from Mrs. Fitz-Martin were increasing. When, she wished to know by returning courier, was her husband coming back to Moyvore?

A day was set for Ranley's departure from Dublin, when Adèle de la Tour-

Vérrière made a startling suggestion: she wished to return with him and live her life at Moyvore. Then they could always be together. Ranley told her nothing on earth would delight him more if it were possible. But it was not. What was he to do about a very-much-alive wife, and four children?

She had a ready answer for that one, too. She would enter his household as a seamstress. She could live in the attics. In describing Moyvore to her, he had told her how generously proportioned the house was; built for the comfort of a large family (he was one of nine children). Surely space could be allotted her.

Ranley threw back his head and roared with laughter. So the talk of the Dublin season, the ravishing Comtesse de la Tour-Vérrière, was to live under the tiles at Moyvore, where he could visit her at night! And how long did she think that would last before scandal swept across the Plains of Meath like a conflagration?

Adèle finally convinced him, however, because she had thought out the whole scheme so carefully and her facile mind matched her determination. He gave in, although a bit fearfully, he admitted. He placed his future in her hands.

With a good deal of fanfare, the Fitz-Martin cavalcade left Dublin. A rather un-wieldy road coach, black, with vermilion wheels, and door panels which displayed the Fitz-Martin arms in gold, swayed drunkenly along the rutted, muddy roads. Four strong-quartered Spanish barbs had all they could do to keep the coach moving.

Ranley and a friend, Sir Calem Barstow, rode in the coach. Following in its wake was a four-wheeled brake, piled high with luggage and presents from Dublin for all the Fitz-Martins. Sitting beside the driver was a small, neatly dressed woman, her dark-brown hair nearly hidden under a high blue mobcap. She was pale, and wore pewter-rimmed spectacles, for her eyes were a trifle weak from sewing. She clutched a small, leather-bound portmanteau. This was the new French seamstress for Moyvore.

Mrs. Fitz-Martin was delighted beyond measure. She was not a whit interested in details. At last, breeches and stockings would be mended. Her own dresses, in a sadly tattered state, would receive attention. The servants at Moyvore were unruly. She had no talent for managing an establishment like this great house.

The quiet little seamstress retired immediately to her rooms in the attics, where two had been set aside for her. They were most charming rooms, comfortably fur-nished, and with a really superb view of the spreading reaches of the romantic River Boyne, flower-strewn Meath, and, in the distance, the first rise of the Dublin Moun-tains. One room, the larger, was fitted as a sitting and sewing room.

The seasons changed. The years passed. The family Fitz-Martin were very well looked after; even breeches for Ranley and the two lumbering boys were kept in trim. Mrs. Fitz-Martin and the girls wore the most beautiful fichus ever seen in Ireland.

Embroidered satin aprons, completely ornamental vanities, became the rage. No one appearing at the Dublin routs had such original aprons as Joanna Fitz-Martin, who sometimes went up to Dublin for a fortnight.

The comtesse, realizing that her sudden disappearance from Dublin at the height of a brilliant social season would be remarked, had had word sent out the day of her departure that she had left for London by the night packet boat, hoping to go to America as a governess. The name on her papers of identity (the one she used until the day of her death) was Mlle. Déprés. Any details of her life she firmly refused to discuss.

Swiftly the years passed at Moyvore. The children grew up. The house was always full to overflowing with guests. Hunting with the Meath brought out large fields. Frequently, during a season, the meet was held in the sweeping, graveled coach yard in front of the portico of the huge white house. Christmas was always very gala at Moyvore, for that was the one day of the year when Mlle. Déprés came into the drawing room of the house. She would help garland the great high-ceilinged rooms with spruce and bayberry boughs. Wreaths of holly and dark-red bog oak hung from crystal chandeliers. The Fitz-Martin children loved Mlle. Déprés. They ran to her in the attic rooms all during their growing-up period. She eased their sorrows, she shared their joys.

Twice during the fourteen years that the enchanting Comtesse de la Tour-Vérrière, bespectacled and bewigged, lived at Moyvore, she went away for a few weeks, once to England to take the waters, once for three months to France. France under Napoleon she had not liked, and was very glad to return to Ireland.

On her return from the Continent, she arrived just in time for the wedding of young Joanna Fitz-Martin to a young cavalry officer from Dublin named Farley. The night before the wedding, Joanna had come to have a last long talk with her adored Mlle. Déprés. She had told her of the big house she would have in County Wicklow.

After Joanna had gone, Adèle de la Tour-Vérrière sat quietly by the window looking away to the Dublin Mountains. What a strange life hers had been, she thought, ever since the day twelve years ago when she had arrived, like a half-drowned rat, in Dublin. Her every thought had been given to Ranley Fitz-Martin since the first moment she saw him. Then, in disguise, she had come to Moyvore, and established herself as his mistress and seamstress to the family Fitz-Martin.

Well, no one had suffered by her living a lie. Quite the reverse. Ranley was assuredly the happiest man in Ireland, and the whole family adored her. Still, it was a strange life for a woman born of the *ancien régime* of France. The one thing she had missed was a house of her own; that, she realized, was always in the back of her mind. Inborn in her was the love of possessions. She had been born and raised in a splendid house. She liked the tending of a house. She loved Moyvore, but it was not hers.

A fit of coughing seized her, something which happened increasingly of late. The mists drifting up from the river after nightfall were bad for her lungs. She knew it, but there was little she could do.

Two years passed. Joanna had her first baby, a huge, red-headed boy, very like his grandfather Ranley. Adèle was coughing more and more, and her chest hurt her now. One night when Ranley had come to her, he found her ill and feverish. Terror stricken, he sent for a doctor to ride over from Moyvalley. The doctor pronounced her condition lung fever, and advised a change of scene, a dry climate, the mountains of Mlle. Déprés' native France, if possible. But it was too late.

On a cold morning in early March, Comtesse Adèle de la Tour-Vérrière, alias Marguérite Déprés, died high up under the tiles of the great Palladian house of Moyvore. The last things she saw were the shell-pink bed curtains of finest Irish linen which she herself had embroidered over a period of fourteen years. In white silk thread she had embroidered field flowers, both Irish and French, birds, butterflies, and a repeated design, a chateau with three towers. A few weeks before, she had embroidered the date of her birth and her age:

Année 1827. Agé 36.

The grief at Moyvore was very great. It swept like a storm from the kitchen quarters into every room in the house. Ranley Fitz-Martin was lost and desolate.

As she had wished, Mlle. Déprés was buried in the family plot, on a slight rise of ground, in a grove of alder trees. A simple white-marble shaft marked her grave.

One day in 1860 a small, agile boy was flying a kite along the banks of the River Boyne near the gates of Moyvore. The Plains of Meath are the answer to every small boy's prayer for this sport. Wide spaces of grassy meadow land, few trees, except around houses, and long, flat runs afford a terrain perfect for kite flying. The big paper birds soar the like of eagles at the end of a lanyard.

There was a terrific pull of wind, and young Patrick Fitz-Martin lost hold of his kite, which wheeled up and away to come finally to rest with its long cord entwined around one of the many chimneys of Moyvore.

The boy raced into the house and up the stairs to the attics. Opening a door, he went through a room that was once used, so he had heard, for a sewing room when the French seamstress who lived at Moyvore was alive. He knew there was a trap door letting onto the roof near the chimney where his kite was caught.

As the boy started to climb up the rafters along the sloping roof, he stopped. In front of the window sat a small woman wrapped in a white shawl. She seemed to be sewing. The figure was rather dim, for the light was poor. The boy spoke a greeting and climbed through the hatch out onto the roof. He reclaimed his kite and returned the same way he had come. On his way down the inside of the roof, the boy noticed something glinting, a sort of shiny box pushed down behind the rafters. He had not noticed it on his upward climb. Taking it down with him, he turned to ask the woman by the window if it was hers. The woman was gone.

When this cedarwood box, bound in silver, was opened by his mother, it was found to contain the lovely painting on ivory of the Comtesse de la Tour-Vérrière which hangs in the drawing room at Moyvore today. It also contained a small packet of letters tied with silver and violet cord.

One of these letters throws light on a question long in dispute. It reads in part:

". . . and my darling Ranley, he is the image of you. Such a strong baby. He is two months old now. I despair at leaving him, but it means coming back to you, and Mme. Colomb will watch over him probably better than I would, who wish to tend no one but you."

This letter was written from Mont St. Michel; the year is 1814.

For a number of years after the death of the comtesse, nothing had happened to show that she visited Moyvore. Then a parlormaid came down from the attics one day and said that she had seen a woman making the bed in the "old Mademoiselle's room." She thought that was strange, for the bed had been turned out for years. After that, no one saw her, nor was there any evidence of her presence, until the day that young Patrick retrieved his kite.

Along about 1890, she began to appear with regularity, always at night. She disturbed no one, simply tended the great house of Moyvore as its chatelaine—something she could never do while she lived.

A small footstool, badly chewed by hound puppies, was covered during the night with an amazingly fine piece of *petit point*, very evidently the work of Adèle de la Tour-Vérrière. A primrose damask curtain in the music room, rent by a spur after a hunt and carelessly hidden from view, was mended with almost impossibly fine stitches. The hearth was swept, a thing seldom done by servants at Moyvore. Withered flowers were removed from vases and fresh flowers added. A large hall clock that had not run for years was oiled and put in perfect running order. Music in the cabinet in the music room was sorted. The violin was polished and showed signs of having been played, though no one reports hearing it. Most important of all is the episode of the painting in oils, a full length, mentioned before in this narrative.

One morning, among the post lying on a salver on the breakfast tray, was a letter addressed simply to Moyvore. It was a large, square piece of paper, folded four times, sealed with rose-colored wax, and stamped with a device of three towers. In the corner, where a stamp should be, if the letter had traveled by post, there was none. Written in violet ink were the words, *N'oubliez pas.*

This happened in 1909. The letter not only showed visual evidence of ancient vintage, but exhaled a pungent, musty odor. Mrs. Gaisford, the grandmother of the Patrick Gaisford who told me this story, was living at Moyvore then. She opened the letter, which read:

"Send to Paris, 22 Rue des Petits Champs, for my portrait. Hang it in the room that used to be occupied by Ranley Fitz-Martin. This is my wish,

Adèle de la Tour-Vérrière."

A member of the Gaisford-Fitz-Martin family went to Paris and sought out the address in Rue des Petits Champs. It proved to be a small bookshop. A Mme. Sautier listened carefully and read the letter, but seemed unimpressed. She nodded, however, and disappeared into the back of the dim shop, returning with a parcel about twenty inches square. It was wrapped in dingy canvas, corded, and sealed with rose-colored wax. A device of three towers was stamped on the wax wafers. As Mr. Gaisford took the parcel, he asked the woman, "When was this left, and by whom?"

She replied, "I do not know. It has been waiting here as long as I can remember."

The shop, he learned, dated from long before the French Revolution.

The Drums of Rathmoy

Rathmoy House

C O U N T Y   S L I G O

RATHMOY HOUSE

The Drums of Rathmoy

STANDING PROUD AND FOURSQUARE, BRACING its bulk against the continuous onslaught of Atlantic gales, stands Rathmoy House. Riding out the years in shuttered silence, for the most part, it is lived in, by members of the Tully family, only one or two months of the year, but not every year. Five or six years may elapse between tenants.

Every once in a while, a lorry, loaded high with bags and boxes, will come out of the east, drive gingerly along the Sea Wall Road, which is very slippery from waves breaking over the retaining wall, and turn in at the keeper-guarded gates. That night lights will be seen moving about inside the huge rooms. Windows blank and long shuttered are opened to the salt breezes. The fishermen from Ardnareel, setting out for the night's catch, will call, one to the other, "Arragh, the great house is alive again. I wonder how long it will be this time before the Drums drive this lot back to where they hail from?"

An answering call will float back across the water, "Great cowards they all are, the lot of them. The old house has lived on its lone too long to want intruders. It'll let 'em know soon enough they're not wanted." It has been proved many times that this unknown voice is right—Rathmoy does not want intruders, whether they be rightful owners or not.

Rathmoy, as it stands today, is a Palladian gesture in architecture, very much on the grand scale. Its history, however, is ancient. Documents in the library in the old city of Sligo tell you it was at one time a "fortified house of renown." It comprised two outer baileys, a keep and dwelling house, two towers, and quarterings for foot soldiers and a "troup of horse" to the number of one thousand.

Later, Rathmoy was abandoned for a time, thirty years, some say. A smaller house was built for the O'Duvenay heiress upon her marriage to Dennis Tully. This was a case where the O'Duvenay dowry, which amounted to a considerable fortune, was instantly put to use in reclaiming Rathmoy from the derelict state into which it had fallen under the improvident and impoverished Tullys.

All this occurred just before Oliver Cromwell sailed along the west coast of

Ireland, sending small scouting parties ashore wherever he sighted a castle or great house standing in its wooded demesne. If the owners of these lonely houses refused to surrender immediately, and most of them did refuse, Cromwell ordered his ships to anchor off shore. Gunners then found the range and reduced each house in question to a heap of ruins. Some houses escaped, but many were so shattered that nothing now remains save turf-grown mounds of stone. Rathmoy House is one that escaped, owing it is said, to the warning of the Drums.

The story of The Drums of Rathmoy and how they aided in protecting the house from obliteration is a tale pregnant with treachery and ghostly doings. Castle Slyne, jutting on its rocky promontory at Slyne Head farther down the coast, was not so fortunate. Unhappy Loughrana Keep was reduced to a smoldering pyre, and under its flame-riven walls, the entire family of Malloy perished.

When word first reached the people of Connaught, Galway, and Sligo that the British invader, Oliver Cromwell, was approaching by slow but deadly stages along the seacoast, they feared, but not too much. They had long expected such a move. They had prepared and were ready. Messengers raced along the old Sea Wall Road spreading news of the oncoming Roundheads.

Burning all before him, Cromwell lay waste the land, from Cork to Liscannor, from Lahinch to Hags Head and Ballyvaughn. After the sacking of Ballyvaughn, the Irish showed their waiting hand. They set up drums along the coast from Blackough to the bleak, walled town of Dumkineely in County Donegal.

These drums were made from huge boiling pots used by the kelp gatherers in the process of extracting iodine from seaweed, an ancient industry which flourishes along the west coast of Ireland. Iodine was called "poor man's gold," for the simple reason that he had only to gather it from the abundant sea, extract the healing fluid at no cost to himself, and sell it to a world-wide market. An answer often heard in County Galway to the question of how one fares, well or ill, is, "I live well the day, thanks to God, the sea, and the boiling pot."

Tyrone oxen were slain, their huge hides roughly cured and stretched across the mouths of the iron pots. The massive thigh bones of the oxen were used as drumsticks. A blow swung against the tautly drawn hide by this bone baton reverberated for miles as a warning and a challenge.

Drums were placed a mile apart. Villages were fairly well populated in those days. Many of them were still walled—"The Walled Towns beyond the Pale." In the early days of the sixteenth century, Connaught was still a kingdom. It comprised all of Galway and was in every sense "beyond the Pale." Connaught was never conquered by the British.

Bands of fishermen, prophets of wind and weather, were counted out in pairs to man the drums. The moment word was brought to each pair that the invader approached, the drum was beaten. As the sharp roll call mounted on the wind, the entire countryside roused to action. Yet the Irish knew full well they had no means with which to combat the cannon on Cromwell's ships lying ever-ready off shore.

One thing that the Irish counted on in their favor, however, was the fact that, after Ballyvaughn, the coastline suddenly became a natural fortress of rocks. There were few bays where a landing party could hope to gain a foothold. The Irish knew each bay; they would be waiting.

The weapons of these countrymen were crude and makeshift, but the fanatical love of their land gave them courage and prodigious strength. It is the eternal trait of the Irish to be able to extricate themselves from a tight place. This time, they were aided by the "gods of wind and weather."

After the plundering of Ballyvaughn, an epic in the ruthless warfare of Oliver Cromwell, the heavens poured down their wrath in a deluge of water. For days the Atlantic, driven by a howling nor'easter, was churned into a living monster. Great waves tore at the hulls of Cromwell's ships. Sails and rigging were ripped loose, and, caught by the tempest, were blown inshore as far as Lisdoonvarna Abbey, ten miles inland in County Clare, where nuns of the order of Poor Clares used the salvaged rope for their Bells of Piety for many years.

We learn that six of Cromwell's ships were sunk and that three others, driven on the rocks off Doonlicka and as far west as the Mullet in County Sligo, broke up on the jagged shale and were abandoned.

It is this story of abandoned ships which bears out the persistent rumor that Rathmoy houses the ghosts of enemy sailors, who were admitted according to plan by a traitor, or, as this class of gentry is called in Ireland, an informer. According to this rumor, it appears the informer, a servant in the house, hoped for gain. But the failure of Cromwell's plans to subjugate the West of Ireland spiked the plans of all traitors.

The week of brutal weather took so large toll among Cromwell's ships and men and did so much damage that the strategy of the entire campaign of the west coast was shattered. It is true, as the gaunt ivy-grown ruins rising like exclamation points along a hundred miles of coast line still show, that Cromwell somehow rallied the remains of his marauding fleet and sailed as far west as The Bloody Foreland off Donegal. But the powder magazines on board his remaining ships, not more than eight in all, had taken such a wetting during the stormy week after Ballyvaughn that, after a few halfhearted attempts to demolish selected targets from off shore failed, the tenacious Roundhead general gave up the fight. Continued rough seas, which threw his gunners hopelessly off range, and lack of men, ships, and ammunition had thwarted his plans utterly.

The drums of iron and oxhide set up along the coast never after came into play to any great extent. They were left in place for a few years lest "The Invader," as the British were always called by the people of Connaught, make another attempt to land. But, save for a few false alarms, when a drum rolled out its warning at dawn or dusk and it was discovered that some overzealous fisherboy had mistaken a clutch of Aran or Clare Island trawlers for an invading fleet, the drums fell into disuse, or were reclaimed by their owners for the boiling of kelp.

In the minds of the west-coast fishermen and farmers living along the Sea Wall Road, however, the reverberating roll of the drums is kept alive by the waves pounding into the many air holes and subterranean caves that honeycomb the rocky headlands from St. Finan's Bay and The Seven Hogs, off the Kingdom of Kerry, all the way to The Bloody Foreland. To many of the inhabitants of this part of Ireland, the dull beat of Atlantic rollers in the caves is a sign and a portent to be ever on the alert, lest "The Invader" spring a surprise. Each lashing storm is an anniversary of the rape of Ballyvaughn.

According to the history of Rathmoy House, one of the last broadsides fired from Cromwell's flagship, the Albion, struck the northmost tower of the keep of Rathmoy. The stonework, old and dry-laid, had been weakened by centuries of Atlantic gales and neglect. It crumbled, bringing down the outer wall of the keep for hundreds of feet. In this state Rathmoy was allowed to remain until the eldest daughter of the O'Duvenay-Tully union built the great Palladian house of Rathmoy as it is today. Lady Elizabeth Tully, as she chose to call herself (though she had married a man named Park from Dundalk, in the County Louth), was by all accounts a woman of iron will, great determination, and a ribald wit. Immediately Lady Elizabeth took possession, buildings sprang up to the right and to the left of her. This frenzy for building she inherited from her Clanricarde grandfather, who almost singlehanded rebuilt the pillaged town of Ballyvaughn after the burning by Cromwell's men.

The rocky promontory from which rise the foundations of Rathmoy is a veritable rabbit warren of caves and blowholes. When the sea is runing high, the crash and boom-boom-boom of the angry waves can be heard for miles up and down the coast.

On nights like these, and the dark coming on fast, shawled women and bearded Sligo men, with a string of glistening fish thrown over their shoulder, pass on the Sea Wall Road, nod a greeting, and say, "The Drums of Rathmoy are up tonight in all their wrath." Then, nodding in the direction of Rathmoy House, looming dark and remote against the cloud-wrack, they add, "Faith and I'd not stay the night in the

old house for all the gold minted in Dublin. The ghost'll be abroad this night, bumpin'
the coffin on the stairs."

The ghostly funeral procession was first heard during Lady Elizabeth's rule over
the demesne of Rathmoy, somewhere about 1764. Actually this procession is thought
by many to date from the Cromwellian siege and the last week of storms that caused
the cessation of his carefully laid plans to conquer the people of Connaught and lay
waste their coast line.

At the time mentioned, there lived at Rathmoy, as kind of caretaker, a cadaverous,
withdrawn individual named McMurty. His Christian name and many facts about
him are lost in the mists of time. They do not matter, but what he is responsible for
does, and that is to be found in the annals of Rathmoy.

McMurty was often seen at night pushing a small black curragh off the beach,
which was only an arc of sand at the foot of the sheer rise of rock on which Rathmoy
stands. He was always alone, he never fished, and his return from these nocturnal
wanderings was so late that no one ever saw him, except for one morning when, a few
days before the sacking of Ballyvaughn, a fisherboy, caught out in the lee of Inishmurray Island by a squall, was very late returning. For the last mile he had rowed
almost abreast of a man in a curragh. It was not until the man pulled into the little
beach underneath Rathmoy that the boy realized who it was. "So! McMurty is a very
late returner," he thought.

The tall, dark McMurty never mingled with the village people at Ardnareel. They
in turn thought him "a dry auld stick," and let it rest there.

The night of the terrible storm, when two ships of Cromwell's fleet were washed
up on the Mullet, some men escaped in the morning. Many were captured during the
day, but one or two were seen to escape into the glens of Nephin Beg, where they
probably starved or were devoured by the savage gray wolves which in those days
infested the Beg. Two others, however, were seen by a farmer to run to the closed
gates of Rathmoy House. After beating on the gates a short while, they were admitted
by the devious McMurty.

Later, farmer Killarn, a respected man from over back of Balcorrick, swore on a
stack of Bibles to what he had seen, which was this:

He was driving along the Sea Wall Road about nine o'clock the morning after the
big blow. It was still raining and a bit of mist about, the class of fog that blows in
great veils across the road, and as suddenly blows away out to sea.

During one of these clear stretches, when he was just in front the big iron gates of
Rathmoy, two men, not Irish surely, staggered along the road. One, the taller of the
two, seemed to be supporting the smaller man, who was matted with blood from head

to foot. His head hanging down, he walked with the halt of a foundering horse.

The tall man picked up a rock lying in the road and beat with it upon one of the iron grilles of the gate. It made a loud clanging sound, and in a minute dour old Mc-Murty had come running to open the gate, himself all wrapped up in a dark ulster. He admitted the two men, who seemed to know him—certainly they had no fear of him, as any Cromwell man would have of an Irishman he did not know.

Just then the veils of thick fog blew in again, blotting out the rest of the picture. Farmer Killarn whipped up his little ass and drove straight to the bailiff at Ardnareel.

About noon the bailiff appeared at Rathmoy House, accompanied by four well-armed stalwarts from the town. For a long while they claimed admittance. Finally, after he had successfully hidden his visitors, McMurty, still wrapped in his volumi-nous ulster, grudgingly admitted the bailiff. McMurty protested every step of the way, but to deaf ears. The bailiff and his men entered under the towering archway into the inner bailey of Rathmoy. All that afternoon and far into the night the five men from Ardnareel searched the winding passages and vaulted rooms of grim Rathmoy Keep, followed by a muttering McMurty. They found nothing but some spots, the remains of hastily wiped-up blood on one of the narrow stairways leading down into the dun-geons under the keep. McMurty explained this by saying he had killed a pig that morning, one which he had kept in the dungeon while fattening on milk and grain. No one believed him, but it was let rest.

When questioned by Lentooley, the bailiff, about his midnight sea journeys alone in a sailing curragh, not returning until dawn cracked the east, the man denied every-thing. He said it was a rough slander against him. Only once had he gone out in the curragh, and then it was for a night's trawling.

For weeks the gates of Rathmoy were carefully guarded. Except for the cannon ball from the Albion leveling the north tower, which, in the light of later develop-ments, was considered to have been a chance or random shot not intended for Rath-moy (whose caretaker had purchased its immunity at a heavy price), all was quiet within the iron grilles straddling the causeway.

After the storms that had saved Connaught from the British had subsided, the weather was fair and calm for weeks. Now and again the drums were beaten by village boys at dusk, just to keep their hand in. Men returned to the harvest. Soon the Invader was forgotten. At least he was laid away in the back of men's minds.

Though Lentooley questioned McMurty many times, his shifty eyes gazed far out to sea, and he divulged nothing which could be used against him. Hide nor hair was seen of the two men he was alleged to have admitted to Rathmoy House. The whole affair died a natural death from lack of interest.

About six weeks after farmer Killarn told of having seen two men hustled inside the gates of Rathmoy by McMurty, a wretched, half-starved man, scratched and torn by briers until he was swollen almost beyond endurance, staggered into the cow byre of a farmer near Glinora, a clutch of houses a few miles in the back country. He was palpably in dying condition. Although he was given food and a salve was rubbed into his wounds to help ease the excruciating pain, he died before nightfall. Before he died, the farmer and his wife were able to piece together some of the hysterical words he seemed possessed to tell them.

The man had been first mate on the Canterbury, second ship of the line in the Cromwellian fleet. Night after night, during fair weather, before the destruction of Ballyvaughn, they had anchored far out, off the coast of Sligo. Each night, after midnight, a tall man, whose name he had caught as McMurty, had come out alone in a little sailing curragh. Coming aboard, the man had been taken directly to the cabin of the captain of the Canterbury.

For hours, the men talked. One night, creeping up and peering through the hatch, he had seen three men, the captain, McMurty, and one of the ship's officers, poring over a map spread out on a table. Obviously, McMurty was a traitor giving secrets of where landing parties might gain a foothold. He also heard McMurty offering the great house of Rathmoy to the British as a fort.

The dying man, whose mother was Irish, hoped he could thus help her people. It was too late, but his dying words were welcome. This information would trap McMurty.

When Lentooley and his men sought entrance to Rathmoy the second time, they found it barricaded. As McMurty was without food, he soon gave up, but in a curious way. Late on the third night, he was seen to leave his hiding place, run crouching along one of the battlements, and leap off onto a roof running parallel a few feet beneath. He disappeared from sight as a wild shriek rent the air, and was never seen again.

Search was made. Nothing of McMurty or the two men who had disappeared months ago was ever found. Years passed. Then Lady Elizabeth took possession and things began to fly.

Italian architects, workers in stucco, upholsterers and cabinet finishers brought to Dublin by Lord Leinster to build and decorate his magnificent Leinster house in the city on the Liffey, and Carton, of three hundred and sixty-five rooms at Maynooth in the springy-turfed County of Kildare, were engaged by Lady Elizabeth to build for her a splendid country house on the foundations of Rathmoy Keep. She loved the wild sweep of the Atlantic spread out before her on three sides. The sunsets along this dramatic stretch of coast are the finest in Ireland, surely, and the air is a renowned tonic. That there is not a tree or bush in sight of Rathmoy mattered not a whit to Lady Elizabeth. If she wanted verdure, she had only to drive three miles inland to one of her numerous farms, and there a perfect eden of greenery prevailed.

Richard Castle, a young Saxon architect, deeply under the influence of Palladio, had designed Carton and Russborough, two of the most splendid of Irish country houses. Lady Elizabeth engaged him to lay out a small village in the classic style. It was to be built a mile from the gates of Rathmoy. The village was to rival Blessington, which had been laid out near Russborough. Lady Elizabeth planned to call it Templetully.

After the enormous cost of building Rathmoy House was met, there was not enough money in the Tully exchequer to finance the building of the village, so for a time the idea was shelved. Meanwhile, things began to happen at Rathmoy which deeply upset its owner.

Night after night the boom-boom-booming of "The Drums" continued, but Lady Elizabeth was of too strong will to give in to a sound which she considered perfectly natural, if one elected to live on a rocky promontory over a nest of blowholes. The oxhide drums to warn against invaders were silent now, she thanked God. But these resounding blowholes would outlast time itself. What really unsettled Lady Elizabeth mightily were cries of anguish coming from the court where the old battlements had stood. Sometimes for an hour or more the most nerve-rending sobbing of a man in mortal agony would rise to ear-splitting crescendo, then die away on the night air.

The ghostly visitation, which came to be known as "The Funeral Procession," first occurred a year or more after Lady Elizabeth had installed herself and some twenty house servants at Rathmoy. She liked to have people of wit and imagination around her, so she planned to entertain extensively.

A large ballroom, painted apple-green and picked out in gold and white, occupied the entire second floor of the south wing. A floor of pearwood was laid in a design of intertwined, five-pointed stars. This was waxed a golden yellow. All was ready for the housewarming of Rathmoy House.

The night before she was to hold her first party to welcome friends to her domicile, Lady Elizabeth sat long at her desk in her sitting room going over last details. Finishing around midnight, she closed the desk, blew out a branch of candles, took a single candle from a table in the entrance hall, and started up the wide staircase to her bedroom. Halfway up the stairs, a sliding noise seemed to come from somewhere in the shadows above. She looked up, puzzled. A heavy object slid past her on the stairs.

Something she could not see knocked her nearly off her feet. The candle she carried fell from her hand, leaving her in total darkness. A chill, as of the grave, rose up all about her.

Now Lady Elizabeth, as has been said, was a woman of strong mind. She just did not scare easily. But this trick on the stairs so unnerved her that she called out loudly for help, forgetting she had sent the servants to their beds early. She called in vain. Not a soul answered her. Becoming a little panicky, she clutched at the wall behind her, hoping that, by clinging as closely as possible to the wall, she might escape touching whatever this ghastly presence was.

Slowly Lady Elizabeth started to climb the stairs, when again she heard the strange sliding sound, only this time it was accompanied by a bump-bump-bump and heavy breathing, as if someone very near exhaustion was trying to lift a heavy box or casket up the stairs. She stood still, really terrified. But the strange invisible crew—for as she listened it seemed as if there were more than one person—went laboriously past her. The cold air swept across her face, and she slipped to the floor in a dead faint.

How long she lay there, she never quite knew, but a serving maid, up and about earlier than the rest, found her mistress about dawn, huddled on the stairs, shivering with a chill. Lady Elizabeth was ill for many days. Finally, when she could sit out on the terrace, she asked various people from Ardnareel to come to Rathmoy and help her, if they could, to find rhyme or reason for this diabolical presence which seemed to inhabit the house.

One very old man said that when he was a boy, he had worked at the old keep, when Mr. Philbin Tully lived there, but he had not stayed long. A wall had fallen in after a terrible winter storm, and in the thickness of the wall a small room was found. In the room were two roughly made coffins, a small table, and a chair. A stub of candle that had guttered in its own wax was stuck into a bottle. The bottle was from Holland, one of the kind used for Holland gin, so much fancied by British sailors, but seldom seen in Ireland.

In one of the coffins was the skeleton of a man, and thrown in a corner was the partial skeleton of another man; as he remembered, no more of it was found. Dried filth littered the place. Mr. Tully had had the tiny stone chamber cleaned and walled up, after burning all that was found in it. So, Lady Elizabeth considered, this was the strange procession she had confronted on its way down the stairs of Rathmoy. Where were they headed? Why did the procession return? She hoped she had witnessed it for the last time.

But this was only the beginning. Over a period of three years, Lady Elizabeth or

273

members of her family saw and were drawn into "The Funeral Procession" at Rathmoy House five different times—the last two times with such dire results that she concluded that the house was too dangerous to be tenantable.

The first of the nearly fatal manifestations occurred on a starry night in May. A garden party had been held in the sunken gardens overlooking the sea. Many guests had departed, but a Miss Caraway from Galway Old City had stayed on for a little music. Later her coach had been announced. She started upstairs to get her bonnet and manteau, when what seemed to her like a cold hand slid down the wall to where she stood, grabbed her by the throat, and choked her. She tried to scream, but in her terror lost all power to make a sound. She fainted and, losing her balance, fell headlong down the stairs. Lady Elizabeth, who was in the hall, turned and saw her. At the same time she heard a sound she well knew, and dreaded—bump-bump-bump—and felt a blast of cold air wipe across her face. Fortunately, Miss Caraway had mounted only a few steps of the stairs, so no bones were broken when she fell. But the shock was acute. She was put to bed in Lady Elizabeth's own room, where she remained for days.

A year later to a day, on just such a May evening of soft breeze and millions of stars, Lady Elizabeth was mounting the stairs at half past ten o'clock, planning to retire. As she reached the top of the stairs, the horrible, gurgling shriek of a man, which she had heard when first she moved into the new Rathmoy, rang out from the direction of the courtyard at the back of the house. Before Lady Elizabeth could step onto the gallery landing, the sliding sound started. It sounded louder tonight, as if the burden was heavier; then the blast of cold air descended with such overpowering force that she was chilled to the bone. A giant hand seemed to materialize from nowhere, pushing her back until it seemed her spine would snap. As she felt herself losing her footing, she had presence of mind enough to clutch the spindles of the balustrade, saving herself from a plunge backward down the full flight of stairs, which would surely have cost her life.

The good fortune which attended Lady Elizabeth on the stairs nearly forsook her as she lay on her bed wracked with chills and fever, sinking, at times, into a terrible abyss of delirium, when she tried to ward off the clammy hand she protested was crushing the life out of her.

One night when Dr. Connoly, Lady Elizabeth's physician, was standing at the door of her bedchamber on the gallery, he heard a scraping sound, then the bump-bump-bump, but as he was not on the stairs, nothing more happened to him, although he felt a distinct chill pervade the place. That settled it, he said. His patient must not stay in this house any longer, for nightly she exposed herself to a danger all the more horrible for being unseen.

A week later, Lady Elizabeth Tully packed her belongings, closed the great house of Rathmoy, so gleaming white on its rock, and went to Dublin to live. She never again returned to Rathmoy.

Every few years a tenant, either in ignorance or to demonstrate the bravery of superior disbelief in the tales told about the house, will install himself at Rathmoy, bag and baggage—but not for long. Sundry excuses are offered, but few will admit hearing "The Funeral Procession," much less admit to leaving on that account. Rathmoy cares not at all *why* these tenants leave, just so they do.

Mostly Rathmoy stands idle, a shimmering Palladian dream so perfect in its proportions that architects come from far and wide to study it. But Rathmoy wishes to live out its existence on its lone. I, for one, believe it will.

The Spanish Fan

The Abbey Farm
Dunbrody Abbey

COUNTY WEXFORD

The Spanish Fan

OUT OF THE WILD BOGS AND THE DARK GLENS of Antrim, there came one day a man who called himself Eoghan (pronounced Owen) Cullen. No one in County Wexford, where he eventually settled. knew anything about the drear-faced man. Most people distrusted him on sight.. Eoghan Cullen made it clear in short order that he hated any man who stood up in shoes. How this class of man ever got the post of overseer at the biggest farm attached to Dunbrody Abbey, no one ever knew. The man who had been there before was killed by the goring of a Beleek bull, and the Abbey Farm had been without an overseer for months. Desperation may have been the reason for hiring Cullen. There was desperation, and to spare, before the farm was quit of his brutal presence. It was said in the neighborhood, after Cullen had been at the Abbey Farm for a few months, "That bull of Moriarity's gored the wrong man. If it'd waited a while, Cullen might have come along."

In any case, unpopular as the man was with his neighbors, the Abbey Farm throve. When sober, he was an able overseer.

Three years after Eoghan Cullen had come to Dunbrody Abbey at Ballyhack, he treated himself to a short holiday. When he returned, he brought with him a wife, a great, hulking woman with not a single feminine attraction to bless herself. She, too, so she said, came from the County Antrim. Her name was Ardath. Ardath Cullen. The fostering of old Gaelic names seemed, if the Cullens were any criterion, to be one of the major pursuits of the County of the Glens.

None of the people who came in contact with Ardath Cullen liked or trusted her, any more than they did her husband. A surly pair, everyone agreed.

For a while, the Cullens worked hard and kept to themselves. Then one night Eoghan went into a pub at Ballyhack and took more than "one over the eight." He got roaring drunk and smashed up the place. Next day he paid his bill for damage done. But from then out every man's hand was against him, and he knew it.

A daughter was born to Eoghan and Ardath Cullen. She was a black, squalling mite who yelled the roof off all during her babyhood. The very sight of her sent

Eoghan into paroxysms of fury. He hated her guts, and said so. Ardath kept her baby out of its father's sight as much as she could, for fear he would bash its brains in, as he plenty of times threatened to do. The baby was named Blanor. This unfortunate name was irony of the first water, for Queen Blanor was one of the most beautiful and radiant of the ancient Gaelic queens, the like of Helen of Sparta, for men's undoing.

Blanor Cullen grew into as queer a specimen as one would see in a week's wandering. She was not precisely ugly, even though she had a long hatchet face of dark brown color. Her mouth was thin lipped as an adder's, and her tongue (when she spoke, which was seldom) was twice as deadly. Masses of unkempt, straggling black hair, as coarse and vibrant as a gypsy's, swung to her shoulder blades. Her eyes were an arresting feature, for they were brown and darting as a forest creature's. So much for Blanor Cullen's face. Few men paid much attention to that. When they encountered Blanor, men forgot she had a face, of such magnificence was her figure.

When Blanor was fifteen, she began to use her superbly modeled body to get a few of the things she wanted in life, things which an almost continuously drunken father and a sadistic mother had denied her. In her smoldering way, Blanor attracted men of rough, seafaring type, men who roamed the world over and took their bought love where they found it, men to whom the "strumpet" kind of woman appealed above any of gentler breed.

When Blanor Cullen was eighteen, she took to walking the quay at Kilmore. Here she had a great pick of sailors of all nationalities, as well as of all shapes and sizes. Within a radius of twenty miles were four big harbors. In the year of this story, 1896, ships, particularly Atlantic steamers and trampers from all ports in the world, plowed up and down this Irish coast. Cobh and Waterford Harbor, Ballymoney and Arklow were all open to the wide. A girl with a figure like Blanor's had it all her own way. Many a scald (bitter insult) was passed about her face, but the sight of her swaying hips called forth another round of drinks on the man lucky enough to buy the use of them for the night. Ah, liane, liane, it was gorgeous, while it lasted ("liane" being Gaelic for extreme amorous ecstasy).

One dirty night, with the wind whipping along the Waterford Parade like all the banshees in Moher, Blanor was breasting the gale on her way to the room she shared with another prostitute named Rosie Mongella. Nicknamed "Rosie the Mongrel" by her chance pickups, the girl was a half-caste Irish-Italian whose mother had had a water-front career a shade more prosperous than her own. Rosie was Blanor's friend, and they shared their days of bad luck together.

Suddenly, out of nowhere, a big stoker barged into Blanor, nearly knocking her into the rain-brimmed gutter. As she was falling, a pair of huge, muscular arms encircléd the girl's waist. Then Blanor Cullen's ferrety eyes looked up into a pair of sullen, black Spanish ones, and her heart was gone from her breast forever.

The Spanish stoker told Blanor his name was Miguel Corbillo. He hailed from Malaga, and was off a Spanish freighter which was now unloading chestnut plankings at Duncannon, up the harbor. The ship would have to reload with pig-iron ingots and sheetings. It would take a fortnight at the very least. Where could they go to spend that time together? At first Blanor had the wild idea of taking Miguel to Dunbrody, to the Abbey Farm. But she knew deep in her heart that her father would kill her if she did—not that he cared how she lived, so long as she kept out of his sight. Then she thought of a small water-front hotel at Ferrycarrig on Wexford Lough Harbor. It was none too fancy, in fact it was dirty and the food was bad. But as long as she and Miguel were together, nothing else mattered.

The plans these two made during their idyl in the soot-laden air of the hotel under the derricks! They might have been lying under the copper beeches at Greenore Head, with the sweep of the Mourne Mountains behind them and the lovely, ivied Castle-bellingham at their feet. Miguel, it seemed, was as much in love with Blanor as she with him. Her heart, for the first time in her beaten life, truly sang.

When his ship sailed, he would sail with it. But this would be the last time. He had saved a little money, one way and another. He knew of a small melon farm near Cadiz. His mother was from Cadiz. They would raise the big, juicy Spanish melons. Life would be great for them. Miguel laughed gaily. Blanor had never known how to laugh. Now she would learn.

The night the boat sailed, Miguel dived down into his duffel bag and came up with a parcel wrapped in oilskin. It was for Blanor. He had meant to give it to her before. He had carried them around for a long time. Them? Yes. Look. Blanor unwrapped the yellow covering. A black Spanish shawl, with long silk fringe, and a black lacquered silk fan. The sticks were red-brown tortoise shell. They clacked, like castanets, when she waved the fan. Miguel showed Blanor how to talk with the fan. To all Spaniards a fan has a language of its own. Open, close—quickly. O-p-e-n, c-l-o-s-e—slowly. So—that was the way. It was a code for lovers. More love-making was done in Spain by the clack, clack, clackety clack than by words.

Miguel's ship sailed at midnight tide. From the very depths of Blanor Cullen's being all that was good went with Miguel.

Blanor never saw Miguel again. No one ever knew why. For years, before her mind began to fog over, she searched the shipping news. She could not read herself, but she got Maggie Shillarn, the barmaid at Casey's Sailor's Rest, to search the shipping columns with her. No news of the Estremadura out of Malaga was ever recorded, except once. According to an item marked "Brazil Ship News," the cargo vessel Estremadura was now on the South American run. That was all Blanor ever heard.

After her father died, Blanor's mother stayed on at the Abbey Farm. She had a great way with her in raising fowls. A small stone house with four rooms was given her to live in. Each night, from her solitary walks along the Duncannon water front, Blanor came home to the cottage at Dunbrody Abbey.

It had now been five years since Miguel had sailed away at midnight tide. All this time Blanor had tended bar at Mike Casey's place in Duncannon. Then her mind began to stray with the weight of her dashed hopes. So she came away out of it and went back to her mother, whom she feared and hated and who despised her. At first she took the black shawl, with the grand, wide fringe, out of its oilskin wrappings only once in a while. She would often practice with the fan, however, for, when Miguel came back, she must tell him—clack, clack, clackety clack, so—how much she had missed him.

One night Farmer Cosgrove, going home through a short cut which took him past the lane leading to Abbey Farm Cottage, was startled to hear a curious noise coming from the thick hawthorn bushes that bordered the bohireen. It sounded like a strong wind in winter branches. Clack, clack, clackety clack, it went. But this was midsummer, and the branches were heavy with foliage. Clack, clack, clack, there it was again. Peering hard into the darkness, Cosgrove was astonished to see that dark-visaged streeler (streetwalker) of a Cullen girl, no longer a girl, surely. She was all wrapped up in a black shawl with long waving fringe. Her eyes were vacant and bloodshot. She smirked in a silly way. All this time the poor, wry creature was opening and shutting a black fan. As Farmer Cosgrove hurried away out of that, down the road towards his farm, he heard, sharply defined in the still night air, clack, clackety, clack—clack.

The world over, young boys with time hanging heavy on their hands will rove the countryside seeking diversion and mischief, which are frequently one and the same. The cruelty that is inherent in the young loves to bait a drunken sot or a lunatic at large. The village idiot has been the butt of ridicule since the beginning of time. The boys of Dunbrody thought, when they first heard that the black Cullen woman was carrying on in the lane, that it would be great sport to bait her. They would get her to clack her fan. One boy would then grab it and break it. Five or six of them tried this little game one night. They, nor any others, ever tried it again.

Blanor was sullen, as was her wont. She was wrapped in her black shawl, waving the lacquered fan. Back and forth she went, bowing to the imaginary crowd in the bohireens. Then the boys swooped down on her. One spalpeen pulled the fringe on her shawl. It was nearly his last move on earth. Like forked lightning, Blanor whirled on the boy. She bared her pointed, yellow teeth, the like of a vixen in a burrow when her cubs are threatened. She grasped his wrist and twisted it with such strength that it broke like a clay pipestem. With a shriek of pain, the boy streaked up the lane with his cronies after him. But even the wildness of their panic did not move Blanor. Brooding and muttering, she continued her marching. Up and down. Up and down. Clackety, clackety, clack.

When Blanor Cullen was in her fortieth year, she died. Walking the bohireen-bordered lanes in all kinds of weather, more than half the time barefoot, had brought on a congestion of the lungs. Even her mother, who cared less than nothing for her "crazed-as-a-loon-bird" daughter, was moved to caring for her at the last. No class of wake was even attempted, for nobody would come except paid keeners, and Mrs. Cullen was not spending good shillings for them.

A cold, narrow grave was dug deep in a clay pit by old Johnny Keeby, who had once enjoyed a favor or two from Blanor in her prime. Into this slit of Mother Earth, he lowered a cheap, cherry-wood box containing all that was left of the woman, Blanor Cullen—the woman who, when a girl, had lived a lifetime in fourteen spellbinding days. With her Spanish lover she had tasted the apples of the Hesperides.

The stone house in which Blanor Cullen lived with her mother for twenty years of her miserable life is no longer lived in by anyone. It has fallen into ruin. The roof is gone entirely, and a gigantic oak, blasted by lightning, waves its branches through the windows of the upper floor. On windy nights the riven branches become the strings of a mighty harp. People who are obliged to travel along the road leading past the lane to the Cullen house, or what is left of it, hurry in the night shadows, for they dislike meeting the woman who is forever trailing a black shawl through the tall grasses of the abandoned lane. She walks up and down, up and down, apparently oblivious to wayfarers. What troubles them is the sound that haunts their dreams later in the night. For as she waves the Spanish fan, it plays a sort of obbligato—clack, clack, clackety, clackety, clackety clack.